My Samsung® Galaxy Tab™ 3

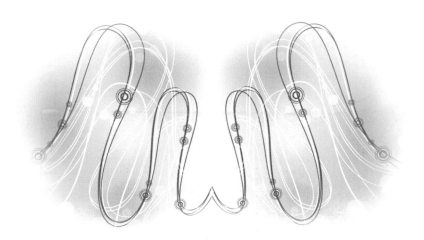

Eric Butow
Lonzell Watson

800 East 96th Street,
Indianapolis, Indiana 46240 USA

My Samsung® Galaxy Tab™ 3

Copyright © 2014 by Pearson Education, Inc.

ISBN-13: 978-0-7897-5193-5

ISBN-10: 0-7897-5193-3

Library of Congress cataloging information is on file.

Printed in the United States of America

First Printing: October 2013

Trademarks

All terms mentioned in this book that are known to be trademarks or service marks have been appropriately capitalized. Que Publishing cannot attest to the accuracy of this information. Use of a term in this book should not be regarded as affecting the validity of any trademark or service mark.

All Galaxy Tab 3 images are provided by Samsung Electronics America.

Warning and Disclaimer

Every effort has been made to make this book as complete and as accurate as possible, but no warranty or fitness is implied. The information provided is on an "as is" basis. The author and the publisher shall have neither liability nor responsibility to any person or entity with respect to any loss or damages arising from the information contained in this book or from the use of programs accompanying it.

Bulk Sales

Que Publishing offers excellent discounts on this book when ordered in quantity for bulk purchases or special sales. For more information, please contact

U.S. Corporate and Government Sales
1-800-382-3419
corpsales@pearsontechgroup.com

For sales outside of the U.S., please contact

International Sales
international@pearsoned.com

Editor-in-Chief
Greg Wiegand

Acquisitions Editor
Michelle Newcomb

Development Editor
Charlotte Kughen

Managing Editor
Sandra Schroeder

Project Editor
Seth Kerney

Indexer
Lisa Stumpf

Proofreader
Jess DeGabriele

Technical Editor
Christian Kenyeres

Publishing Coordinator
Cindy Teeters

Book Designer
Anne Jones

Compositor
Mary Sudul

Contents at a Glance

Chapter 1	The Galaxy Tab Universe	3
Chapter 2	Meeting the Samsung Galaxy Tab 3	17
Chapter 3	Setting Up the Galaxy Tab 3	47
Chapter 4	Customizing Android to Your Liking	59
Chapter 5	Adding Widgets to Your Home Screens	79
Chapter 6	Browsing the Web	103
Chapter 7	Sending Email and Instant Messages	119
Chapter 8	Finding Widgets	149
Chapter 9	Using Productivity Apps to Simplify Your Life	179
Chapter 10	Connecting to Devices and the Cloud	215
Chapter 11	Using Apps for Learning, Creating, and Sharing	239
Chapter 12	Playing Music and Video	269
Chapter 13	Reading and Managing Books and Magazines	317
Chapter 14	Capturing and Managing Photos	347
Chapter 15	Using Maps, Navigation, Local, and Location Sharing	367
Chapter 16	Finding and Managing Apps	391
Chapter 17	Adding New Hardware	419
Chapter 18	Troubleshooting Your Galaxy Tab 3	425
	Index	443

Online Material

Appendix A	Finding Galaxy Tab 3 Accessories
Appendix B	Glossary of Terms

Table of Contents

1 The Galaxy Tab Universe   3

First, a Look at Android...4

The Newest Members: The Galaxy Tab 3 Family.......................5

    The Galaxy Tab 3 7.0...5

    The Galaxy Tab 3 8.0...7

    The Galaxy Tab 3 10.1 8

Comparing the Tab 3 to Other Tabs.....................................9

    Galaxy Tab 7.0 9

    Galaxy Tab 7.0 Plus...10

    Galaxy Tab 7.7 10

    Galaxy Tab 8.9 11

    Galaxy Tab 10.1 12

    Galaxy Tab 2 7.0 and 10.1 12

    Galaxy Note 8.0 and 10.1 13

2 Meeting the Samsung Galaxy Tab 3   17

Investigating the Galaxy Tab 3 Unit....................................18

    Physical Features of the Galaxy Tab 3 8″..........................19

    Physical Features of the Galaxy Tab 3 10″.........................23

The Galaxy Tab 3 Buttons and Switches..............................26

    The Three Galaxy Tab 3 Buttons......................................27

    The Power Button..29

    Volume Control Buttons 30

Galaxy Tab 3 Screens 32

    The Lock Screen (Galaxy Tab 3 8″)...................................32

    The Lock Screen (Galaxy Tab 3 10″) 33

    The Apps Screen (Galaxy Tab 3 8″)..................................34

    The Application Screen (Galaxy Tab 3 8″).........................35

Manipulating the Screen...35

    Tapping an Element 36

    Pinching 36

    Dragging and Flicking 36

Interacting with Android..38

   Sliders..38

   Settings Menus..38

   Button Bar 39

   Tab Areas 39

Using the Keyboard 40

   Using Special Keyboards and Characters 42

3 Setting Up the Galaxy Tab 3   47

Getting Details About the Galaxy Tab 3 48

Setting Up Your Network 50

Syncing the Galaxy Tab 3 55

4 Customizing Android to Your Liking   59

Password-Protecting the Galaxy Tab 3.........................59

Changing Your Password 62

Setting Parental Restrictions..64

Changing the Date and Time 65

Modifying Your Wallpaper 68

Setting Alert Sounds..69

Changing Keyboard and Voice Settings.......................71

Modifying More Settings 74

5 Adding Widgets to Your Home Screens   79

Accessing the Widgets Screen 79

Taking a Tour of Available Widgets 81

Adding a Widget to a Home Screen 90

Creating a New Home Screen 97

Removing a Widget... 100

6 Browsing the Web   103

Browsing to a URL 103

Searching the Web 105

Viewing Web Pages 107

Bookmarking Websites 110
Returning to Previously Visited Pages 111
Deleting Bookmarks 113
Filling in Web Forms... 115
Copying Text and Images from Web Pages............................ 116

7   Sending Email and Instant Messages   119

Configuring Email 119
Reading Email.. 124
Composing a New Message.. 127
Creating Your Own Signature... 129
Deleting Messages 130
Searching Through Email.. 131
Configuring Email Settings 133
Sending and Receiving Instant Messages 137
Configuring Google Hangouts Settings 142
Reading Email Messages Using the Email Widget............... 145

8   Using Galaxy Tab 3 Widgets   149

Finding the Widgets 150
Using the Widgets 153

9   Using Productivity Apps to Simplify Your Life   179

Staying Up to Date 180
Managing Contacts 194
Managing Your Busy Schedule 203
Use Calendar Views.. 207

10   Connecting to Devices and the Cloud   215

Connecting Using Wi-Fi Direct 215
Printing Wirelessly 217
Sharing Files.. 222
Sharing Music and Video 230
Copy Files with Windows Media Player............................ 230

Connect as a Mass Storage Device 232

Samsung Kies for PCs and Macs 234

11 Using Apps for Learning, Creating, and Sharing   239

Staying Up to Date with Google Now.. 239

Using ChatON.. 245

Connecting to Google+.. 249

Creating Documents and Presentations with
Polaris Office... 255

12 Playing Music and Video   269

Downloading Movies and TV Shows 269

Playing Videos 276

Viewing YouTube Videos 282

Recording Video 286

Purchasing Music.. 291

Use the Samsung Music Hub 291

Playing Songs.. 303

Creating Your Own Playlists 310

Adding a Podcast App 312

13 Reading and Managing Books and Magazines   317

Using Google Play Books 318

Using Google Play Magazines.. 331

Shopping for Book and Magazine Readers............................ 344

14 Capturing and Managing Photos   347

Using the Camera 348

Navigating Image Viewer... 353

Tips for Capturing Photos.. 356

Working with Gallery... 356

Creating Screen Captures 364

15 **Using Maps, Navigation, Local, and Location Sharing 367**

    Enabling GPS 368

    Getting Around with Maps... 368

    Getting Voice-Command Directions.. 376

    Getting to Know Local 380

    Sharing Locations with Friends 382

16 **Finding and Managing Apps**   **391**

    Getting Apps in the Google Play Store 392

    Managing Apps Through Your Home Pages............................ 402

    Adding Useful Apps 407

17 **Adding New Hardware**   **419**

    Galaxy Tab 2013 USB Connection Kit 420

    Bluetooth Keyboards.. 420

    Pairing Bluetooth Devices 420

    MicroSD Cards... 422

18 **Troubleshooting Your Galaxy Tab 3**   **425**

    Maintaining Your Galaxy Tab 3.. 425

    Updating Galaxy Tab 3 Software.. 426

    Backing Up and Restoring Your Galaxy Tab 3......................... 427

    Syncing and Using Manual Backup... 429

    Extending Battery Life.. 429

        Utilize Sleep Mode 432

    Solving Random Galaxy Tab Issues 434

        Difficulty Turning Your Tab On or Off................................. 434

        Touchscreen Becomes Unresponsive 435

        Battery Does Not Charge.. 436

    Troubleshooting Wi-Fi Accessibility

        Problems... 438

        Make Sure Wi-Fi Is Activated 438

        Check Your Range.. 439

x

Getting Technical Help.. 440

Contact Your Cellular Provider or Samsung...................... 441

Index **459**

Online Materials

A **Finding Galaxy Tab 3 Accessories**

Protective Cases

Screen Protectors

Chargers and Adapters

B **Glossary of Terms**

About the Authors

Eric Butow began writing books in 2000 when he wrote *Master Visually Windows 2000 Server*. Since then, Eric has authored or coauthored 21 other books. Those books include Addison-Wesley's *User Interface Design for Mere Mortals*, Amacom's *How to Succeed in Business Using LinkedIn*, Wiley Publishing's *Droid Companion*, Que Publishing's *My Samsung Galaxy Tab 2*, and, most recently, Que Publishing's *Blogging to Drive Business*, Second Edition.

Eric lives in Jackson, California. He has a master's degree in communications from California State University, Fresno, and is the owner of Butow Communications Group (BCG), an online marketing ROI improvement firm.

Website: http://butow.net

LinkedIn: http://linkedin.com/in/ebutow

Lonzell Watson is the author of other popular titles including *My Samsung Galaxy Tab 2, My HTC EVO 3D, Teach Yourself Visually Digital Video, Teach Yourself Visually Final Cut Pro*, and the *Canon VIXIA Digital Field Guide*.

Dedication

To my father: May 10, 1938–November 10, 2012
—Eric Butow

To Antonio Tapia. Thank you so much for your guidance and insight. For this, I am forever grateful.
—Lonzell Watson

Acknowledgments

Eric Butow: My thanks as always to my family and friends. I want to thank my awesome literary agent, Carole Jelen, as well as Cindy Teeters, Christian Kenyeres, Charlotte Kughen, Seth Kerney, Todd Brakke, Greg Wiegand, and especially Michelle Newcomb. I'd also like to thank everyone who gave me permission to use their information, particularly the parents of my mother's daycare children for letting me take their pictures for the book.

Lonzell Watson: I would like to give special thanks to Michelle Newcomb, without whom this project would not have been possible. I would like to thank Antonio Tapia for all of his hard work and insight. Special thanks go to Laura Clor, to my lovely wife, Robyn, to Shannon Johnson, and Danya and Sean Platt.

We Want to Hear from You!

As the reader of this book, *you* are our most important critic and commentator. We value your opinion and want to know what we're doing right, what we could do better, what areas you'd like to see us publish in, and any other words of wisdom you're willing to pass our way.

We welcome your comments. You can email or write us directly to let us know what you did or didn't like about this book—as well as what we can do to make our books better.

Please note that we cannot help you with technical problems related to the topic of this book.

When you write, please be sure to include this book's title and author as well as your name, email address, and phone number. We will carefully review your comments and share them with the author and editors who worked on the book.

Email: feedback@quepublishing.com

Mail: Que Publishing
          ATTN: Reader Feedback
          800 East 96th Street
          Indianapolis, IN 46240 USA

Reader Services

Visit our website and register this book at quepublishing.com/register and enter the ISBN (9780789751935) for convenient access to any updates, downloads, or errata that might be available for this book.

Review the different versions of
Android

Meet the newest members of the
Galaxy Tab family: the Galaxy Tab 3
7.0, 8.0, and 10.1

Learn how the Galaxy Tab 3 compares
to other Galaxy Tab models

In this chapter, you're introduced to the different versions of Android and the different models of the Galaxy Tab including the Galaxy Tab 3. Topics in this chapter include:

→ The three different versions of the Android operating system

→ The three models of the Galaxy Tab 3

→ A comparison of Galaxy Tab 3 and other models in the Galaxy Tab family

The Galaxy Tab Universe

If you're brand new to the Galaxy Tab 3, start with this chapter so you can learn more about your new tablet and also learn more about the Android operating system that the Galaxy Tab 3 uses. If you want to get started right away, proceed to Chapter 2, "Meeting the Samsung Galaxy Tab 3."

First, a Look at Android

The Galaxy Tab 3 runs the Android operating system that is produced and maintained by Google. As of this writing, the latest IDC report that tracked mobile operating system marketing share stated that in the first quarter of 2013 Android commanded 75 percent market share, well above the second place iOS used on iPhones and iPads (www.idc.com/getdoc. jsp?containerId=prUS24108913).

There are several versions of Android currently available that run on various smartphones and tablets. Each version is best known by the nicknames Google gives it. Since version 1.5, Google has given the name of a sweet treat to every new version; version 1.5 was known as Cupcake. (There were two previous versions before Cupcake that didn't have a nickname, so Google decided to give the third release of Android a nickname starting with the third letter of the alphabet.)

Galaxy Tab models run one of the following Android versions:

- Version 2.2, or Froyo (short for frozen yogurt), runs on the original Galaxy Tab 7.0. You can learn more about using Froyo on the Galaxy Tab 7.0 in Que's 2011 book, *My Samsung Galaxy Tab* (ISBN 978-0-7897-4797-6).

- Version 2.3, Gingerbread, was the most widely used version of Android as of early July 2012 (http://developer.android.com/about/dashboards/index.html). In addition to including user interface improvements, Gingerbread was designed for use on extra-large screen resolutions and provided improved network performance.

- Version 3, Honeycomb, was the first version optimized for use with tablets. It included more user interface improvements, support for video chat using Google Talk, and the ability to encrypt all user data.

- Version 4, Ice Cream Sandwich, included more improvements to the user interface, improved features, such as real-time speech-to-text dictation, and new apps, such as a photo editor. You can learn more about using Ice Cream Sandwich on the Galaxy Tab 2 in Que's 2012 book, *My Samsung Galaxy Tab 2* (ISBN 978-0-7897-5038-9).

- Version 4.1, Jelly Bean, included a new interface layout for tablets with smaller screens, such as the Galaxy Tab 3 7.0, Google Chrome as the new web browser; and the Google Now personalized search app.

- Version 4.2, which is also called Jelly Bean, includes everything in Version 4.1 as well as the ability to place widgets on your Lock screen, a redesigned Camera app, and a Gesture Keyboard that predicts what you're trying to type as you glide your fingers over the keys. The text and screenshots in this book are based on the latest version of Jelly Bean (as of this writing), Version 4.2.2.

You find out more about the versions each Galaxy Tab model uses later in this chapter.

What About Android 4.3 (Jelly Bean) and 4.4 (KitKat)?

In July 2013, Google introduced Android 4.3, also called Jelly Bean. This version is only available on Google Nexus smartphones and tablets. The bigger news came in September 2013 when Google announced Android 4.4, which wasn't named Key Lime Pie as expected. Instead, Google named its next release after the Kit Kat chocolate wafer bar from Nestlé.

As of this writing, there wasn't any news about KitKat features, a release date, or its availability on the Galaxy Tab 3. When KitKat is available, articles about the new version of Android and related articles will be available on the Que Publishing website at www.quepublishing.com.

The Newest Members: The Galaxy Tab 3 Family

Before we talk more about all the Galaxy Tab models Samsung offers, it's important to talk about the subject of this book and the three newest additions to the Galaxy Tab family: The Galaxy Tab 3 7.0, 8.0, and 10.1. All three models were released at the same time, run Jelly Bean, and play the latest audio and video files. However, each model has differences you should know about.

The Galaxy Tab 3 7.0

The Galaxy Tab 3 7.0 has a 7" screen, which explains how it got its name. The Tab 3 7.0 only comes with 8GB of total data storage, but it does contain a microSD slot that can bring your total storage capacity to 64GB. The Tab 3 7.0 also includes

- Wi-Fi connectivity

- 1024 × 600 pixel screen resolution

- 1.3 megapixel front camera

- • 3.0 megapixel rear camera

- • 10.58 ounces (0.66 pound) total weight

- • A 4,000mAh battery

What Does mAh Stand For?

A milliampere-hour, better known by the acronym mAh, denotes the battery power capacity. A higher number indicates more capacity and thus longer battery life. However, the amount of time you can run the Tab 3 on a single battery charge is determined by the apps you run. For example, playing video takes up more battery power than checking your email messages.

If you prefer to hold a tablet in one hand comfortably but you also want more screen space than a smartphone then consider the Tab 3 7.0. Unlike some of the e-readers out there (such as Amazon's Kindle), the Tab 3 7.0 comes with the full version of Jelly Bean as well as the Kindle app.

The Galaxy Tab 3 8.0

The Galaxy Tab 3 8.0 has an 8.0" screen and has Wi-Fi connectivity. The Tab 3 8.0 also includes

- 1200 × 800 pixel screen resolution

- 16GB of data storage with a microSD slot that can bring total storage to 64GB

- 1.3 megapixel front camera

- 5.0 megapixel rear camera

- 10.9 ounces (0.68 pound) total weight

- A 4,450mAh battery

As with the Galaxy Tab 3 7.0 model, you can hold the Galaxy Tab 3 8.0 in one hand comfortably, but you get more screen space than the Tab 3 7.0. You also get a higher screen resolution and more battery capacity in exchange for a larger and slightly heavier unit.

The Galaxy Tab 3 10.1

The Galaxy Tab 3 10.1 is so named because of its 10.1" screen, which is one of the largest screens you can find on a tablet. The Tab 3 10.1 also includes

- Wi-Fi connectivity

- 16GB of data storage with a microSD slot that can bring total storage to 64GB

- 1200 × 800 pixel screen resolution

- 1.3 megapixel front camera

- 3.2 megapixel rear camera

- 17.99 ounces (1.12 pound) total weight

- A 6,800mAh battery

You can hold the Galaxy Tab 3 10.1 in one hand, but it's usually safer to hold it with both hands. If you want to have the most screen space available so you can use it for tasks that you've previously done on your laptop (such as taking notes or watching movies) then the Tab 3 10.1 might be the right tablet for you.

If you want to learn more about each Tab 3 model and the differences between them, skip ahead to Chapter 2.

Comparing the Tab 3 to Other Tabs

There are now a total of seven different Galaxy Tabs, including the Tab 3 family. What's more, the Galaxy Note is a smartphone/tablet hybrid that's included in this discussion.

Galaxy Tab 7.0

This is the original Galaxy Tab that Samsung produced. The Tab 7.0 was originally positioned as a smaller alternative to the iPad, which came in only one size at the time the Tab 7.0 was first released. Samsung decided that their Tab models would run various versions of Google's Android mobile operating system so the Tab would be compatible with other Android phones just as the iPad is compatible with the iPhone. The Tab 7.0 runs Froyo.

Though the Tab 7.0 Plus was designed to eventually replace the Tab 7.0, the original Tab 7.0 is still offered by AT&T, Sprint, Verizon, and T-Mobile. You can also buy a Wi-Fi only model. Prices vary between the carriers and the Wi-Fi version.

Galaxy Tab 7.0 Plus

The Tab 7.0 Plus is a sleeker version of the original Tab 7.0 that runs Honeycomb and has some more hardware and software features than the original Tab. Therefore, the Tab 7.0 Plus doesn't have the buttons below the screen like the original Tab 7.0 or the Galaxy Note. Instead, the Tab 7.0 Plus works like its larger siblings, the Tab 8.9 and Tab 10.1. The Tab 7.0 Plus is only offered by T-Mobile or as a Wi-Fi model. If you choose the Wi-Fi model, there are several different online vendors that sell it.

Galaxy Tab 7.7

The Tab 7.7 is not only a bit larger than the 7.0 models but it also boasts some interesting features. The screen is based on AMOLED technology with a 1200 × 800 pixel resolution. (AMOLED stands for active-matrix organic light emitting diode.) The Tab 7.7 includes a more powerful battery—5,100mAh compared to 4,000mAh on the 7.0 Plus—that results in longer usage times on a single charge. And unlike other Tab models, you can make and receive voice calls with the Tab 7.7.

Galaxy Tab 8.9

The Galaxy Tab 8.9 not only has a larger screen and a larger footprint, it also has a 1280 × 800 pixel screen. Like the 7.0 Plus, 7.7, and 10.1 models, the 8.9 runs Honeycomb. The Tab 8.9 is only offered by AT&T with 16GB of memory, although you can also buy a 16GB or 32GB Wi-Fi model from several online vendors.

Galaxy Tab 10.1

If you're looking for the largest Tab model, or a larger Tab that's offered by more carriers, then you should consider the Tab 10.1. Like the Tab 8.9, the Tab 10.1 includes a screen that has 1280 × 800 pixel resolution and a screen size of 10.1". This screen is not only larger than the iPad 2 screen but also has greater resolution. The battery (7,000mAh) is the most powerful of any Tab and provides 9 hours of usage on a single charge.

Like the Tab 8.9, you can buy a Tab 10.1 with 16GB or 32GB of memory. The Tab 10.1 is offered by Verizon and T-Mobile but also comes in a Wi-Fi model as well. As of this writing, the Tab 10.1 was not being sold because of a patent dispute between Apple and Samsung. What's more, the Tab 10.1 was effectively replaced by the Tab 2 10.1, which Samsung is selling as of this writing.

Galaxy Tab 2 7.0 and 10.1

The Galaxy Tab 2 was the successor to the original Tab family, just as the Tab 3 family is the successor to the Tab 2 family. However, just as with the Tab 7.0, the Tab 2 7.0 and 10.1 models are still available on the Samsung website (www.samsung.com) if you want to purchase them. The Tab 2 7.0 is so named because of its 7" screen and you can purchase the unit from Verizon or in a Wi-Fi version.

The Tab 2 10.1 is so named because of its 10.1" screen. You can purchase the Tab 2 10.1 in a Wi-Fi version and also from a variety of carriers including AT&T, Verizon, Sprint, and T-Mobile.

You can get more information about the Tab 2 series on the Samsung website and in the Que book, *My Samsung Galaxy Tab 2* (ISBN: 978-0-7897-5038-9).

Galaxy Note 8.0 and 10.1

In late 2011 and early 2012, Samsung released the 5.3" version of its Galaxy Note "phablet," which is a device that's larger than a phone but smaller than a tablet and has features of each. For example, the Note has buttons below the screen—as the Tab 7.0 does—because the Note runs Gingerbread. The Note comes with a stylus called an S Pen so you can manipulate screen elements, handwrite notes, and draw on apps created for use with the Note.

Samsung subsequently created the Note 8.0 and 10.1 models to replace the original Galaxy Note, but both new models still come with the S Pen. These new Note models, however, run Android 4.1 (the first version of Jelly Bean) and cost more than the Tab 3 8.0 and 10.1.

Choosing from all these models can be confusing, but you can't say that Samsung doesn't have an offering for nearly every potential tablet user. You can learn more about the Galaxy Tab and Note family and get updated information by visiting Samsung's website (www.samsung.com).

See the differences between the Galaxy Tab 3 7.0, Galaxy Tab 3 8.0, and the Galaxy Tab 3 10.1

Take a tour of the physical buttons and switches on your Galaxy Tab 3

Familiarize yourself with what the four menu icons at the bottom of the Galaxy Tab 3 screens do

View three important screens on your Galaxy Tab 3, including the home screen

Understand how to manipulate the screen

Learn how to interact with Android

In this chapter, you discover the different hardware and the common screens on the Galaxy Tab 3. Topics covered in this chapter include:

→ Features on the front, back, and sides of the unit

→ Galaxy Tab 3 icons for manipulating the screen

→ Three important screens you need to know

→ How to manipulate the Galaxy Tab 3 screen

→ Configuring email settings

→ How to interact with Android

Meeting the Samsung Galaxy Tab 3

This book covers two models of the Galaxy Tab 3: the 8" Tab and the larger 10" version.

The 8" unit, called the Galaxy Tab 3 8.0, runs version 4.2.2 of Google's Android operating system, also called Jelly Bean.

The 10" unit, called the Galaxy Tab 3 10.1, also runs Jelly Bean. Both models connect to the Internet and/or a network using a Wi-Fi connection. (As of this writing, no cell phone carrier has offered the Galaxy Tab 3 with its data network plans.)

Many tasks throughout the book include information for one model or the other, and if there are any differences between the models then there are separate tasks for each. The headers for each section (or subsection) indicate in parentheses the model name, such as (Galaxy Tab 3 10"). If you don't see an area in parentheses in the section (or subsection) name, the information applies to both models.

What About the Galaxy Tab 3 7.0?

There aren't many differences between the Galaxy Tab 3 7.0 and the other models. The Tab 3 7.0 has many of the same physical features (except for the screen size, of course).

Investigating the Galaxy Tab 3 Unit

Before you work with your Galaxy Tab 3, it's important to take it out of the box and examine it so you can learn where all the controls and features are on the unit. If you've used (or tried) another tablet computer in the past, you might already be familiar with some of the features. If this is your first time using a tablet computer or the Galaxy Tab 3, though, take time to read this chapter and enjoy learning about it.

It's Not All Good

WHY DO THE GALAXY TAB UNITS LOOK DIFFERENT BETWEEN PHOTOS?

Each of the three Galaxy Tab 3 models comes in two colors: White and Gold Brown. The figures show the two different colors of all the models (mostly the Tab 8.0 and 10.1) in photos throughout this book. Some screens may also look different because of app updates or the screen orientation. For example, on the Tab 3 8.0 the permanent icons on the Home screens appear at the bottom of the screen in vertical screen orientation but appear on the right side of the screen in horizontal screen orientation.

Physical Features of the Galaxy Tab 3 8"

The front of the Galaxy Tab 3 8" includes the LCD touch screen for viewing information as well as a brightness sensor and a camera so you can take photos and/or record video of yourself.

You learn more about using the cameras to record video in Chapter 12, "Playing Music and Video," and to take photos in Chapter 14, "Capturing and Managing Photos."

Brightness sensor

Camera viewfinder

Touch screen

The back of the unit has only one feature: a second camera that includes a flash so you can take photos and record video using your Galaxy Tab 3. (Otherwise, the function of the back is to rest in your hand, of course.)

Camera

There are four buttons included on both the Galaxy Tab 3 8" and the Galaxy Tab 3 10". Those buttons are covered later in the chapter in the "The Galaxy Tab 3 Buttons and Switches" section. Aside from those four, the Galaxy Tab 3 8" contains a number of features on the sides of the unit:

- A headphone and microphone jack on the top side of the unit so you can either listen to audio privately or record audio into a microphone.

Headphone/ Microphone jack

Headphone/Microphone Jack on the Galaxy Tab 3 7.0
The headphone/microphone jack on the Galaxy Tab 3 7.0 model is on the top left side of the unit.

- A MicroSD memory card slot on the left side of the unit.

MicroSD memory card slot

- The audio speakers on the bottom side of the unit.

- A dock/charge and sync cable connector that is also on the bottom side of the unit. You learn more about docking, charging, and syncing your Galaxy Tab 3 in Chapter 3, "Setting Up the Galaxy Tab 3."

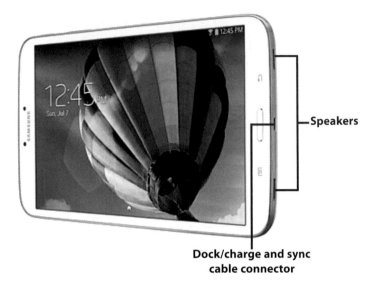

Speakers

**Dock/charge and sync
cable connector**

- The power button on the right side of the unit.

- The volume control slider also on the right side of the unit.

- An infrared (IR) blaster also on the right side of the unit. The IR blaster controls a device that accepts infrared commands from a remote device such as your television and your cable box.

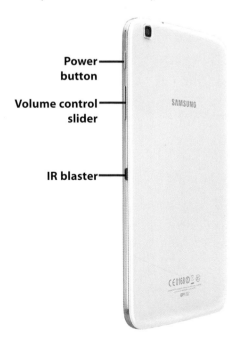

Power button

Volume control slider

IR blaster

Physical Features of the Galaxy Tab 3 10"

The front of the Galaxy Tab 3 10" includes the LCD touchscreen for viewing information and a camera so you can take photos or record video of yourself.

You learn more about using the cameras to record video in Chapter 12 and to take photos in Chapter 14.

Brightness   Camera
sensor   viewfinder   Touchscreen

The back of the unit has only one feature: a second camera that includes a flash so you can take photos and record video using your Galaxy Tab 3.

Camera

There are three buttons included on both the Galaxy Tab 3 8" and the Galaxy Tab 3 10". Those buttons are covered later in the chapter in the "The Galaxy Tab 3 Buttons and Switches" section. Aside from those three, the Galaxy Tab 3 10" contains a number of features on the sides of the unit.

- A headphone and microphone jack on the left side of the unit so you can either listen to audio privately or record audio into a microphone.

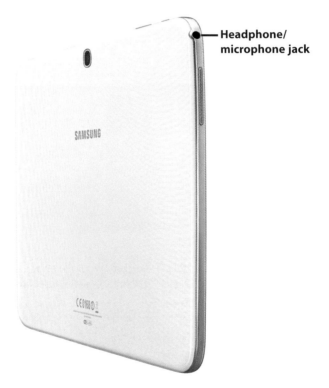

Headphone/
microphone jack

- The audio speakers on the left and right sides of the unit. The speaker on the left side of the unit appears below the headphone and microphone jack.

The speaker on the right side of the unit

- A dock/charge and sync cable connector that is on the bottom side of the unit. You learn more about docking, charging, and syncing your Galaxy Tab 3 in Chapter 3.

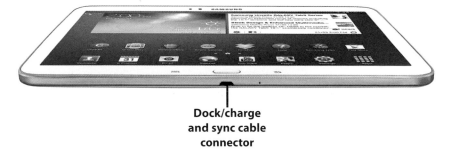

Dock/charge and sync cable connector

- The power button on the top of the unit.

- The volume control slider on the top of the unit.

- A MicroSD memory card slot on the top of the unit.

- An IR blaster at the top of the unit. The IR blaster controls a device that accepts infrared commands from a remote device such as your television and your cable box.

IR blaster——

MicroSD memory——
card slot

Volume control slider——

Power button——

The Galaxy Tab 3 Buttons and Switches

Both models of the Galaxy Tab 3 feature two touch buttons on either side of a physical Home button. All three are below the touch screen. The power button and volume slider are on one side of the unit.

Setting Up Your Galaxy Tab 3

When you start your Galaxy Tab 3 for the first time, you go through a series of steps to get your Tab 3 up and running including setting up your wireless connection. The four icons appear on your Home screen after you set up the Tab 3. This book presumes that you have already set up your Tab 3 using the documentation that came in your Tab 3 box. If you need help with setting up a Wi-Fi network then you can find that information in Chapter 3.

The Three Galaxy Tab 3 Buttons

There are three buttons below the touch screen that you use frequently to manage the device and applications on it. They are (from left to right) Menu, Home, and Back.

Menu   Home   Back

- **Menu**—The Menu touch button opens a pop-up menu at the bottom of the screen so you can access different functions. For example, if you're on the Home screen and touch the Menu button, you see a menu in the middle of the screen that gives you options to add apps and widgets, set your wallpaper, and more. Tap a menu option to open the associated screen or window. Close the menu by tapping the Menu touch button again.

- **Home**—The fact that the Home button is a physical button signifies its place of importance with regard to how the Tab 3 functions. It's probably the button you will use most often because it's the one you press to get out of a specific application, such as the Galaxy Tab 3 web browser, and move back to the Home screen so you can open another application.

If you want to hide an application and go back to the Home screen, pressing the Home button is the way to go. Pressing the Home button hides the application you currently have open.

WHAT ABOUT THE TASK MANAGER?

The previous two models of the Galaxy Tab had a separate Task Manager icon on the screen. On the Tab 3, you access the Task Manager screen by holding your finger on the Home button to see apps that are open currently. Open the app on the screen by tapping the app thumbnail screen in the Task Manager app list.

Task Manager screen

- **Back**—The Back touch button moves you back to the previous screen. For example, if you're on the Home screen and touch the current time at the bottom right of the screen to bring up the Settings area, you might decide that you don't want to change settings. Close the settings area at the bottom of the screen by tapping the Back icon.

The Power Button

The Power button performs a number of important functions on your Galaxy Tab 3:

- Turns on the unit when you press the button. The Power button is on the right side of the Galaxy Tab 3 8" unit and on the top of the Galaxy Tab 3 10" unit. The Galaxy Tab 3 boots up and is ready for you to use in about 20 seconds.

- Turns off the unit when you press the button for about two seconds.

- If you press and hold the button for a few seconds while the unit is on, the Galaxy Tab 3 automatically restarts.

- If you press the button and immediately release your finger, the screen turns off and the Galaxy Tab 3 enters sleep mode.

Power button on the Galaxy Tab 3 8"

Power button on the Galaxy Tab 3 10"

What Happens if I Don't Turn Off the Galaxy Tab 3?

If the Galaxy Tab 3 is idle for a long period of time, the unit goes into sleep mode automatically. Sleep mode drains very little battery power, so if the Galaxy Tab 3 is frequently in sleep mode, you don't need to recharge your battery as often. Refer to Chapter 18, "Troubleshooting Your Galaxy Tab 3," for information about expected battery life and strategies for extending that lifespan.

Volume Control Buttons

There are two volume control buttons on the left side of the device—one that turns up the volume and one that turns down the volume. What device the buttons control depends on what you have connected to the Galaxy Tab 3.

**Volume control buttons
on the Galaxy Tab 3 8"**

**Volume control buttons
on the Galaxy Tab 3 10"**

If you're listening to audio through the Galaxy Tab 3 speakers, the unit remembers the volume settings for the external speakers and sets the volume accordingly. If you decide to connect headphones to the unit, the Galaxy Tab 3 adjusts to the headphone volume the unit has in memory. When you remove the headphones, the unit readjusts the volume to the speaker volume.

You might want to check your volume settings for your headphones and external speakers so you don't get any nasty surprises. You learn more about setting the volume in Chapter 3.

Galaxy Tab 3 Screens

There are three important screens that are mainstays of your Galaxy Tab 3 experience no matter which Galaxy Tab 3 model you use.

The Lock Screen (Galaxy Tab 3 8")

The lock screen is the default state of the Galaxy Tab 3 when it first boots.

The lock screen shows the current date and time as well as the Wi-Fi con-nectivity status and battery charge status in the upper-right corner of the screen. It also includes the Smart Stay feature icon (it looks like an eye), which indicates that this feature is on. Smart Stay is a new feature in Jelly Bean that detects if you're looking at the screen. When the Tab 3 detects that you are looking at it, the device won't go to sleep.

All you have to do to unlock your Tab 3 is to hold your finger anywhere on the screen and then swipe your finger in any direction. If your Tab 3 is password-protected then you need to type your password in the password box. You learn more about password-protecting your Galaxy Tab 3 in Chapter 3.

The Lock Screen (Galaxy Tab 3 10")

The lock screen is the default state of the Galaxy Tab 3 when it first boots.

The lock screen shows the current date and time, the current status of your Bluetooth and Internet connections, and the amount of charge you have in your battery. It also includes the Smart Stay feature icon (it looks like an eye), which indicates that this feature is on. Smart Stay is a new feature in Jelly Bean that detects if you're looking at the screen. When the Tab 3 detects that you are looking at it, the device won't go to sleep.

All you have to do to unlock your Tab 3 is to hold your finger anywhere on the screen and then swipe your finger in any direction. If your Galaxy Tab 3 is password-protected, the password box appears on the screen. You must tap the password box, type your password, and then tap the OK button to open the Home screen or the application you were working on before you put the unit to sleep. You learn more about password protecting your Galaxy Tab in Chapter 3.

The Apps Screen (Galaxy Tab 3 8")

The applications screen is your command center where you can access all the applications available on the Galaxy Tab 3. Tap the Apps icon to view the applications screen.

The Apps icon on the Home screen

When you tap an application icon, the application launches. If you have more than one page of application icons on the applications screen, dots appear at the bottom of the screen. You can scroll between pages by clicking one of the buttons or dragging or flicking left and right. You learn more about dragging and flicking later in this chapter.

Two buttons on the bottom of the screen

The Application Screen (Galaxy Tab 3 8")

After you press an application button on the applications screen, the application launches and takes up the entire screen. For example, if you open the My Files application, a list of files and folders on your Tab 3 appears on the screen.

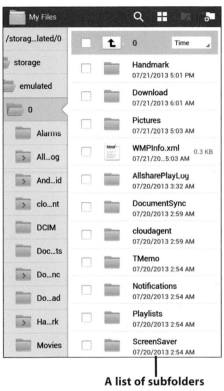

A list of subfolders within the 0 folder

Manipulating the Screen

Like many tablets these days, the Galaxy Tab 3 doesn't come with a stylus (essentially a stick) for manipulating elements on the screen. Instead, you use your fingers and change the orientation of the Galaxy Tab 3 itself to make it do what you want. Although the examples in this section are for the Galaxy Tab 3 8", you manipulate elements on the Galaxy Tab 3 10" screen in the same way. If there are different instructions for manipulating the screen for the Tab 3 10" model, we note them in a different subsection.

Tapping an Element

Unlike a desktop or laptop computer, you don't have a mouse installed on your Galaxy Tab 3, so there is no cursor that you can see. However, when you quickly tap an element with your finger, the Galaxy Tab 3 performs an action. For example, when you tap an application icon, the Galaxy Tab 3 launches the application.

You can also double-tap, which is two quick taps in the same location, to perform a specific function. For example, you can double-tap an image to zoom in and double-tap again to zoom out.

Pinching

Apple set the standard for multitouch screen gesture requirements with its iPad, and the Galaxy Tab 3 follows the same standard. A multitouch screen can recognize different gestures that use multiple finger touches. One such gesture is the pinching gesture.

You pinch when you touch the screen with both your thumb and forefinger and bring them together in a pinching motion. This is also called pinching in, and it has the same effect as zooming in. For example, you can get a closer view of a web page in the browser by pinching. You can also pinch outward, which has the same effect as zooming out, by touching the screen with your thumb and forefinger together and moving them apart.

Dragging and Flicking

You can drag up and down the screen (or even left to right if an app allows it) by touching the top of the screen and moving your finger to drag content the length of the screen. If you want to move more content down the screen, remove your finger, touch the top of the screen, and drag your finger down the length of the screen again. You can drag a page of content up by touching the bottom of the screen and dragging your finger upward.

Dragging can become cumbersome, though, if you have to drag through a long document such as a web page or spreadsheet. The Galaxy Tab 3 makes it easy for you to drag through large chunks of content by flicking. That is, after you touch the top (or bottom) of the screen, move your finger quickly down (or up) and then lift your finger at the last moment so the content scrolls after you lift your finger. You can wait for the content to stop scrolling when you reach the beginning or end of the content, or you can touch anywhere on the screen to stop scrolling.

Screen Rotation and Orientation

Your Galaxy Tab 3 has two screen orientation modes—vertical and horizontal—and it knows which way it's oriented. By default, the Galaxy Tab 3 screen orientation changes when you rotate the unit 90 degrees so the screen is horizontal, or you can rotate it another 90 degrees so the screen is vertical again. Nearly all default apps, such as the Browser, use both orientations. However, there might be times when you don't want the Galaxy Tab 3 to automatically change its screen orientation when you move the unit. For example, you might want to view a web page only in vertical orientation.

You can set the autorotation setting on or off as you see fit.

1. Open the Quick Settings and Notifications screen by holding your finger at the top edge of the screen and then swiping downward.

Hold your finger and swipe downward at the top edge of the screen

2. Tap the Screen rotation button. The bar at the bottom of the button turns gray to signify that orientation lock is on.

3. Tap the Screen rotation button again to turn off orientation lock. The next time you rotate the unit 90 degrees, the screen rotates automatically.

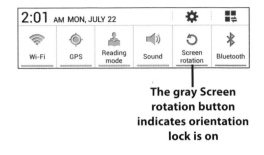

The gray Screen rotation button indicates orientation lock is on

Interacting with Android

Android is a fun operating system to use; it includes a number of common elements, including sliders and switches, as well as the keyboard that you can use to enter and edit text in your Galaxy Tab 3.

Sliders

A slider is a button that requires a bit of effort for you to activate. Android uses sliders to prevent you from doing something that can lead to unintended consequences. For example, if you open the Quick Settings and Notifications screen, you see the Brightness slider so you can adjust the brightness of the screen.

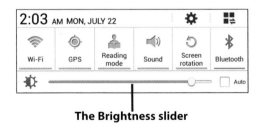

The Brightness slider

Settings Menus

When you tap the Menu touch button below the screen, you may be able to access a settings menu by tapping Settings in the pop-up menu. For example, in the Google Play app, tap the Menu button and then tap Settings in the pop-up menu that appears in the lower-right corner of the screen. Then you see the Settings screen, from which you can change various Google Play options.

The Settings menu option

Button Bar

You might see a button bar in different locations on the screen depending on the app you're using. For example, if you read a message in the Gmail app, you see some icon buttons in the bar at the top of the screen that enable you to perform certain tasks, such as putting the message in the trash.

A button bar at the top of an email message

Tab Areas

Some apps have a Tab area that contains a set of buttons that control the app. The area location and buttons vary depending on the app; if the app doesn't have a Tab area, you won't see one. For example, if you tap the Downloads app you see a Tab area in the center of the screen that enables you to view Internet downloads or any other type of download.

Internet downloads	Other downloads
∧ Yesterday	
ps_logo2.png www.google.com Complete 25.57 KB	07/21/2013

**A tab area that appears when you tap
the Download app in the Apps screen**

Using the Keyboard

The Galaxy Tab 3 doesn't come with a physical keyboard like you find on
many smartphones. Instead, you type in the text with something that looks
similar to a computer keyboard. The keyboard appears at the bottom of the
screen automatically when you want to enter text.

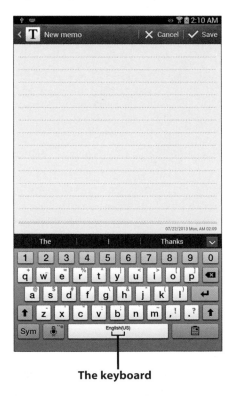

The keyboard

You can type the letter by tapping the letter key. For example, if you tap the letter *a* on the keyboard, the lowercase letter *a* appears on the screen.

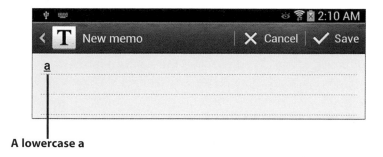

A lowercase a

HOW DO I CAPITALIZE A LETTER?

>>>Go Further

There are two ways you can capitalize a letter:

- Tap one of the two Shift keys and then tap the letter you want to capitalize. Notice that after you tap the Shift key that all the keys on the keyboard become capitalized.

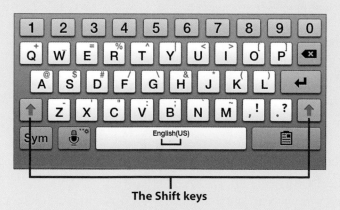

The Shift keys

- You can capitalize more than one letter by tapping the Shift key twice. The Shift key turns blue; this denotes that the Shift key is locked. You can unlock the Shift key by tapping the key again. You know the Shift key is unlocked not only because the white light on the Shift key is off, but also because all the letter keys on the keyboard are back to lowercase.

Using Special Keyboards and Characters

It's not easy typing on a screen that's only 8" wide (or even 10"), especially with an onscreen keyboard, but Android has a trick to make it a bit easier to add information.

You can't access special characters from the standard Tab keyboard, but you can access those special character keys by tapping the Sym key to see a variety of symbols.

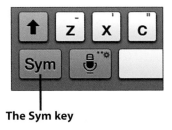

The Sym key

If the symbol you need isn't on the keyboard that displays, then you can access an extended symbols keyboard by tapping the 1/2 key on the numbers and symbols keyboard. After you tap this key, the key label changes to 2/2, which signifies that you are on the second of two extended keyboards. When you're on the second extended keyboard, you can return to the numbers and symbols keyboard by tapping the 2/2 key.

The 1/2 key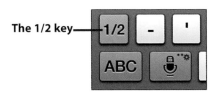

My Keyboard Doesn't Look the Same!

Your keyboard options might change somewhat depending on the app you're in. For example, if you're typing an email message in the Gmail app, you see the @ key to the left of the spacebar because that's a key that you use often when typing an email address.

If you hold down a key on the keyboard, the letter appears, and if there are any related characters, such as a letter with an umlaut (such as ü), you see a character window above the letter key. Hold and drag your finger to the character you want to insert and then release your finger. One of the special character options is the character that's visible in the upper-right corner of the letter's key on the regular keyboard. For example, the left caret symbol (<) is in the upper-right corner of the u key. When you open the u character's pop-up window, the left caret symbol is one of the available options.

A button list of special characters

What Does the Clipboard Key Do?

To the right of the spacebar you see a key that has a clipboard on it. When you tap the key the Clipboard area appears and shows you the eight most recent text and images you have in the Clipboard. Each text snippet and image appears in its own box. Edit or delete the snippet by tapping the Edit button or save the snippet to a file by tapping the Save button. When you're finished, tap the down arrow button to close the Clipboard area and return to the keyboard.

Copy and Paste Data

Android makes it pretty easy to copy and paste text from one app to another. In this example, you learn to copy a term from the Browser app and paste it into the Search app so you can search for the term not only on the Web but also throughout the Galaxy Tab 3.

1. Tap Internet on the Home screen.

2. This example starts on the Google website. Type a search term into the Google search box.

3. Hold down your finger on the search box for a couple of seconds and then release your finger. The search term is highlighted and bracket bars appear below and on each side of the term.

4. Tap Copy in the Edit Text pop-up menu that appears above the selected text.

5. Tap the X at the right side of the Search box to clear the contents of the box.

6. Hold down your finger on the Google box until the Edit Text pop-up menu appears below the Search box and then release your finger.

7. Tap Paste in the Edit Text pop-up menu to insert the copied text.

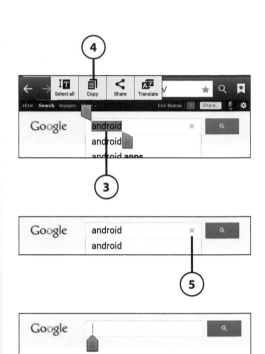

Learn how to get details about the Galaxy Tab 3

Learn how to set up your network

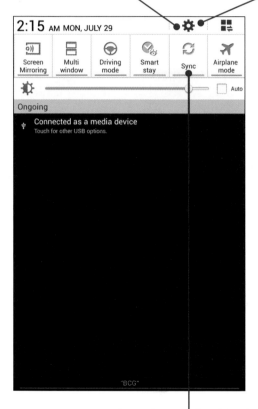

2:15 AM MON, JULY 29

Screen Mirroring | Multi window | Driving mode | Smart stay | Sync | Airplane mode

Auto

Ongoing

Connected as a media device
Touch for other USB options.

"BCG"

Learn about synchronizing the Galaxy Tab 3 with other computers

In this chapter, you discover more about your Galaxy Tab 3 and how to connect it with other computers and networks, including:

→ Getting details about the Galaxy Tab 3

→ Setting up your network

→ Syncing the Galaxy Tab 3

Setting Up the Galaxy Tab 3

You can easily find information about the Galaxy Tab 3 so you can make changes as needed. When you finish making general changes to the Galaxy Tab 3, it's time to set up the network so your Galaxy Tab 3 can connect with the Internet. Finally, you find out how to synchronize your Galaxy Tab 3 with other devices, such as your desktop or laptop PC.

Getting Details About the Galaxy Tab 3

If you want to get information about the features in your Galaxy Tab 3 from one place, you can use the About Device section within the Settings app.

1. Open the Quick Settings and Notifications screen by tapping and holding your finger on the top edge of the screen and swiping your finger down.

2. Tap the Settings icon.

3. Scroll down the Settings list and then tap About Device.

4. See the model number for your Galaxy Tab 3.

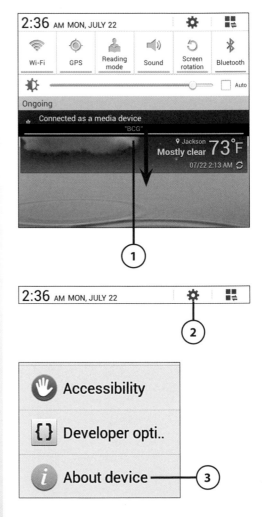

5. See the Android and Kernel versions.

6. Scroll down (if necessary) to see the build number for your Galaxy Tab 3.

7. Scroll back up and tap Status.

8. View the status of your Galaxy Tab 3, including battery status and battery charge level, IP address, your Wi-Fi MAC address, Bluetooth address, and the current up time (that is, how long your Galaxy Tab 3 has been on continuously).

9. Tap the Back touch button.

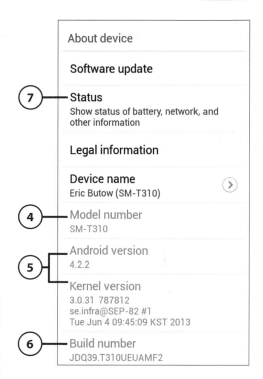

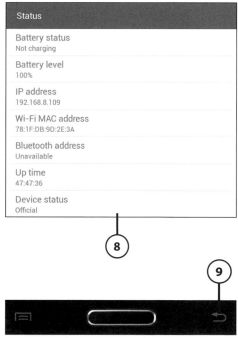

10. Tap Legal Information to view a
menu that shows Galaxy Tab 3
legal information, privacy information, and license settings.

Setting Up Your Network

Now that you're familiar with the details about your Galaxy Tab 3 and accessing the Settings app, you need to use the Settings app to do one very important setup task: connect your Galaxy Tab 3 to the Internet. Depending on
the phone carrier you use, you can connect with the Internet through a Wi-Fi
connection. You also can connect to other devices and networks using a
Bluetooth connection or through a Virtual Private Network (VPN).

I Don't Have a Wireless Network...What Do I Do?

If you don't have a Wi-Fi network but you do have a high-speed Internet connection through a telephone (DSL) or cable (broadband) provider, you have several
options. First, call your provider and ask for a new network modem that enables
wireless connections. Second, ask how much the modem costs—some providers might give you a free upgrade.

Another option is to keep your current box and add a wireless base station of
your own, such as ones offered by Apple and Microsoft.

Set Up Wi-Fi

1. On the Home screen, tap Settings.

2. Tap Wi-Fi if Wi-Fi is not selected
already.

3. If Wi-Fi is turned off, you see a
slider button within the Wi-Fi
entry in the settings list. Turn
Wi-Fi on by sliding the button to
the right.

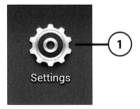

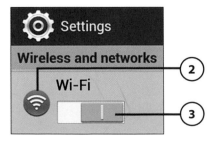

4. Tap Add Wi-Fi Network in the list of Wi-Fi devices on the right side of the screen. You might need to scroll down the list of Wi-Fi devices to view the Add Wi-Fi Network entry in the list.

5. Type the network SSID.

6. Tap the Security field to set the security level.

7. Select the security level; the default is None.

8. Tap Connect.

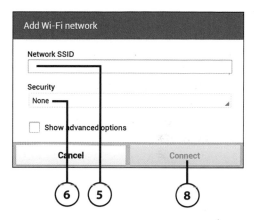

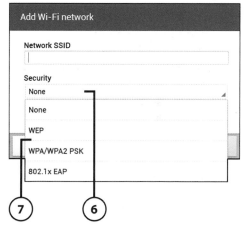

It's Not All Good

BE SECURE FIRST!

Your wireless network equipment should have security enabled. You know that security is enabled on the Wi-Fi network when you view the Wi-Fi Settings screen and see a padlock next to the Wi-Fi network in the list. When you select the Wi-Fi network for the first time, you should be asked to supply a password.

If you don't require a password, strongly consider adding one because unsecured networks send unencrypted (plain text) data—such as passwords and credit card numbers—through the air. Anyone else who has a Wi-Fi connection can tap in to your unsecured network and see what you're doing online. If you need more information, consult your network equipment documentation and/or manufacturer's website.

>>>Go Further

DISABLE WIRELESS CONNECTIONS ON A PLANE

When you're flying, the flight attendants always remind you to turn off your wireless devices during takeoffs and landings. You can quickly disable your wireless connections until you get to a safe flying altitude and the pilot gives you permission to turn on wireless devices again. Here's how:

1. Tap Settings on the Home screen.

2. Tap More Settings.

3. Tap Airplane Mode.

The check box contains a green checkmark to inform you that wireless connections are disabled. Tap Airplane Mode again to enable wireless connections.

Set Up Bluetooth

1. Tap Settings on the Home screen.

2. Tap Bluetooth.

3. Turn on Bluetooth by sliding the Bluetooth slider button to the right.

4. Tap the check box to the right of the device name if you want your Galaxy Tab 3 to be discovered by other computers and/or devices that you can connect to using a Bluetooth connection. The Galaxy Tab 3 scans for available devices.

5. If the Galaxy Tab 3 doesn't find one, turn on the Bluetooth device to which you want to connect and then tap Scan in the Settings toolbar.

6. Tap a found device to connect with that device. You can rescan for devices by tapping Scan.

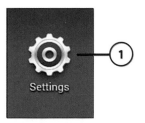

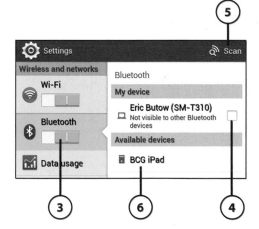

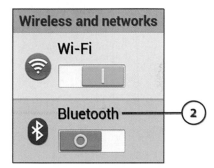

Set Up a VPN

A VPN enables users in a public network (such as the Internet) to transfer private data by making it appear to the users that they're in a private network of their own. For example, you can set up a VPN between yourself and your boss at the office so you can securely send private company data.

1. Tap Settings on the Home screen.

2. Tap More Settings.

3. Tap VPN. If your Tab 3 is not protected by a password or similar encryption method, you see a dialog box that tells you to set a screen unlock pattern, PIN, or password. Open the Screen Unlock Settings screen and add a password, pattern, or PIN by tapping OK. Refer to Chapter 4, "Customizing Jelly Bean to Your Liking," for more information about how to add a password, pattern, and PIN.

4. Tap Add in the Settings menu bar.

5. Enter the VPN information including the VPN name, type, and server address.

6. Tap Save.

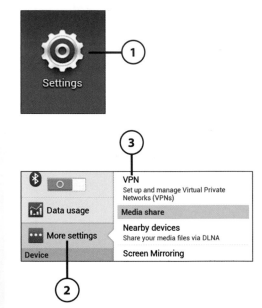

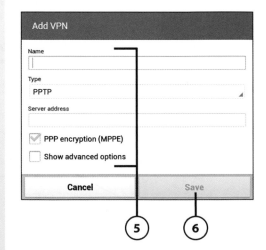

7. Tap the VPN name in the list.

8. Type the VPN username in the Username field and the password in the Password field.

9. Tap Connect.

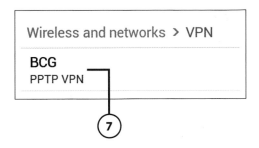

How to Disconnect from Your VPN

You can begin the VPN disconnection process by opening the Quick Settings and Notifications screen that is covered earlier in this chapter. On the screen, a notification in the list informs you that you're connected to the VPN. Disconnect from the VPN by tapping the notification in the list and then tapping Disconnect.

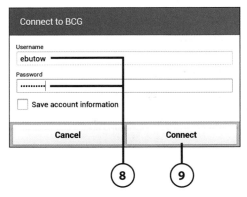

Syncing the Galaxy Tab 3

Synchronizing your Galaxy Tab 3 with your desktop or laptop computer has a number of advantages.

The Galaxy Tab 3 stores a backup of its contents on your desktop or laptop every time you sync both devices, so if you lose your data on the Galaxy Tab 3—or lose the Galaxy Tab 3 itself—you can restore the data from the backed up copies on your computer. What's more, if you have music, photos, or video on your computer, you can choose and copy a selection of those files onto your Galaxy Tab 3.

Android prefers Windows when it comes to syncing, and that's no surprise considering that Windows is the leading operating system for desktop PCs by far. This chapter describes how to sync music with the Galaxy Tab 3 in Windows. Later chapters cover how to sync other types of data, such as contacts.

Can I Sync Between the Galaxy Tab 3 and the Mac OS?

Syncing music from iTunes on the Mac OS to the Galaxy Tab 3 requires that you download additional software for your Mac. JRTStudio (www.jrtstudio.com) produces iSyncr, a utility that syncs what you have in iTunes with Android devices. As of this writing, the main app costs $3.99 in the Google Play Store, and that app enables you to sync your Tab 3 with iTunes on your Mac by connecting your Tab 3 to your Mac using the Tab 3 cable.

It's easy to sync music files in Windows Media Player, the default music and multimedia player in Windows, to any model of the Galaxy Tab 3.

1. Connect the Galaxy Tab 3 to your computer with the USB cable that came with your Galaxy Tab 3, if you haven't done so already. After a short while, your Windows PC informs you that it has installed the drivers to connect with your Galaxy Tab 3.

2. Launch Windows Media Player on your Windows PC. On the right side of the window the Galaxy Tab 3 sync area appears.

3. Click the folder in the tree that contains the files you want to sync with the Galaxy Tab 3.

4. Select the file(s) you want to move and then click and drag the files to the sync area.

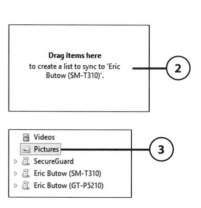

5. Click Start Sync.

6. After Windows Media Player syncs with your Galaxy Tab 3, open the app associated with the type of file(s) you synced on the Galaxy Tab 3. For example, if you synced image files, open the Gallery app; the Pictures tile shows one of the images you synced. You find out how to use the Gallery app in Chapter 13, "Capturing and Managing Photos."

SYNC WITH ITUNES

>>>Go Further

It's also easy to sync your Galaxy Tab 3 with iTunes. You can mount the USB drive on the Galaxy Tab 3; then, on your computer, you can drag songs from iTunes and drop them to that drive. You can also sync to iTunes wirelessly by downloading the TuneSync app from the Android Market or from Fireleap Software (www.tunesync.com) for only $5.99. Fireleap also makes a free Lite version if you want to check it out first, but this version limits playlists to 20 songs.

Learn how to set
parental restrictions

Learn how to password-protect your Galaxy Tab 3

Learn about modifying screen wallpaper

Learn about setting alert sounds

Learn how to change keyboard settings

Your Galaxy Tab 3 isn't just a static system that forces you to work with it. It's malleable so you can change many attributes of the system to work the way you prefer. The topics in this chapter include the following:

→ Password-protecting the Galaxy Tab 3

→ Setting parental restrictions

→ Changing the date and time

→ Modifying your wallpaper

→ Setting alert sounds

→ Changing keyboard settings

Customizing Android to Your Liking

Password-Protecting the Galaxy Tab 3

One of the first things you should do when you set up your Galaxy Tab 3 is password-protect it so that unauthorized persons can't use it or gain access to the data stored on it.

1. Tap Settings on the Home screen.

2. Scroll down the Settings list and then tap Security.

3. Tap Encrypt Device.

4. Tap Set Screen Lock Type.

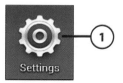

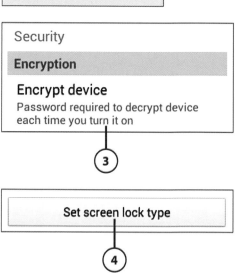

5. Tap Password.

6. Type your password in the Select Password screen. The password must be at least four characters. A couple of seconds after you tap the letter, the letter turns into a dot to hide what you just entered. Tap Continue.

7. Retype the password in the Confirm Password screen and then tap OK.

The next time you log in to your Galaxy Tab 3, you are prompted to type in your password in the password box. If the keyboard doesn't appear on the screen right away, open the keyboard by tapping on the Enter Password box.

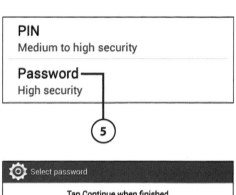

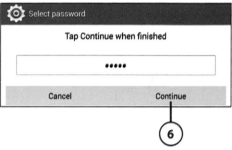

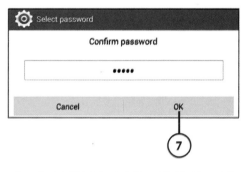

Type your password in the Enter Password box

>>>Go Further

WHAT IF I CAN'T REMEMBER MY PASSWORD?

If you can't remember your password, your only recourse is to reset your Galaxy Tab 3 so that you wipe all the data from it and start from scratch. Unfortunately, this means that all your other data is wiped off the unit as well. Use the following steps to reset your Tab.

1. Turn your Galaxy Tab 3 off if it isn't already. You might need to remove the battery to turn off the unit.

2. Press and hold the Power and Volume Up buttons.

3. When you see the Samsung Galaxy Tab 3 logo, release the Power button but continue to hold the Volume Up button.

4. When the recovery screen appears, tap the Volume Down button until wipe data/factory reset is highlighted.

5. Press the Power button.

6. In the next screen, press the Volume Down button until Yes—Delete All User Data is highlighted.

7. Press the Power button.

8. After the Galaxy Tab 3 wipes the system data, press the Power button to reboot the system.

Changing Your Password

It's a good idea to change your password regularly so you have the peace of mind of knowing that you're keeping one step ahead of potential thieves.

1. Tap Settings on the Home Screen.

2. Tap Lock Screen.

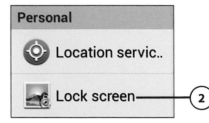

3. Tap Screen Lock.

4. Type your password in the Confirm Password screen and then tap Continue.

5. Tap Password.

6. Type your password in the Select Password screen. The password must be at least four characters. A couple of seconds after you tap the letter, the letter turns into a dot to hide what you just entered. Tap Continue.

7. Retype the password in the Confirm Password screen and then tap OK. The next time you log in to your Galaxy Tab 3 you are prompted to type in your new password.

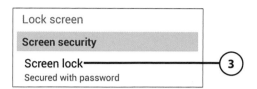

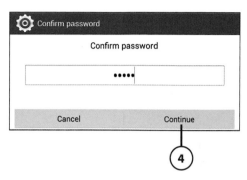

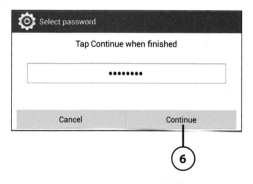

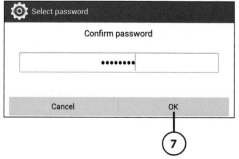

>>>Go Further

ENTER A PATTERN OR NUMERIC PIN

The Galaxy Tab 3 gives you one of three options for password-protecting your unit: a text password, a numeric PIN (such as the one you use for an ATM card), or a pattern that you can draw on the screen. In the Screen Unlock Settings screen, tap Pattern or PIN to create a new pattern or numeric PIN, respectively. Then follow the step-by-step instructions to set the PIN.

Setting Parental Restrictions

Android 4.2.2 doesn't include parental restriction settings for specific applications aside from the pattern, PIN, or text password used for full access to the Galaxy Tab 3.

However, you can find parental control apps in the Google Play Store. Search for "parental control" or "parental controls," read the user reviews for each app, and then decide whether you want to download an app to see if it works for you.

Change Your Content Filter Settings in the Google Play Store

You can determine what types of apps are shown to anyone who uses your Galaxy Tab 3 by setting the content filtering settings within the Google Play Store. You can show all apps or you can show apps by maturity level. You find out more about how to do this in Chapter 16, "Finding and Managing Apps."

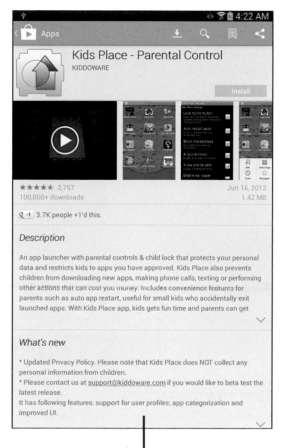

**An example of a parental control
app in the Google Play Store**

Changing the Date and Time

You can set the date and time for your Galaxy Tab 3, change the time zone, change the date format, and display whether you want to display the time as standard 12-hour or 24-hour (military) time.

1. Tap Settings on the Home screen.

2. Scroll down the Settings list and then tap Date and Time.

3. Tap Set Date.

4. Tap the month, date, or year to change the date information. You can also tap the up and down arrow buttons above and below the month, date, or year to move the information up or down one month, one date, or one year, respectively.

5. Tap Set.

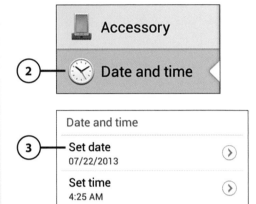

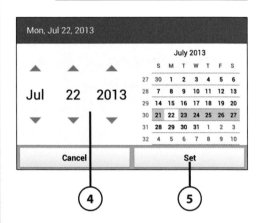

6. Tap Set Time.

7. Tap the hour and/or minute to change the time information. You can also tap the up or down arrow buttons above and below the hour or minute to move the hour or minute by one hour or one minute, respectively.

8. Tap the AM or PM arrows to change the time of day between AM and PM.

9. Tap Set.

10. Tap Use 24-hour Format to change the format to 24-hour time. Note that the time on the Notification bar reflects the change. You can return to 12-hour time by tapping Use 24-hour Format again.

11. Tap Select Date Format.

12. Tap one of the three format options to change the date format. If you don't want to change the date format, tap Cancel.

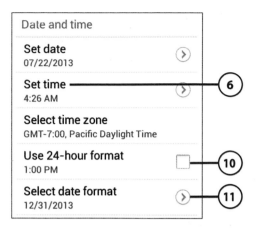

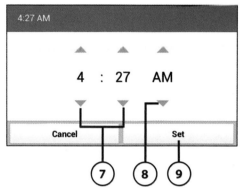

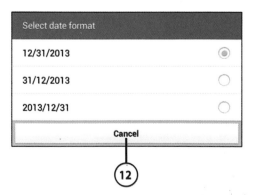

Modifying Your Wallpaper

The standard wallpaper appears behind both the lock screen and the Home screen. Android makes it easy for you to change the wallpaper to whatever you want.

1. Tap the Menu touch button while you're on the Home screen.

2. Tap Set Wallpaper.

3. Tap Home Screen, Lock Screen, or Home and Lock Screens depending on where you want to display your wallpaper. This example uses the Home and Lock Screens option.

4. Select where you want to get the wallpaper by tapping Gallery, Live Wallpapers, or Wallpapers.

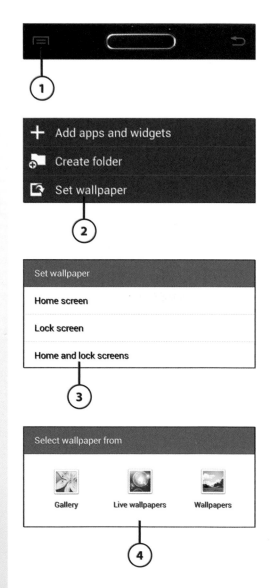

5. Scroll through the thumbnail images of wallpapers. The current thumbnail image appears above the Set Wallpaper button and a larger version of the image appears above the thumbnail images.

6. When you find wallpaper you want, tap Set Wallpaper. The new wallpaper appears on your Home and lock screens.

The Difference Between Wallpaper and Live Wallpaper

So what makes wallpaper "live" on the Galaxy Tab 3? The difference is animation. For example, if you select the Bubbles live wallpaper then you see the bubbles move around and fade in and out in the background screen. Regular wallpaper doesn't have any animated features.

Setting Alert Sounds

If you want the Galaxy Tab 3 to make noise when you perform different actions, such as when you tap something on the screen, you can change the alert sounds. If you prefer, you can turn them off entirely.

1. Tap Settings on the Home screen.

2. Tap Sound.

The One Guaranteed Solution for Silence

The Galaxy Tab 3 makes certain noises by default. For example, the unit plays tones when you use the dial pad on the phone.

If you really want to ensure that the unit doesn't make any noise, the one foolproof solution is to turn off the Galaxy Tab 3 unit.

3. Tap Volume.

4. Change the volume for music, video, games, and other media, notifications, and system sounds by dragging the appropriate slider bar to the left (lower volume) or right (higher volume).

5. Tap OK.

6. Tap Notifications.

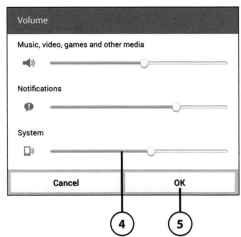

7. Set the notification ringtone from the menu. This ringtone plays whenever you receive a notification. If you don't want a ringtone, scroll to the top of the list and tap Silent.

8. Tap OK.

9. Tap Touch Sounds to turn off the feature that plays a sound when you make a screen selection. Turn on this feature again by tapping Touch Sounds.

10. Tap Screen Lock Sound to stop playing sounds when you lock and unlock the screen. Turn on this feature again by tapping Screen Lock Sound.

11. Tap Adapt Sound to open the Adapt Sound screen and fine tune the sound output of your earphones. You need to connect your earphones to the headphones/ microphone jack on your Galaxy Tab 3 to use Adapt Sound.

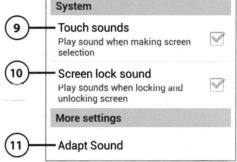

Changing Keyboard and Voice Settings

The Galaxy Tab 3 7" and 8" come with the Samsung keyboard only. The Galaxy Tab 3 10" gives you two input options: the Samsung keyboard and the Swype keyboard.

The examples in this book use keyboard settings for the Samsung keyboard, which is the default keyboard the Galaxy Tab 3 uses when you type text, as well as built-in keyboard settings that apply to all keyboards.

1. Tap Settings on the Home screen.

2. Scroll down the Settings list and then tap Language and Input.

3. Because the default is the Samsung keyboard, open the Samsung Keyboard Settings screen by tapping the settings icon to the right of Samsung Keyboard.

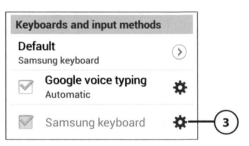

4. Tap Input Languages if you want to change the default keyboard input language.

5. Slide the Predictive Text slider to off (the slider turns from a green bar with an I to a gray bar with a O) if you don't want the Galaxy Tab 3 to guess what you're typing and provide suggestions for words so you don't have to keep typing all the time. This is similar to the auto-complete feature in word processors.

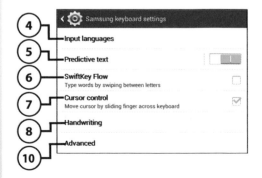

6. Tap SwiftKey Flow to enter text by sliding the finger across the keyboard to type words. After you release your finger, the word that the Galaxy Tab 3 thinks you're trying to type appears on the screen.

7. By default, you can move a cursor on the screen by sliding your finger across the keyboard. You can turn this feature off and move the cursor only with the keyboard by tapping Cursor Control. Turn the feature back on by tapping Cursor Control.

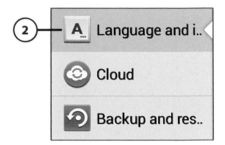

8. If you purchased a stylus with your Galaxy Tab 3 then you can use the built-in Handwriting feature to write words on the screen and use the stylus for actions such

as deleting a word. Tap Handwriting to open the Handwriting
screen and change the recogni-
tion type, the time it takes the
Galaxy Tab 3 to recognize that
you're writing something, the pen
thickness, and the pen color.

9. Return to the Samsung Keyboard
Settings screen by tapping the
left arrow at the left side of the
menu bar at the top of the screen.

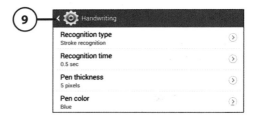

10. Tap Advanced to open the
Advanced screen and change
more settings.

11. Tap Auto Capitalization to turn
off auto-capitalization for words.
By default, the Galaxy Tab 3
auto-capitalizes the first word in
a sentence. If the Galaxy Tab 3
recognizes a punctuation mark
and a space, the next letter is
capitalized automatically unless
you tap the Shift key to turn it off.
(There are exceptions to this rule,
such as when you type in the To
box when you compose a new
email message.) You can turn the
feature back on by tapping Auto
Capitalization.

12. Tap Auto Spacing to turn off the
automatic insertion of a space
between words. By default, the
Galaxy Tab 3 monitors your words
as you type and automatically
inserts a space between words.
Turn the feature back on by tapping Auto Spacing.

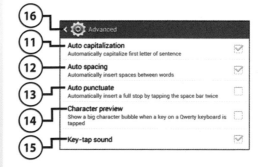

13. Tap Auto Punctuate to automatically insert a full stop after a word
by double-tapping the space bar.

14. Tap Character Preview to display the character you're typing on the keyboard in a box above the key for about a second after you tap the key.

15. Tap Key-Tap Sound to have the Galaxy Tab 3 make no sound each time you press a key. Turn on the key-tap sound feature by tapping Key-Tap Sound.

16. Return to the Samsung Keyboard Settings screen by tapping the arrow at the left side of the menu bar at the top of the screen.

17. Tap Help to view quick and easy tutorials about how to use the keyboard in the Help screen.

18. If you change your mind after you make settings and decide you want the default settings instead, tap Reset Settings.

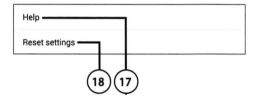

Modifying More Settings

There are too many settings in Android to cover in this book, but here are some of the more important settings that you should know about.

1. Tap Settings on the Home screen.

2. Scroll down the Settings list if necessary and then tap Display.

3. Set the brightness level by tapping Brightness and then move the slider in the Brightness window to change the brightness level.

4. When you finish changing the brightness level, tap OK.

5. Tap Screen Timeout.

6. Select the period of inactivity after which the screen times out and goes dark. The default is one minute. If you don't want to change the time interval, tap Cancel.

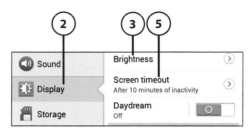

Powering Up Your Screen

After the screen goes dark, you can easily start it again by tapping the screen or pressing the Power button. If your Galaxy Tab 3 is password-protected (or PIN or pattern-protected), you must type your password (or PIN or pattern) to start using the Galaxy Tab 3 again.

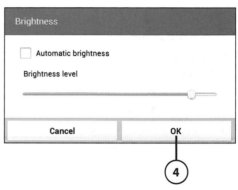

7. Set the font style and size by tapping Font Style and Font Size, respectively, in the Font area. When you select the font style you can choose from the built-in fonts or you can search for, purchase, and download fonts from the Google Play Store.

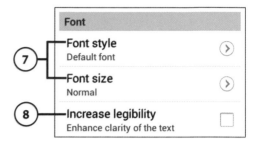

8. If you find that the text isn't legible enough, you can enhance clarity of the text by tapping Increase Legibility.

9. Tap OK in the Enable Increase Legibility window, which tells you what the Increase Legibility setting will do.

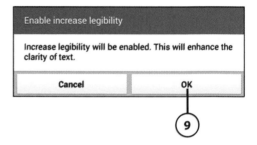

10. The screen goes blank with the exception of the Status Bar at the top of the page. After a second or two, the Home screen displays with enhanced text clarity to see if you like it. You can turn off the increased text legibility by opening the Settings screen again, tapping Display in the Settings list, and then tapping Increase Legibility.

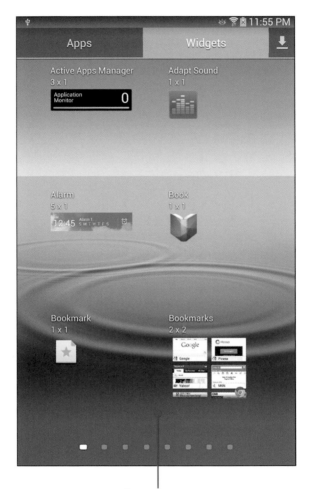

Learn how to
browse widgets
and add a widget to
your Home screen

Widgets are a truly valuable aspect of the
Android platform. A widget is a small, portable
piece of code that you can interact with like
a miniature application. Your Galaxy Tab 3 has
quite a few widgets for you to choose from that
can make your Tab experience even more convenient. This chapter covers the following:

5

→ Accessing the Widgets screen
→ Taking a tour of available widgets
→ Adding a widget to a Home screen
→ Creating a new Home screen
→ Removing a widget

Adding Widgets to Your Home Screens

Accessing the Widgets Screen

You can find widgets on the Widgets screen, where 48 preinstalled
widgets for different tasks are listed. Tapping a widget can provide
you a variety of information such as stock market news or the
weather. (By default, you have a weather widget on your Home
screen.) A widget can also act as a world clock or initiate functionality from a parent app, such as Maps, when you tap it. Though
you can apply widgets to a Home screen, some widgets must be
configured.

1. Tap Apps on the Home screen.

2. Tap Widgets.

3. Scroll left and right through the pages of widgets. The number of pages depends on the Galaxy Tab 3 model you have and your screen orientation.

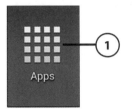

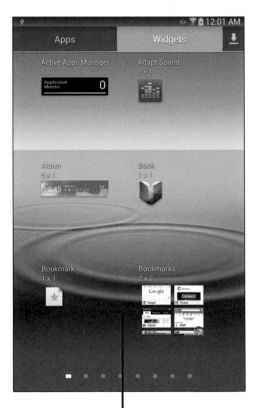

Widgets

Taking a Tour of Available Widgets

Each widget on the page contains the name of the widget, the size of the widget (width by height in number of grid spaces), and a thumbnail-sized graphic that shows you how the widget will appear on the Home screen. Note that if you want to see how big a 1 × 1 icon is, the Books widget icon that belongs with step 4 in the next task is sized at 1 grid space wide by 1 grid space high.

All the widgets listed in this section are available on all Galaxy Tab 3 models. On the Galaxy Tab 3 8", which is used for the screenshots in this section (and throughout most of this book), six widgets appear on each of the eight pages within the Widgets screen.

Examine the Page 1 Widgets

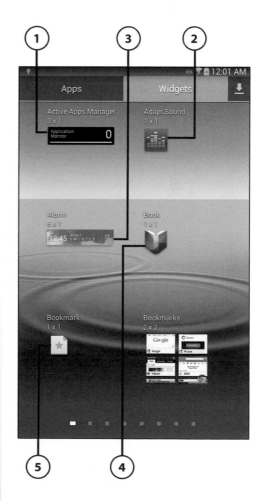

1. **Active Apps Manager:** Opens the Task Manager screen so you can see all active applications, view downloaded apps, and manage memory and storage.

2. **Adapt Sound:** Opens the Adapt Sound app so you can test and fine-tune the sound level of the earphones you plug into the Galaxy Tab 3.

3. **Alarm:** Enables you to create an alarm in the Alarm app and display the alarm on the Home screen. You find out more about setting an alarm using the widget in Chapter 8, "Using Galaxy Tab 3 Widgets."

4. **Book:** Opens the Google Play Books app and shows you a list of all books you've downloaded.

5. **Bookmark:** Opens the Internet app so you can select a book-marked website on the Choose a

Bookmark screen. After you select the bookmark in the appropriate folder, the bookmarked website appears as an icon on the Home screen. View the website in the Internet app by tapping on the bookmark icon.

6. **Bookmarks:** Places a larger widget on the screen so you can select a bookmark from directly within the widget. Swipe up and down within the widget to view folders and then tap a folder name; after you find the bookmark you want within the folder you tap it. The website appears in the Internet or Chrome app. When you return to the Home screen, you can navigate to and open a bookmark from within the widget.

Choosing Your Browser

After you open a bookmark from the Bookmark or Bookmarks widget, you may see the Complete Action Using window so you can choose between opening the website in the Internet app or in the Google Chrome app. Tap the icon that signifies the app you want to use (Internet or Chrome) and then tap the Always button to open websites using that app in the future or the Just Once button to open the website using your selected app that one time. If you tap the Just Once button then the next time you open the bookmark you will have to choose the browser app in the Complete Action Using window again.

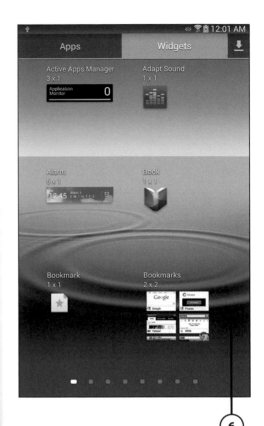

6

Examine the Page 2 Widgets

1. **Briefing:** Displays your upcoming events and top news stories from Yahoo! News so you can get your information and news stories at a glance from your Home screen.

2. **Calendar:** Displays a small calendar for the current day that shows a brief list of your appointments that day.

3. **Clock (Digital):** Opens a digital clock that shows the current time and date.

4. **Clock (Modern):** Shows a modern-looking analog clock that displays the current time.

5. **Contact:** Opens the Contacts window app so you can select the contact to display in the widget. After you select the contact, the picture of the contact appears on the Home screen. Tap the contact picture to open the contact window.

6. **Directions & Navigation:** Opens the Directions & Navigation app so you can enter your destination address from your current location to get turn-by-turn directions.

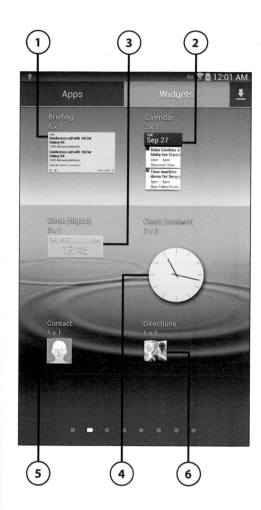

Examine the Page 3 Widgets

1. **Dropbox Folder:** Places a Dropbox folder link on your Home screen. You have to open the Dropbox app and log in before you can add this widget. After you log in, you can select the folder to which you want to link in the Create Shortcut window.

2. **Dual Clock (Analog):** Shows times in two separate cities as analog clocks.

3. **Dual Clock (Digital):** Shows times in two different cities as digital clocks. The current date appears below the time for each city.

4. **Email:** Shows the most recent five email messages that are aggregated from all your inboxes. After you add the app to a Home screen, set up the Samsung Email widget app by tapping the widget.

5. **Flipboard (Medium):** Enables you to access your Flipboard social aggregation website data when you tap the widget. This widget takes up half the Home screen, which explains the Medium designation. The full screen widget appears by default on a Home screen. Read Chapter 8 for more information about the Flipboard widget.

6. **Flipboard (Small):** Places a small version of the Flipboard widget on the Home screen so you can open the Flipboard app by tapping the widget.

Examine the Page 4 Widgets

1. **Game Hub:** Opens the Game Hub app. This widget appears on one of the Home screens by default.

2. **Gmail:** Shows the most recent three messages you received in your Gmail inbox. When you add the app to a Home screen, the Choose Folder window appears so you can select the folder that contains messages you want to read. After you tap the folder name, the most recent messages within that folder appear on the Home screen.

3. **Gmail Label:** Adds a Gmail Label, which acts as a shortcut that opens a Gmail folder. When you add the app to your Home screen, the Choose Folder window appears and asks you to select a Gmail folder. The Name Label Shortcut window appears so you can accept the folder name as the shortcut name or type a new name. Tap Done in the window to view the Gmail Label widget on the Home screen.

4. **Google Now:** Displays basic Google Now app information such as a brief weather forecast and information about your next appointment. Open the Google Now app and get more information by tapping on the widget on the Home screen.

5. **Google Play Books:** Opens the most recent book you read in the Google Play Books app. The cover

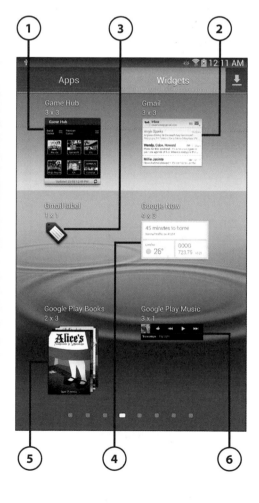

of the most recent book you read appears in the widget icon.

6. **Google Play Music:** Plays the next song in your Google Play Music playlist when you tap the Play button in the Google Play Music widget. Open the Play Music app by tapping the thumbnail-sized image on the left side of the widget.

Examine the Page 5 Widgets

1. **Google Search:** Adds a transparent Google Search box to the home page; this widget box appears on the main Home screen by default.

2. **Google Search (smaller version):** Adds a smaller, white Google Search box to the Home screen.

3. **Google+ Posts:** Displays your latest Google+ posts within the widget. Open the Google+ app and view the most recent post by tapping the widget in the Home screen.

4. **Memo:** Enables you to write a new memo that will be easily accessible on your Home screen. When you add the memo to the Home screen, the Memo window displays so you can type your memo. After you save the memo, the memo icon appears on the Home screen so you can open it quickly.

5. **Music Hub:** Shows the latest music within several categories in the Music Hub app. Tap the

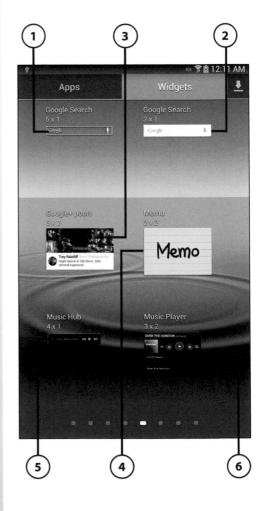

widget to open the Music Hub app and shop for songs.

6. Music Player: Displays the Samsung Music Player app that enables you to play songs stored on your Galaxy Tab 2 within the widget itself. For example, you can tap the Play button within the widget to play the song at the top of the list.

Examine the Page 6 Widgets

1. Music Playlist: Opens the Play Music app window so you can select a playlist that contains the songs you like. After you tap the playlist you want, the playlist icon and name appear on the Home screen. Tap the playlist icon to start playing songs within that playlist.

2. Picture Frame: Displays one or more of your selected pictures stored on your Tab 2 within an area on the Home screen.

3. Play—My Library: Shows contents of one or all of the Google Play apps. For example, the My Books library shows covers of the most recent books you read. Read the book in the Play Books app by tapping the book cover.

4. Play Recommendations: Displays Google Play Store recommendations in one category (for example, Apps) or in all categories. View the recommended app or multimedia file by tapping the widget.

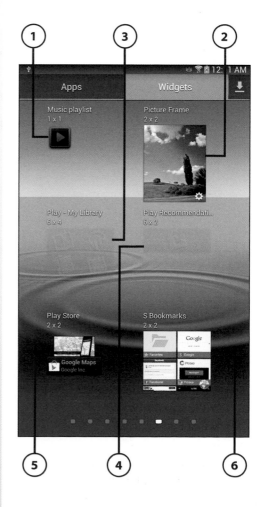

5. Play Store: Displays a slideshow of new and interesting apps in the Google Play Store. Open the Play Store app by tapping the widget.

6. S Bookmarks: Displays your website bookmark folders. Open the list of bookmarks by tapping the bookmark folder and then tap on the bookmark tile to open the website in the Browser app.

Examine the Page 7 Widgets

1. S Planner (Mini Today): Displays a list of all your events for the day stored in the S Planner app. Tap the arrows to the left and right of the date to move backward or forward one day, respectively. You can also tap the widget to add a new event in the S Planner app screen; you can read more about this in Chapter 8.

2. S Planner (Month): Displays events for the entire month on an entire Home screen. You can also view different months from within the widget and add an event. Read more about how to use this app in Chapter 8.

3. Settings Shortcut: Opens the Settings screen from the Home screen. This shortcut is available on every Home screen by default.

4. Software Update: Opens the Software Update screen from the Home screen.

5. Story Album: Enables you to create digital picture albums of

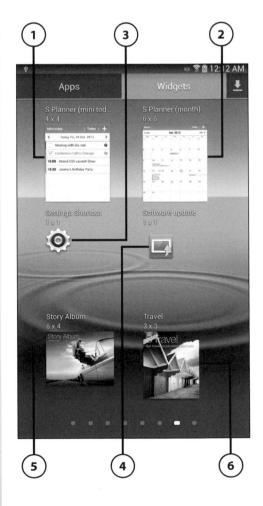

various events to share. You can also publish those albums as hard copy books. Read more about using Story Album in Chapter 8.

6. Travel: This widget displays travel recommendations in case you're looking to get away. Read more about how to use this widget in Chapter 8.

Examine the Page 8 Widgets

1. User Manual: View the user manual within the Internet app by tapping the User Manual widget. After you select the language in which you want to view the manual, you see the manual on the screen so you can view information from learning the basics to troubleshooting your Galaxy Tab 3. You can also search for user manual topics based on one or more keyword(s).

2. Video Player: Places a link to a selected video on the Home screen; the title appears in the widget. Play the video in the Video Player app by tapping on the widget.

3. Weather: Displays the current weather for your location on the Home screen. This widget appears on the main Home screen by default.

4. Yahoo! Finance: Displays your latest stock quotes on your Home screen from Yahoo! Finance. You can get more information within

the Yahoo! Finance app by tapping the widget in the Home screen.

5. Yahoo! News: Shows the top news stories from Yahoo! News on your Home screen. You can read the entire story in the Yahoo! News app by tapping the widget in the Home screen.

6. YouTube: Displays a slideshow of the most recent YouTube videos within various categories such as Most Popular. View the featured video in the slideshow within the YouTube app by tapping the image of the video in the widget.

Adding a Widget to a Home Screen

It's easy to add a widget from the Widgets screen to an existing Home screen or a new one that you create. When you add a Widget to a Home screen you can specify where that widget—either an icon or the widget area—will reside on the Home screen. If you decide that you want to move the widget to a different location on the same or a different Home screen, you can drag the widget to that new location on the current Home screen, another existing Home screen, or a new Home screen that you create.

Some widgets also enable you to change the size of the widget before you place it on your desired Home screen. If the widget you're trying to add to an existing Home screen won't fit on that Home screen then Jelly Bean adds a new Home screen automatically and places the widget on that new Home screen.

Place a Widget on a Home Screen

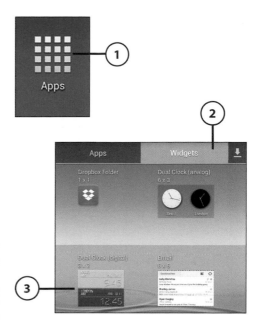

1. Tap Apps on the Home screen.

2. Tap Widgets at the top of the Apps screen.

3. Navigate to the page that contains the Dual Clock (Digital) widget used for this example.

4. Press and hold your finger on the Dual Clock (Digital) widget. The Edit Home screen appears; the Home screen appears in a smaller area of the screen and the widget you're moving appears as an outline on the screen.

5. Move the outline over the Home screen to which you want to add the widget. The Home screens appear as small thumbnail buttons at the bottom of the screen and each button contains different elements as they appear on the Home screen. The Home screen buttons appear in a row of three and the main Home screen (the one that opens when you start your Galaxy Tab 3) appears second from left in the row.

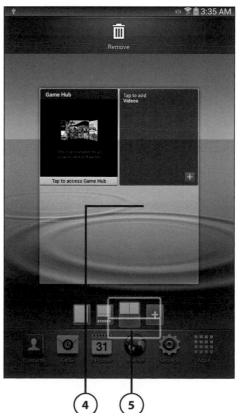

6. Release your finger. The widget appears at the top left of the screen by default. If any other widgets appear on the screen then the Dual Clock (Digital) widget appears to the right of the widget or on the left side of the screen underneath a row of widgets.

7. The Dual Clock (Digital) widget lets you configure the information that it displays. Tap the plus sign to set the city.

8. Swipe down the list of cities and tap one. For example, perhaps a friend has traveled to Rome for the summer and you don't want to call her in the middle of the night. Swipe down the list of cities and then tap Rome.

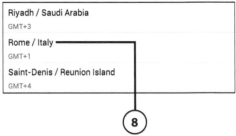

9. Rome is added to the clock, and now you know the current time for the city where your friend is staying.

10. Tap either city to change to a different city. You can search for a city by typing the city name in the Search Cities box.

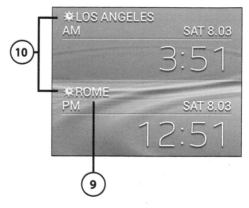

Move a Widget on a Home Screen

You can move a widget to a different location on the same Home screen by tapping and holding the widget within the Home screen. This example shows how to reposition the Dual Clock (Digital) widget.

1. The widget outline appears on a smaller version of the Home screen so you can see where you can move the widget.

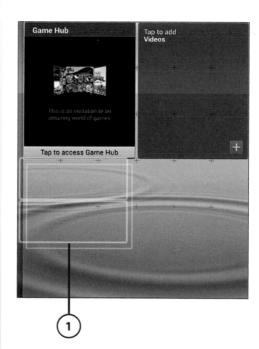

2. Drag the widget to the new location on the Home screen. The Home screen is ordered in a grid format, and + signs within the Home screen denote grid corners. As you move the widget to the new location, a lighter copy of the outline appears below and to the right of your widget outline. This lighter outline copy denotes where your widget will reside on the screen. If there's a widget that already resides in the location you want, the widgets reposition themselves on the screen to accommodate your desired location for the widget.

3. Release your finger. The widget appears in your desired location.

Move the Widget to a Different Home Screen

If you want to move a widget to a different Home screen, drag the widget outline to one of the Home screen thumbnail buttons as described earlier in this chapter. You can also add the widget to a brand new Home screen by dragging the widget outline over the Home screen thumbnail button at the right side of the button row (it has a + in the button). After you add the widget to the Home screen you want, you can open that Home screen and move the widget to your desired location within that Home screen.

Resize a Widget

Some widgets come in a preset size. Others allow you to change the size of the widget when you add it to the Home screen. You can also change the size of an adjustable widget after you add the widget to a Home screen. This example describes how to add the Email widget.

1. Tap Apps on the Home screen.

2. Tap Widgets at the top of the Apps screen.

3. Navigate to the page that contains the Email widget.

4. Press and hold your finger on the Email widget. An overlay of the Home screen that you chose appears and the widget you're moving appears as an outline on the screen.

5. Move the outline over the Home screen to position the widget within the screen. When you're satisfied with the location of the widget on the Home screen, release your finger.

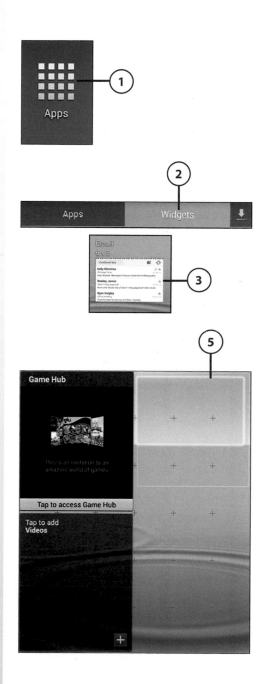

6. The widget appears on the Home screen with an orange box around it. Orange circles, or handles, appear on all four sides of the box.

7. Resize the widget by tapping and holding on one of the handles and then dragging left and right or up and down depending on the handle you're moving. For example, if you drag the bottom handle up and down then you change the height of the widget. If your widget size is too large for the available area on the Home screen then the box and handles turn red to tell you that the widget is too large for the available space.

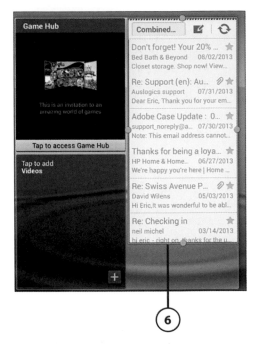

6

7

8. Release your finger. The resized widget appears on the Edit Home screen. If the widget is too large for the area you want, Jelly Bean automatically resizes the widget to fill the available width or height.

9. Tap the Back touch button. Your widget appears on the Home screen at your desired size.

Resize and/or Move the Widget Again

If you decide that you want to resize the widget, tap and hold on the widget. The Edit Home screen appears so you can resize the widget on the Home screen, move the widget around on the Home screen, or move the widget to a different Home screen.

Creating a New Home Screen

A task earlier in this chapter describes how to create a new Home screen when you add a new widget. There are two other ways to create a new Home screen: from within an existing Home screen and in the Home screen menu.

1. Tap and hold your finger on a blank area of the Home screen until the Home Screen window appears. A blank area is an area that isn't occupied by another feature such as a widget or icon.

2. Tap Page in the menu.

3. The new Home page appears on the screen and the selected Home page appears at the right side of the Home page button row.

4. Press the Menu touch button and then tap Edit Page in the menu.

5. Tap the Add Page button in the Edit Page screen.

6. The button for the new Home page appears on the screen. Open the new Home page by tapping the button.

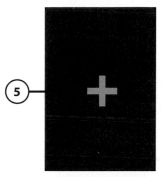

HOW DO I REMOVE A HOME SCREEN?

It's easy to remove a Home screen if you don't want the Home screen and any icons or widgets on that screen. Start by pressing the Menu touch button and then tapping Edit Page in the menu. In the Edit Page screen, tap and hold the button with the Home page you want to delete and then drag the button to the Remove icon at the top of the screen. When the button you're dragging turns red, release your finger. The Home screen button disappears from the Edit Page screen.

If your Home page has icons or widgets in it when you delete it, the Remove Home Screen Page window appears reminding you that the Galaxy Tab 3 will remove the Home screen and all items within it. Delete the Home screen by tapping the OK button.

Removing a Widget

It's easy to remove a widget from a Home page if you decide that you don't want it any longer.

1. Navigate to the Home page that contains the widget you want to remove. Tap and hold on the widget.

2. Within the Edit Home Page screen, drag the outline of the widget to the Remove icon at the top of the screen. When the Remove icon is highlighted in red, release your finger.

3. The Home screen appears and no longer contains the widget you removed.

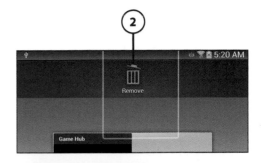

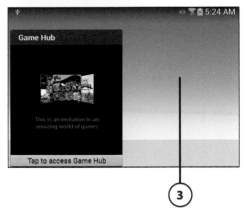

Learn how to browse the Web
and view websites using the
built-in Internet app

The Galaxy Tab 3 is a great tool for viewing web pages, whether you're at home or you're on the go. No matter which Galaxy Tab 3 model you use, the screen is much larger than a mobile phone, so you can see more on the Galaxy Tab 3's screen. Because you can touch the screen, you can interact with web content in ways that a computer typically cannot. This chapter covers the following:

6

→ Browsing to a URL
→ Searching the web
→ Viewing web pages
→ Bookmarking websites
→ Returning to previously visited websites
→ Deleting bookmarks
→ Filling in web forms
→ Copying text and images from web pages

Browsing the Web

Browsing to a URL

It's likely that you already know how to browse to different web pages in your favorite web browser on your computer. The built-in Internet app in Android works much the same as the browser on your computer, but there are some differences.

1. Tap Internet on the Home screen.

2. Tap the Address field at the top of the screen. The keyboard opens at the bottom of the screen so you can type a Uniform Resource Locator (URL), which can be a website name or a specific page in a website. You can also select from one of the search sites in the list that appears below the Address field.

3. Start typing a URL, such as samsung.com or play.google.com.

4. Tap Go on the keyboard when you finish typing.

Smarter Searching

As you type, terms that match the letter(s) you've added appear in the list below the Address field. As you type more letters, Android updates the list to give you what it thinks is a more accurate list of possible terms you're looking for. You can stop typing at any time and scroll down the list to view the terms and then tap the term to open the web page. For example, as you type the first five letters of "android" (without the quotes), you see that you get terms for android and a number of other results.

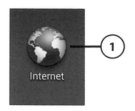

Tips for Typing a URL

The Internet app doesn't require you to type the "http://" or the "www." at the beginning of the URL. For example, if you type samsung.com or www.samsung.com, you still go to the Samsung home page. However, there might be some instances when you need to type in "http://" or even "https://" (for a secure web page) at the beginning of the URL. If you do, the Internet app lets you know so you can type in the "http://" or "https://" in the Address field.

☆ **Android SDK | Android Developers**
developer.android.com/sdk/index.html

Q android | +

Q android apps | +

Q android market | +

Q android sdk | +

Q android file transfer | +

Q android tablet | +

Q android 4.3 | +

Q android central | +

Q android versions | +

Search results when you start typing the word "android" in the Address field

Searching the Web

The Internet app makes it easy for you to search the Web, so you don't need to know every URL of every web page out there (which is good considering there are literally billions of web pages). As you type, the Internet app suggests search terms you've used in the past as well as search terms that you might be looking for.

1. Tap Internet on the Home screen.

2. Tap the Search field at the top of the screen. The keyboard opens at the bottom of the screen so you can type the URL. Start typing your search term. As you type, a list appears underneath the address bar with suggestions. You can stop typing at any time and scroll down the list to find your search term; tap the search term to select it and start the search.

3. If you haven't found what you're looking for, open the Google search page by tapping Go in the keyboard.

4. The results display in a Google search results page. Tap any link to go to a page; you can also tap one of the links at the bottom of the screen to view more results.

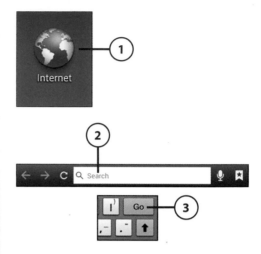

TIPS FOR SEARCHING THE WEB

>>>Go Further

You can search deeper within Google itself. For example, if you put a + in front of a search term, you're telling Google that you require the word in the search results. If you put quotes around a search term ("term"), you're telling Google that you want to search for results that contain that term. Scroll to the bottom of the search page and then tap Search Help to get more information about how you can get the most from your Google searches.

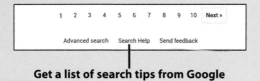

Get a list of search tips from Google

If you look at the top of Google's search results page, you see links so you can search for more than text terms, including Images and Videos. If you click the More link, a pop-up list displays so you can search a variety of other areas within Google.

**A list of more areas in which to
search within Google**

Viewing Web Pages

After you open a website, you can control what you view on the web page in several ways. These techniques enable you access the entire web page and navigate between web pages in the Internet app.

1. Navigate to a web page using one of the two methods described in the previous tasks in this chapter.

2. As you view a page, you can drag up and down the page with your finger. You can also flick with your finger to scroll quickly. After you flick, the screen scrolls, decelerates, and then comes to a stop.

3. Zoom in by double-tapping an area on the screen. Zoom out by double-tapping again.

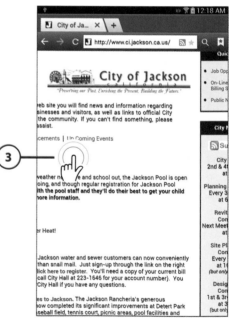

4. While you're zoomed in, you can touch and drag left and right to view different parts of the web page.

5. Move to another web page from a link in the current web page by tapping a link. Links are usually an underlined or colored piece of text, but they can also be pictures or images that look like buttons.

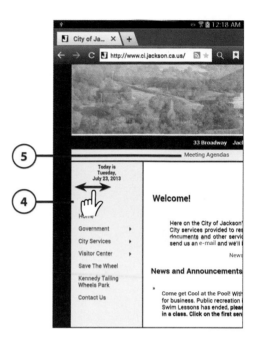

Hunting for Links

Unfortunately, it isn't always easy to figure out which parts of a web page are links and which ones aren't. Back in the early days of the Web, all links were blue and underlined. As web page elements have become more enhanced over time, it's now more common to find links in any color and any text style. What's more, graphics that are links aren't underlined, either.

On a computer's web browser it's easy to find out which element is a link when you move the mouse pointer over the link because the pointer changes shape. In Android, there is no cursor, so you can't find out if a web page element is a link unless you tap it and see what happens.

Bookmarking Websites

As you browse websites, you might want to save some of the websites in a list of your favorites so you can go back to them later. In browser parlance, this saving process is called bookmarking.

1. Navigate to any page in the Internet app.

2. Tap the Add Bookmark button at the top of the page.

3. In the Bookmarks list, tap the Add Bookmark button.

4. Edit the title of the bookmark. The official title of the web page is filled in for you, but you can change the name by tapping the Name field and using the keyboard.

5. Select the folder you want to place the bookmark into by tapping Bookmarks.

6. Select the folder into which you want to place the bookmark. The default is the Bookmarks folder, but you can also select another folder or save the bookmark to the Home screen.

7. Tap OK.

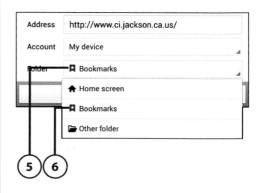

8. The new bookmark appears in the list.

Should I Edit a Bookmark Title?

Because the titles of web pages are usually long and descriptive, it's a good idea to shorten the title to something you can recognize easily in your bookmarks list. Every bookmark also includes a thumbnail picture of what the web page looks like so you can identify the bookmark more easily. If you would rather view your bookmarks by title, press Settings and then tap List View in the menu.

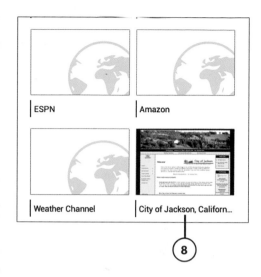

Returning to Previously Visited Pages

It's easy to return to the last page you visited in the Internet app—just tap the Back icon to the left of the Address bar. As you keep tapping the Back icon, you keep going back to pages you visited. In the History page, the Internet app also keeps a list of all web pages you've visited during your browsing session.

Browsing Forward

Like any web browser, you can browse more recent pages you've viewed in your current browsing session by tapping the Forward button, which is the right-arrow button immediately to the right of the Back button.

1. Visit several web pages in the Internet app if you haven't done so already.

2. Tap Bookmarks.

3. Tap the History tab. The list of web pages you visited for the current date appears under the Today heading.

4. You can view web pages you visited on an earlier date by tapping the date range (such as Yesterday), and the list of web pages you visited displays underneath the date heading. You can also view the web pages you've visited most often by tapping Most Visited; the list displays on the right side of the screen.

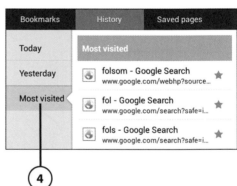

Tips for Using History

If you want to hide the history for a specific day so you can see history for another day, tap the header for the specific day. For example, if you want to hide all the web pages for today, click the Today header above the first web page in the Today list. The Today header is still visible, but you won't see the web pages. You can view the web pages again by tapping the Today header.

You can also clear the entire history database by tapping the Menu touch button and then tapping Clear History in the pop-up menu.

Deleting Bookmarks

If you find there are websites that you don't visit anymore or that go to obsolete or missing web pages, you need to cull your bookmark list. You can delete a bookmark from the Bookmarks list or from the History list.

Delete from the Bookmarks List

The first method uses the Bookmarks list to delete a bookmark.

1. Tap the Bookmarks button at the top of the Internet screen. The thumbnail list of bookmarks appears.

2. Tap and hold your finger on the bookmark you want to delete until the pop-up menu window appears.

3. Scroll down the menu (if necessary) until you see Delete Bookmark and then tap it.

4. A dialog box asks if you want to delete the bookmark. Tap OK to delete the bookmark instantly.

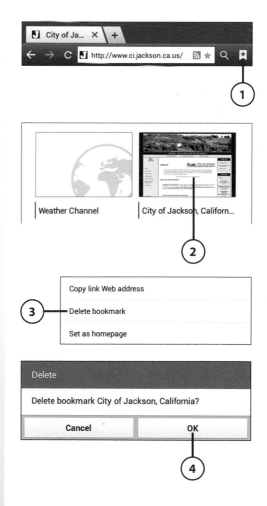

Delete from the History List

The second method uses the History list to delete a bookmark.

1. Tap the Bookmarks button at the top of the Internet screen. The thumbnail list of bookmarks appears.

2. Tap the History tab. This brings up a list of web pages you've viewed recently.

3. The bookmarked page is denoted by a yellow star to the right of the website name. Tap and hold your finger on the website in the History list until the pop-up menu window appears.

4. Tap Remove from Bookmarks. The window closes and the yellow star next to the website name is now gray, which signifies that the website is no longer bookmarked.

Sync Your Bookmarks

You can sync the bookmarks in your favorite web browser on your desktop or laptop computer with the Internet app so you have maximum control over your bookmarks. You can read more about syncing your Galaxy Tab 3 in Chapter 3, "Setting Up the Galaxy Tab 3."

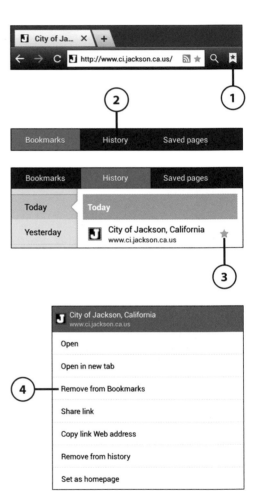

Filling in Web Forms

On many web pages you are asked to fill in forms, such as for signing up for a company's email newsletter or to get more information about a product. Filling out web forms on your Galaxy Tab 3 is similar to filling out forms on a computer's web browser, but there are differences.

1. Navigate to a page that you know contains a form. (The sample page is at http://code. google.com/p/android/issues/ entry?template=Feature%20 request.)

2. Tap in a text box.

3. The keyboard appears at the bottom of the screen. Use the keyboard to type text into the box. Tap the Go button when you finish typing.

4. Select an item in a pull-down menu by tapping the field.

5. Tap an item in the menu to select it. If the menu list is long, touch and drag up and down to view more selections.

6. The selected item appears in the field.

Special Menus

Some websites use special menus that are built from scratch. In these cases, the menu looks exactly like the one you get when you view the web page on a computer. If the web page is well constructed, it should work fine on the Galaxy Tab 3. However, it might be a little more difficult to make a selection.

Copying Text and Images from Web Pages

The Internet app treats web pages like other documents. That is, you can copy text and images from a web page you view in a browser to another app.

Copy a Block of Text

You can select text from web pages to copy and paste into other documents such as email messages or your own text documents.

1. Navigate to a web page in the Internet app if you haven't done so already.

2. Hold down your finger on the first word in the block of text and then release your finger. The first word is highlighted in blue with "handles" at the beginning and end of the word.

3. Hold down your finger on the bottom handle (the one on the right side of the word) and drag over the text you want to copy. When finished, release your finger. The selected text is highlighted in blue.

4. In the pop-up menu that appears above the selected text, tap Copy.

5. Android informs you that the text has been copied to the clipboard. You can now go to another application, such as Email (or an email form on another web page), and paste the text into a text area.

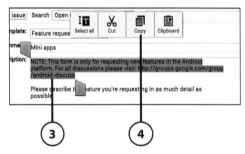

Copy an Image

In addition to being able to copy and paste text from the Internet app, you can also copy images from a web page and save them to an email message or a photo collection.

1. Go to a web page that includes an image on the page.

2. Tap and hold your finger on that image for a couple of seconds and then release your finger.

3. A pop-up menu for the image appears. Tap Save Image. This saves your image to the Galaxy Tab 3 so you can view and use it in any app where you select images from your photo albums.

4. The downloaded file appears as an icon in the Status bar.

5. Hold your finger on the Status bar and swipe down to open the Quick Settings and Notifications screen.

6. Scroll down the notification area and then tap the image filename to open the file in the Gallery app.

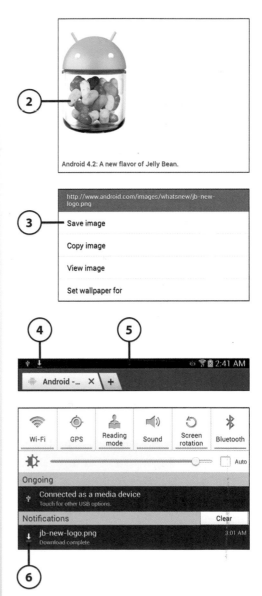

Android 4.2: A new flavor of Jelly Bean.

http://www.android.com/images/whatsnew/jb-new-logo.png

Save image

Copy image

View image

Set wallpaper for

Send and receive email from
your ISP or an email service

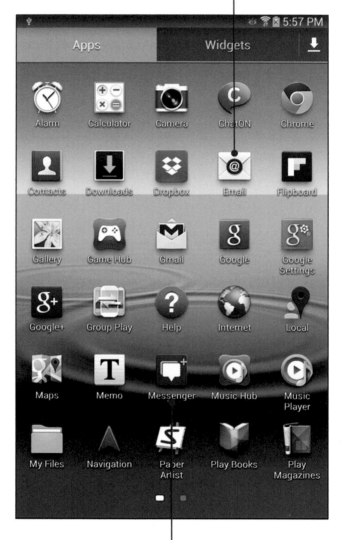

Send and receive
instant messages

Your Galaxy Tab 3 makes it easy for you to read and respond to email messages when you're on the go. Before you start, though, you need to configure your email account(s) and then figure out how to use the built-in Email app. Email isn't the only way to communicate. The Galaxy Tab 3 also contains a built-in Messaging app so you can configure your instant message settings to communicate using standard text message (SMS) and multimedia message (MMS) services. This chapter covers the following topics:

7

→ Configuring and reading email
→ Composing a new message
→ Deleting and moving messages
→ Searching through email
→ Configuring email settings
→ Sending and receiving instant messages
→ Reading email messages with the Email widget

Sending Email and Instant Messages

Configuring Email

The following is a complete checklist of the information you need to set up your Galaxy Tab 3 to use a traditional email account. If you have an email service such as Exchange, Google Gmail, or Yahoo! you won't need all this. However, if you don't configure the email settings, you can't use webmail services in other apps (like Gmail) to do things such as email web page links or photos, so you need some of the following information no matter what:

- Email address
- Account type (POP or IMAP)
- Incoming mail server address
- Incoming mail user ID
- Incoming mail password
- Outgoing mail server address
- Outgoing mail user ID
- Outgoing mail password

DO I USE POP OR IMAP?

If you're not sure whether to use POP or IMAP as your account type, keep the following in mind:

Post Office Protocol, or *POP*, retrieves and removes email from a server. Therefore, the server acts as a temporary holding place for email. If you receive email using both your Galaxy Tab 3 and your computer, it's more difficult to share your email messages using POP. You need to either set up your email to go to one device and some to another device, or you need to set up one device so it doesn't remove email from the server so another device can retrieve the email as well.

Internet Message Access Protocol, or *IMAP*, makes the server the place where all messages are stored. Your Galaxy Tab 3 and computer display all email messages on the server. This is the better situation if you have multiple devices retrieving email from the same account.

1. Tap Email on the Home screen.

2. Type the email address in the highlighted Email Address field. When you start typing, the keyboard appears at the bottom of the screen.

3. Tap Next in the keyboard.

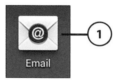

4. Tap the password for your email account in the Password field. As you type in the password characters, they become dots so the password is hidden right away.

5. Tap Done in the keyboard.

6. Tap the button that corresponds to the account type you have.

7. Type the incoming server settings into the appropriate fields.

8. Tap Next.

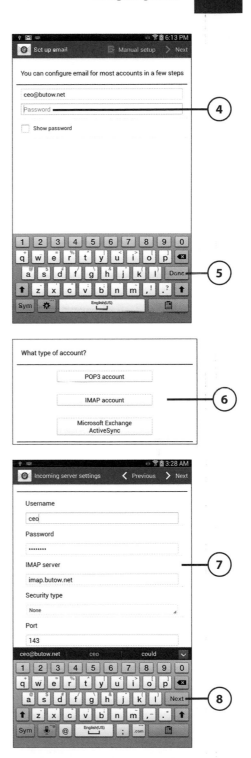

9. After the Galaxy Tab 3 checks your incoming server settings, type the outgoing server settings into the appropriate fields.

10. Tap Next.

11. Tap the check box to automatically download files attached to email messages. You can also uncheck the Notify Me When Email Arrives box if you don't want to be notified when you have new messages.

12. Tap the Sync Schedule field to change the checking frequency at which your Tab 3 checks for new messages. The default frequency is to check your inbox every 15 minutes. You can have the Tab check for new email as often as every 5 minutes. If that's too often, you can have the Tab check every 10 minutes, 15 minutes, 30 minutes, every hour, every 4 hours, or once per day. You can set the time yourself by tapping Manual.

13. Tap the checking frequency in the list.

What's the Peak Schedule?

The Peak Schedule field reflects how often the Email app checks for new messages during working hours—every 15 minutes, which is the same as the Sync Schedule. Working hours are 8:00 a.m. to 5:00 p.m. by default. The "Configuring Email Settings" section later in this chapter explains how to change these hours.

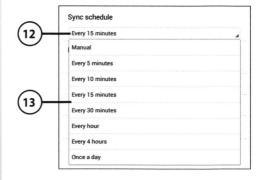

14. Tap Next.

15. Type an optional name into the Give This Account a Name field.

16. Type your name as you want it to be displayed in outgoing messages.

17. Tap Done. A list of your email messages appears in your Inbox screen.

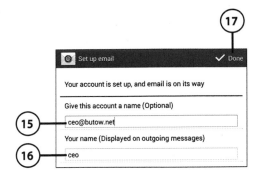

What Happens if the Settings Won't Verify?

If your settings don't verify, a dialog box displays, asking you to tap the Edit Details button to return to the previous screen and double-check all the information you entered. When something is wrong, it often comes down to misspelled information, such as a misspelled word or a letter that needs to be capitalized, or other incorrect information, such as a different outgoing server port number.

The Refresh icon

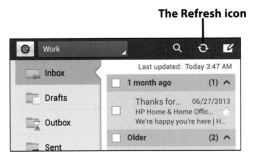

Can I Still Check My Mail Even if the App Never Checks Mail Automatically?

You can still check your mail list by tapping the Refresh icon in the Inbox screen as shown in the figure. After you tap the Refresh icon, the app checks for new messages. Any new messages appear at the top of the Inbox.

Reading Email

You use the Email app to navigate, read, and type your email messages.

1. Tap Email on the Home screen. Your list of Inbox folder messages displays with a list of folders to the left of the message.

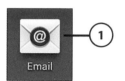

2. Tap a message in the list to view it. New, unread messages appear in the list with a white background; read messages have a gray background. A folder you're currently in is highlighted in blue in the folder list and the number of new messages appears to the left of the Inbox folder name.

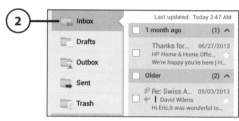

3. Tap the envelope icon at the top-left corner of the screen to return to your list of messages and folders.

4. Tap the sender's name at the top of the page.

5. Tap Create Contact to add the sender to your list of contacts.

6. Tap Device and then select the account to which you want to add the contact.

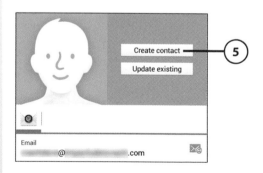

7. Type information into the Create Contact screen fields if you want. (You learn more about adding a contact in Chapter 9, "Using Productivity Apps to Simplify Your Life.") Tap Save to save the new contact and return to the message list.

8. View another account (if you have more than one account in the Email app) by tapping the email account name in the upper-left corner of the screen and then tapping the account name in the list.

9. Scroll down the folder list to view folders within the Inbox and tap a folder to view messages within that folder.

10. The number of messages in the folder appears to the right of the folder name and the list of messages within that folder appears to the right of the folder list.

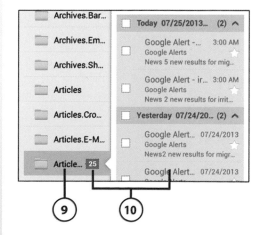

11. Scroll up the folder list until you see the Inbox folder. Tap it.

12. Tap the Refresh icon to refresh the message list on the left side of the screen. Any new messages that have come in appear at the top of the list and the Last Updated text at the top of the message list reflects the new time the Email app checked for messages.

How Do You Create Folders?

You can't create folders inside your mailbox in the Email app. If you use an IMAP mail server, you can go to the web interface for that server and create a new folder there so it appears in the Email app. Unfortunately, if you use a POP email server, you cannot add folders to the server—all you have is Inbox, Sent, and Trash.

How Do I Combat Spam?

The Galaxy Tab has no spam filter built in. However, most email servers filter spam at the server level. If you use a basic POP or IMAP account from an ISP, unfortunately you might not have any server-side spam filtering. If you use an account at a service such as Gmail, you get spam filtering on the server, and spam mail goes to the Junk folder, not your Inbox.

Composing a New Message

The process for composing a new message and composing a reply to a message is similar. This section covers composing a message from scratch.

1. Tap the New Mail icon in the Email app.

2. Enter the recipient's address in the To field.

3. Tap Cc/Bcc to enter an address so you can copy (Cc) or blind copy (Bcc) the message to another recipient.

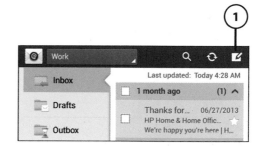

4. Tap +Me if you'd like to send a copy of the message to your own email address so that you have a record of what you sent.

5. Tap in the Subject field and then type a subject for the email.

6. Tap below the Subject field in the body of the email and then type your message.

7. Tap Send.

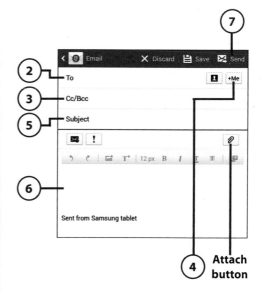

Add Attachments

If you've copied text or images to your clipboard, you can add that text or image as an attachment, just as you can with any email program on your computer. Just tap the Attach button, which has a paper clip icon and is located underneath the subject line near the far right of the window. Then you can pick your text, image(s), contacts, or location from the Attach window.

>>>Go Further

HOW DO I REPLY OR FORWARD A MESSAGE?

When you're reading a message, you can choose to reply to the sender or forward the message to another recipient.

At the right side of the menu bar that appears above the message, you see a series of four icons. The Reply icon appears as an arrow pointing left. After you tap the icon you see the reply message screen so you can type your response to the message. The Subject field contains the RE: prefix that denotes you're replying to the original message. View the original message by swiping down the screen. Send the message by tapping Send in the menu bar.

The Forward icon appears as an arrow pointing right. After you tap the icon you see the forward message screen. You can type the recipient in the To field as well as any recipients you want to copy or blind copy in the Cc/Bcc field. You can also type a message to the recipient within the body of the email. Any attachments that came with the original message are also attached to the forwarded message. You can view the original message by swiping down the screen. When you finish composing your forwarded message, tap Send in the menu bar.

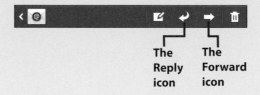

The
Reply
icon

The
Forward
icon

Creating Your Own Signature

You can create a signature that automatically appears at the end of your messages. You create your signature in the Email app.

1. Tap Email on the Home screen.

2. Tap the Menu touch button below the screen.

3. Tap Settings.

4. Tap your account name in the list.

5. Tap Signature. You can disable the signature field in your email messages by moving the slider from right to left. The slider button turns gray and displays an O (for Off), but you can turn it back on by sliding the bar to the right so the button turns green and displays an I (for On).

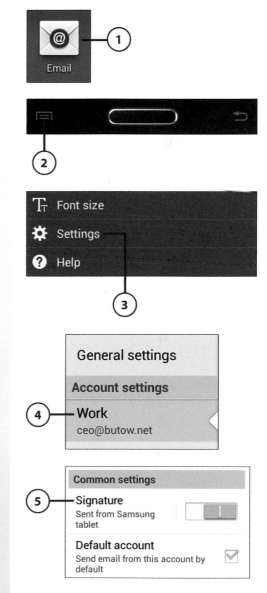

6. Type what you want the signature to say (such as your full name) in the Signature screen.

7. Tap Done.

8. The signature as it will appear in your Message Composition field appears under the Signature heading.

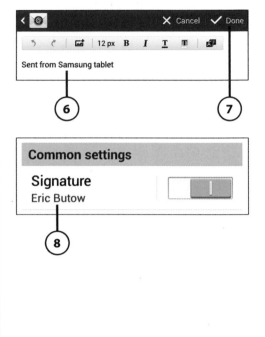

Can I Have Multiple Signatures?

You can have only one signature per email account on your Galaxy Tab 3, so technically you can't have multiple signatures. However, the signature is placed in the editable area of the Message Composition field, so you can edit it like the rest of your message and create multiple signatures that way.

Deleting Messages

When you view a message, you can tap the Delete icon and move the message to the trash.

1. In the Email app, go to any mailbox and any subfolder, such as your Trash folder.

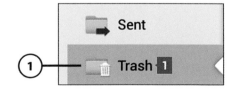

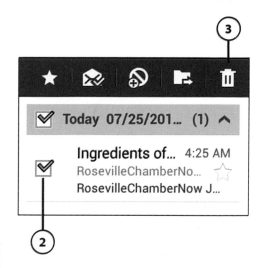

2. Tap a check box at the left side of the message entry that you want to delete. You can select multiple check boxes if you want to delete multiple messages.

3. Delete the messages by tapping the Trash icon.

Can I Move Messages to Other Folders?

Unfortunately, you can't move messages in the Email app from one folder to another. If you use an IMAP server, you can log in to the web interface for that server and move messages around there. The next time you log in to the Email app, the app reflects the changes you made in the IMAP server. If you're using a POP server, though, the only way you can move messages is to do so in another email program like one on your desktop or laptop computer.

Searching Through Email

By default, the Galaxy Tab 3 doesn't let you search through your email messages. You can change this quickly and then search text in your email messages.

1. Tap Email on the Home screen.

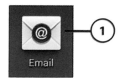

2. Open a folder or subfolder and then tap the Search icon.

3. Tap All and then choose whether you want to search for the term in the entire message (All), just the sender name, or just the title of the message. All is the default, but use Sender for this example.

4. Type the search term into the Search field.

5. As you type, updated results display below the field. In my example, I opened the Chambers. Folsom subfolder and typed `fols` into the field. A message from a Folsom Chamber of Commerce representative appears in the list so I can open it by tapping on the message.

6. If you don't find the search results you want, continue searching for messages that match your search term(s) in the email server by tapping Continue Searching on Server.

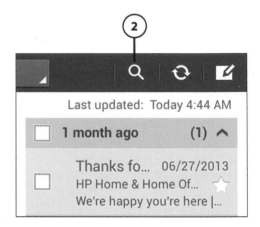

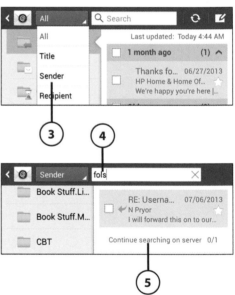

What's the Continue Searching on Server Link?

If you use an IMAP server, you can search other locations on your server (such as other email accounts) for the search term you entered by tapping the Continue Searching on Server link. After you tap this link, more results (if any) appear underneath your original search results. If you use another type of email service, such as POP, you won't see this link.

Configuring Email Settings

The Galaxy Tab enables you to update your email account settings as needed.

1. Follow the steps from earlier tasks in this chapter to open the Email app if you aren't there already. Then tap the Menu touch button.

2. Tap Settings.

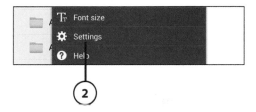

3. Tap your account in the Account Manager list if there is more than one. If not, your account appears on the screen automatically.

4. Tap Email Notifications to specify whether the Galaxy Tab 3 should notify you when email arrives. This feature is activated by default. Deactivate it by tapping the check box.

5. Tap Select Ringtone to select a ringtone or to designate that there should be no ringtone at all. Select the ringtone from the Select Ringtone pop-up window. The default ringtone is Postman.

6. The Sync Email check box is checked by default. You see the date and time the app last checked for email appears to the left of the check box. Disable email syncing by tapping the check box to clear it.

7. Tap Sync Schedule.

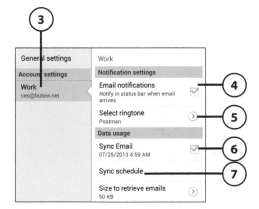

8. Tap Sync Schedule and then select the time interval in the Sync Schedule window as described in the "Configuring Email" section earlier in the chapter.

9. Tap the Peak Schedule check box if you don't want to set a separate email syncing schedule. When you clear the check box, the app disables all the options in the Peak Schedule section underneath the checkbox.

10. Tap Peak Schedule to change the peak schedule syncing interval in the Peak Schedule window. Tap the appropriate interval for syncing during the peak schedule. (Each interval is the same as in the Sync Schedule field.)

11. By default the peak days are Monday through Friday, and the peak days are highlighted in blue. Tap a day to select or deselect it to add or delete it from the peak schedule, respectively.

12. Change the peak start time by tapping Peak Start Time.

13. Change the time by tapping on the up and down arrows above (from left to right) the hour, minute, and AM/PM settings.

14. When you finish setting the time, tap Set.

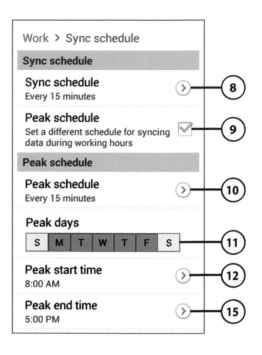

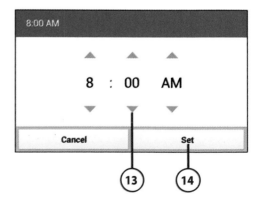

15. Your new peak start time appears. Change the peak end time by tapping Peak End Time.

16. Change the peak end time in the window as you did with the peak start time. The new peak end time appears.

17. Go back to the main Settings screen by tapping the Email app icon in the menu bar.

18. Tap Size to Retrieve Emails to open the pop-up window and change the default amount of data you can receive in an email message. When you receive messages, the Email app only downloads the first 50KB of data in a message by default. If the message has more than 50KB of data then at the bottom of the message the app asks if you want to download the rest of the message. You can choose from 2KB to 100KB. Scroll down to view more options.

19. Tap the Signature field to change your signature. Read the "Creating Your Own Signature" task earlier in this chapter for more information about signatures.

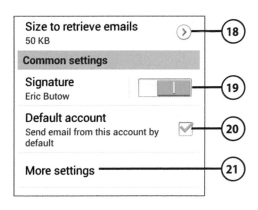

20. The Default account check box is checked when the Email app sends and receives email automatically from the account you're viewing. If you don't want to send email from that account, clear the check box by tapping Default Account.

21. Tap More Settings.

22. Tap Account Name to change your account name.

23. Tap Your Name to add or change your name.

24. Tap Always Cc/Bcc Myself and then select Cc or Bcc in the pop-up window if you always want to add your email address in the Cc or Bcc box.

25. Turn off the feature that always includes attachments with forwarded messages by tapping the Forward with Files check box; otherwise, that feature is turned on.

26. Tap Show Images to automatically show images in a message when you view it.

27. Tap Recent Messages and then select the number of recent messages in the pop-up window. You can choose from 25 messages, which is the default, up to all messages in the folder.

28. Tap Auto Download Attachments to download file attachments in a message to the app automatically.

29. Tap Auto Resend Times to change the number of times you automatically resend a message if it doesn't go through the first time. Then tap the number of times (1, 3, 5, or 10) you want the Email app to resend the unsent message before giving up. The default is No Limit.

30. Set advanced security options by tapping Security Options. In the Security Options screen that appears, you can encrypt all outgoing email, sign all outgoing email, and create and manage encryption keys for keeping your email messages private.

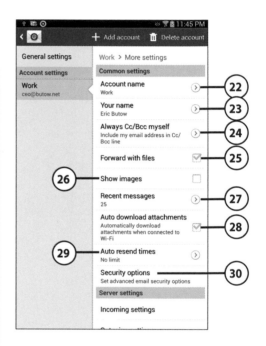

31. Change your incoming settings (as you did with a new account earlier in this chapter) by tapping Incoming Settings.

32. Change your outgoing settings (as you did with a new account earlier in this chapter) by tapping Outgoing Settings.

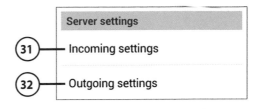

Sending and Receiving Instant Messages

You can send and receive instant messages using one of two built-in apps: The Messenger app and the Google Talk app. However, these two apps have now been replaced with the Hangouts app, but you have to upgrade Messenger and Google Talk to Google Hangouts the first time you use Messenger or Google Talk. This example shows you how to upgrade to Google Hangouts from within the Messenger app.

Use the Messenger App the First Time

The first time you use the Messenger app, you see different screens than what you'll see after you set up the app.

1. Tap Apps on the Home screen.

2. Tap Messenger.

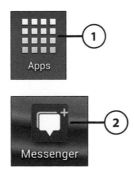

3. If you already have an existing Google account, tap the account name in the list within the Select an Account window. The Messenger app logs you in, and you might be asked to choose an account if you have more than one Google+ account assigned to your name. If you do then tap the appropriate account in the Choose Account list before tapping the Next button.

4. Tap the check boxes to turn off the default options to add your Google+ connections to your Contact app database and also allow Google to make suggestions based on who you communicate with on your tablet most often on your Galaxy Tab 3.

5. Tap Next.

6. The Over Wi-Fi only button is selected by default so you can back up any photos and videos you receive in the Messenger App to Google+. If you don't want to back up photos and videos from Messenger, tap the Not Now button.

7. Tap the Also Back up Existing Photos & Videos check box to turn off the function to back up existing photos and videos stored on your Galaxy Tab 3.

8. Tap Done.

9. Close the app because you will update the Messenger app to the Hangouts app.

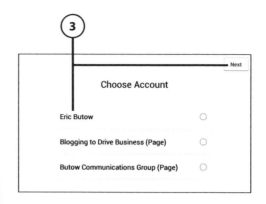

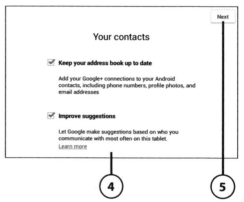

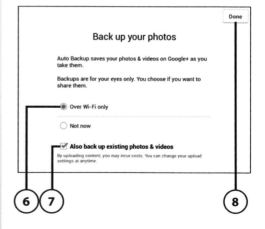

Upgrade To and Use Google Hangouts

The next time you open Messenger after you set it up and close the app, Messenger invites you to upgrade to Google Hangouts.

Do I Need a Google+ Account to Use Google Hangouts?

Yes, you need to have an existing Google+ account that is tied to your primary Gmail account. If you don't have a Google+ account, Google Hangouts has you set up your Google+ account before you continue setting up Google Hangouts.

1. Tap Messenger in the Apps screen.

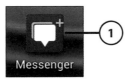

2. The Update to Hangouts message informs you that Messenger functionality has been moved to the new Google Hangouts app. Download the app by tapping Get the App.

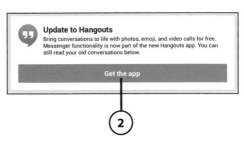

3. Tap Update to install the Hangouts app from the Play Store.

4. Tap Accept to accept the permissions the app is requesting.

5. Tap Open to open the app after the Play Store installs Hangouts.

6. Tap the plus icon to select the circles or names in the Add People screen.

7. Tap the recipient field and then type the name of the person with whom you want to chat.

8. As you type, matches appear in the drop-down list underneath the field. Tap the name of the person with whom you want to chat.

9. Continue typing names of people you want to include in the conversation or you tap the Back menu button, scroll down the list of users or Google+ groups in the window, and then add the user or group to recipient field by tapping the user or group name.

10. Delete a person's name from the conversation by tapping the person's name box in the recipient field and then tapping the X button within the name box.

11. Tap Message to send a message to the recipient(s).

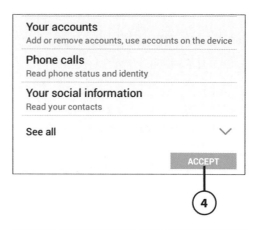

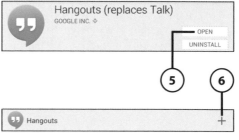

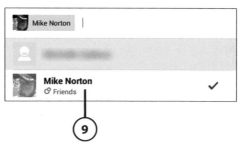

12. Type your message in the Send a Message box.

13. Add an emoticon to better convey the meaning of your message by tapping the emoticon icon to the left of the Send a Message box.

14. Swipe down the section of emoticons and then tap the emoticon you want. The emoticon appears at the end of your message.

15. Tap the send icon to send your message.

16. Your message appears above the Send a Message field. If you receive a message from the recipient, your message will be moved up and you will see the recipient's response above the Send a Message field.

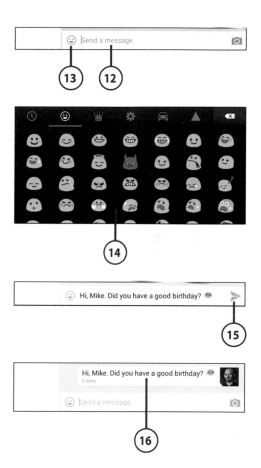

What if I Don't Use Either Google+ or Google Talk for Instant Messaging?

If you use a different instant messaging service then visit the Google Play Store by tapping Play Store on the Home screen. Then search for the instant messaging app you're looking for. If you use Skype, for example, there is a Skype app for Android available that you can download free of charge. You discover more about downloading apps in Chapter 16, "Finding and Managing Apps."

Configuring Google Hangouts Settings

You can change your Google Hangouts settings so you can manage your messages to your liking, determine how you want to be notified of new messages that come into your message Inbox, and change your Google+ profile.

1. Tap Hangouts in the Apps screen.

2. Tap the Menu touch button below the screen.

3. Tap Settings.

4. Tap Profile Photo to change your Google+ profile photo. You can take a photo using the Camera app or you can choose a photo within the Gallery app.

5. The Notifications and Hangout Request check boxes are checked by default so you receive notifications about new Google Hangouts (which are live video chats) started by one of your contacts and when you receive a request to join a Google Hangout. If you don't want to be notified about any hangouts, tap Notifications to clear the check box.

6. Tap Sound to open the Sound window and set a tone that notifies you when someone has joined your Hangout or you have received a request for someone to join your Hangout. By default you will only see a message on the screen.

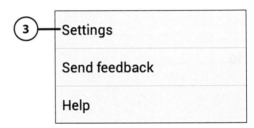

Settings

Send feedback

Help

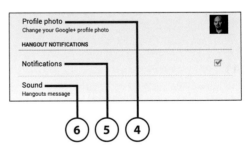

Profile photo
Change your Google+ profile photo

HANGOUT NOTIFICATIONS

Notifications

Sound
Hangouts message

7. Select from the preselected silent mode, the default ringtone, or a number of other ringtones. Scroll up and down the list to view the entire list and tap the button to the right of the tone so you can listen to the sound.

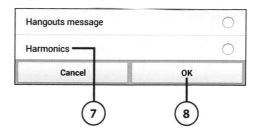

8. Tap OK when you've selected a sound. The name of the selected sound appears within the Sound entry in the Hangout Notifications section.

9. Tap Hangout Requests to clear the checkbox and tell the Hangouts app not to notify you when the app receives requests from another Google+ user to join your Hangout. Turn on hangout request notification again by tapping Hangout Requests.

10. Tap Sound in the Video Calls section to have the Google Hangouts app play a sound when you receive a video. You can keep the default silent mode or select a new sound as you did with the Hangout Notifications sound in Steps 6–8.

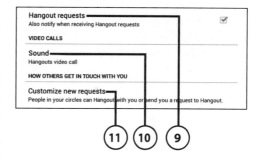

11. Tap Customize New Requests to determine who can join your Hangouts.

12. In the Customize New Requests screen, you can determine the circles that can join a Hangout with you or request that you accept them as a Hangout partici- pant. Circles include ones that you created in Google+ as well as the default Public circle that includes all Google+ users. Change how users in each circle can request Hangout participation by tapping the circle name in the list. In the window that appears, you can tap Hangout With You or Request Only.

13. After you change the request type, the type appears under- neath the circle name.

14. Return to the main Settings screen by tapping the Google Hangouts log at the left side of the menu bar.

15. Tap Google+ Profile to change your Google+ profile settings within the Internet browser app.

16. Tap Blocked People to view a list of blocked users. In the Blocked People screen that appears, you see a list of users (if any) that you blocked in Google+.

17. Tap Sign Out to sign out of Google Hangouts and close the Hangouts app.

18. Tap About Hangouts to read more information about Hangouts, including the privacy policy and terms of service.

19. Return to the Hangouts screen by tapping the Google Hangouts icon at the left side of the menu bar.

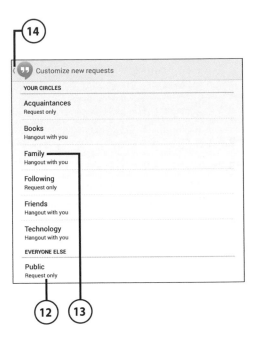

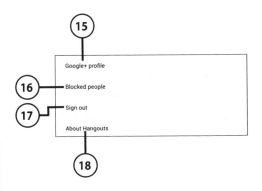

Reading Email Messages Using the Email Widget

Chapter 5, "Adding Widgets to Your Home Screens," explains how to add widgets to your Home screens to perform certain tasks. In this task you see how to add the Email widget to a Home screen so you can view your latest email messages without having to open the Email app.

1. Tap Apps on the Home screen.

2. Tap Widgets.

3. Swipe on the Widgets screen from right to left until you see the Email widget.

4. Tap and hold on the widget and then add the widget to the home screen you want as you learned to do in Chapter 5.

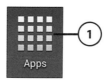

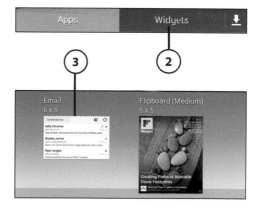

5. The number of messages you see in the widget depends on the size of the widget on your Home screen. In this example, the three most recent messages in my Inbox folder appear in the widget. View a message in the Email app by tapping the message within the widget.

6. By default, you see all messages from all email accounts that you set up in the Email app. If you want to view email in a specific account, tap the Combined button. The button label changes to reflect one of your accounts and the list of messages changes to display the most recent messages in that account's Inbox folder. Tap the button again to view Inbox folder messages in another account.

7. Tap the Write icon to write a new message in the Email app as described in this chapter.

8. Tap the Refresh icon to have the widget check for new messages in the Inbox folder.

Use widgets designed
for Jelly Bean and the
Galaxy Tab 3

Chapter 5 describes how to add a widget to a Home screen. Your Galaxy Tab 3 comes with a number of preinstalled widgets you can use. Some of these widgets are new with the latest version of Jelly Bean and others are unique to the Galaxy Tab 3. The widgets include the Flipboard social aggregation widget, the Google Now personal assistant widget, and more. This chapter covers the following topics:

8

→ Finding widgets on the Galaxy Tab 3
→ Getting weather information
→ Using Flipboard
→ Accessing the Game Hub
→ Adding and viewing videos
→ Having Google Now assist you
→ Sending and receiving instant messages
→ Using the S Planner calendar
→ Creating a Story Album
→ Getting travel tips with S Travel

Using Galaxy Tab 3 Widgets

Finding the Widgets

By default, five widgets appear on the three default Home screens:

- The primary Home screen contains the Weather widget at the top of the screen. This widget displays the current date and time as well as the current weather conditions for your location. Underneath the Weather widget, the Google Search widget enables you to set up the Google Now app so you can get information you need without having to launch a browser app.

- Swipe from left to right on the primary Home screen to view the Flipboard app on the Home screen. Note that this widget is also available in smaller versions from within the Widgets screen that's covered in Chapter 5, "Adding Widgets to Your Home Screens." Examples in this chapter use the full screen version of Flipboard that's already installed.

The Weather widget

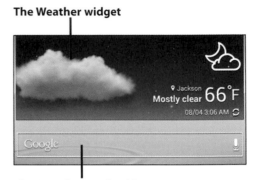

The Google Search widget

The Flipboard widget

- Swipe from left to right on the primary Home screen to view the Game Hub and Videos app on the Home screen. These widgets enable you to access the Game Hub app from the Home screen and add videos that you can view from within the Video Player widget.

The Game Hub widget

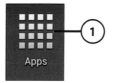

The Video Player widget

Find Widgets on the Widgets Pages

The widgets covered in this chapter are also within the Widgets screen pages. Some of them are already on Home screens by default, but it's useful to know where the widgets are within the Widgets screen in case you remove a widget and want to place it on a Home screen again.

1. Tap Apps on the Home screen.

2. Tap the Widgets tab at the top of the screen.

3. Swipe from left to right to view the Flipboard widgets. These two widgets are smaller than the default Flipboard widget that is already on one of the Home screens by default.

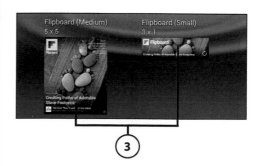

4. Swipe from right to left to open Page 4 of the Widgets screen and view the Game Hub widget that is already on one of the Home screens by default.

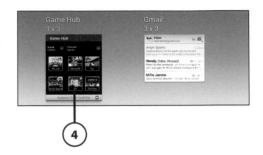

4

5. Swipe from right to left to view the Google Search widget on Page 5 of the Widgets screen. This widget is on the primary Home screen by default, although you can add a smaller Google Search widget if you want.

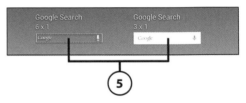

5

6. Swipe from right to left to view Page 6 in the Widgets screen that contains the Picture Frame widget. Then swipe from right to left to view page 7 in the Widgets screen.

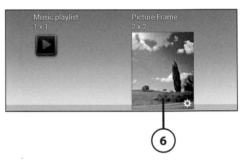

6

7. The S Planner (Mini Today) and S Planner (Month) widgets appear at the top of the screen. Read more about using these widgets in the "See Your Calendar at a Glance Using S Planner" section later in this chapter.

8. The Story Album and Travel widgets appear at the bottom of the screen. Read more about these widgets in the "Tell Your Story in Story Album" and "Get Travel Tips in S Travel" sections later in this chapter.

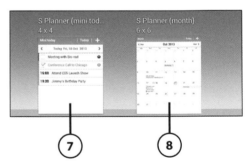

7   **8**

9. Swipe from right to left to view
    Page 8, the last page in the Wid-
    gets screen. The Video Player
    and Weather widgets, which are
    located on the Home screens by
    default, appear on this page.

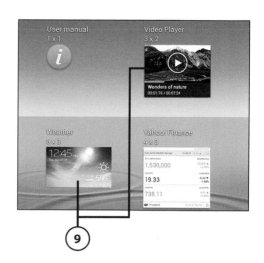

Where Should I Put These Widgets?

You can place these widgets
anywhere on Home screens (as
described in Chapter 5), and it's
presumed that you have added
the widgets discussed in this
chapter to a Home screen. For the
purposes of this chapter, widgets
that are not on Home screens
by default appear on their own
Home screens.

Using the Widgets

All widgets enable you to open the related app on the screen to view more
information and make changes to the app. Some widgets have controls contained within the widget to update and/or change information you view in
the widget.

Let's begin by viewing the widget that appears on the primary Home screen:
the Weather widget.

Learn What It's Like Outside with the Weather Widget

1. On the Home screen, update the current temperature and sky conditions for your area by tapping the Refresh icon. After a few seconds, the sky conditions image and text as well as the current temperature appear on the screen. The time and date of your last refresh appear to the left of the Refresh icon.

2. Open the Weather app by tapping an area inside the widget other than the Refresh icon.

3. Four areas comprise the Weather app screen. The top of the screen displays current weather information including the current sky conditions for your area, the current temperature, the forecast high and low temperatures for the day, and the sunrise and sunset times.

4. The middle of the screen includes an extended weather forecast for the next six days.

5. Check the bottom of the screen to see the date and time the information was last updated. Tap the Refresh icon to get the most current weather information that appears at the top of the screen.

6. Tap the left arrow icon to the right of the extended forecast to display the extended forecast in temperature graph view.

7. Tap the right arrow icon to the left of the extended forecast to display the extended forecast in text view.

8. Tap More to view more weather information for your area in either the Internet or Chrome app.

9. The AccuWeather.com page appears and displays current information for your area. Swipe up and down the screen to view the current wind speed, humidity level, and the amount of cloud cover in the sky.

10. Return to the Weather widget screen by tapping the Back touch button.

11. View a current weather map by tapping Weather Map.

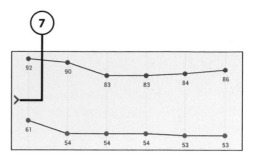

12. A Google map of the larger area around your location appears on the screen with current conditions for many different cities nearby in black boxes. Your current location appears in the center of the map; in this example it's Jackson, California.

13. Return to the Weather widget screen by tapping the Back touch button.

Menu icon

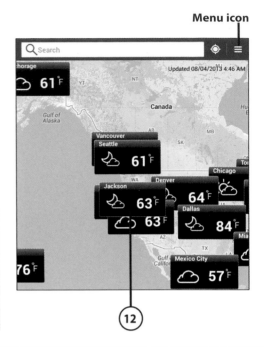

CAN I GET WEATHER FOR ANOTHER CITY OR AREA?

You can add another city or area to check by tapping the Menu icon at the upper-right corner of the screen. In the Setup screen, add a new city by tapping the plus icon. In the Search screen that appears, type a city to find a city in the AccuWeather database. After you select the city, it appears in the list within the Setup screen. View weather information for that city by tapping the city in the list.

Plus icon

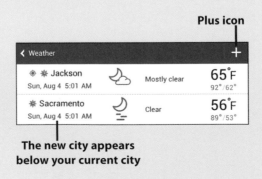

The new city appears below your current city

Get Social Network Updates with Flipboard

The Galaxy Tab 3 has the Flipboard widget installed by default on a Home page. This social media aggregation service enables you to get updates from all the social media websites you use within one app.

1. Go to the Home screen that contains the Flipboard widget.

2. Tap anywhere in the widget.

3. Swipe from right to left in the screen to start setting up Flipboard.

4. Tap a content category tile in the list that you want to add. A selected category contains a check mark in the tile.

5. Tap Build Your Flipboard.

6. Tap Next in the Welcome to Flipboard window until you reach the last page and then tap Done.

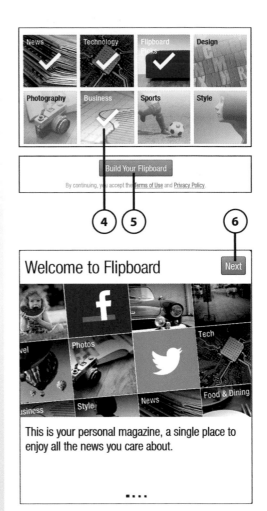

7. You can tap a tile to read the story on the screen, or you can swipe to the left and right to view more Flipboard pages that contain more news items.

8. Press the Home button to return to the Home screen that contains the Flipboard widget. Now that you have set up the Flipboard app, the latest cover story appears within the widget.

⑦

Refresh the Cover Story in the Widget

You can refresh the cover story within the Flipboard widget by tapping the Refresh icon at the lower-right corner of the widget.

⑧

Refresh icon

Access the Game Hub App

If you want to shop for games to play on your Galaxy Tab 3, you don't have to go into the Apps screen to open the Game Hub app. Instead, you can tap the Game Hub widget on one of the Home screens.

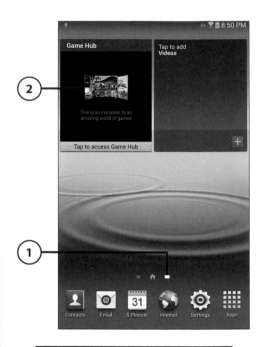

1. Go to the Home screen that contains the Game Hub widget.

2. Tap anywhere in the widget.

3. If you see the Disclaimer screen, tap the Do Not Show for 90 Days check box so this screen won't appear for the next 90 days.

4. Tap Confirm.

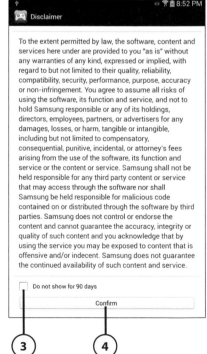

5. Shop for games in the Game Hub app. Read Chapter 16, "Finding and Managing Apps," to get more information about finding apps.

6. Return to the Home page that contains the Game Hub app by pressing the Home button. The Game Hub widget now contains tiles with popular games so you can see the latest and greatest games available for you to play.

7. Refresh the list by tapping the Refresh icon in the widget.

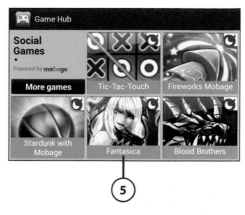

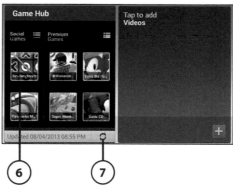

Add Videos to the Video Player Widget

You can view videos directly from within the Video Player widget, which appears on the same Home screen as the Game Hub widget. The most recent video you viewed appears within the widget, but if the Video Player app can't find a video, then the widget invites you to tap the widget to add a video.

1. Go to the Home screen that contains the Video Player widget.

2. Tap anywhere in the widget.

3. When you start the Video Player app, the screen tells you that there are no videos. You can drag and drop videos from your computer using Windows Media Player or another media player that you learned about in Chapter 3, "Setting Up the Galaxy Tab 3," or you can record a video with the Camera app. (Find out how to record video in Chapter 12, "Playing Music and Video."

4. For this example, I switched to the Camera app to record a brief video of a picture of my grandfather, a U.S. Navy Commander who was the Commander of a naval base in Kodiak, Alaska in the early 1950s. When I opened the Video Player widget again, the video I took played continuously in a thumbnail tile on the screen.

5. Tap Thumbnails in the menu bar.

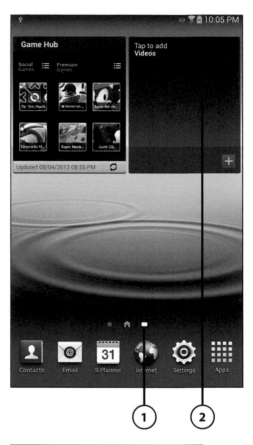

6. You can view a list of videos that shows a thumbnail image of the photo as well as file information, view a list of videos along with the folder in which the file is contained, and scan for videos on connected devices such as a smartphone.

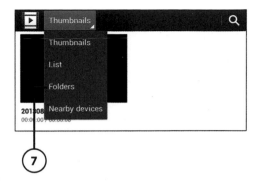

7. Tap Folders.

8. The folder name appears in the folder list on the left side of the screen and the video thumbnail image and file information appear on the right side of the screen. View the video in the AllShare Play app by tapping the thumbnail image.

Search icon

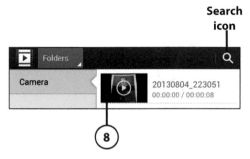

Can I Search for Files?

If you don't see the video file you're looking for, you can search for it by tapping the Search icon at the right side of the menu bar that appears at the top of the screen. You can then type in your search term(s) and then tap the Search button in the keyboard.

View Pictures in the Picture Frame

The Picture Frame widget enables you to view one or more pictures stored on your Tab 3 within the widget area on a Home screen.

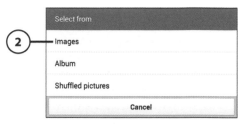

1. Add the Picture Frame widget to your desired Home screen if you haven't done so already. The Select From window opens as soon as you add the widget to the Home screen.

2. In the window you can select from images stored on your device, an album file that contains images, or shuffled pictures that you view within the widget as a slideshow. For this example, tap Images. In the Gallery window, images in various folders display on the screen.

3. Tap the folder with the images you want to add to the Picture Frame app. This example uses the Download folder.

4. Select the image to add to the Picture Frame widget by tapping the check box at the upper-right corner of the image tile.

5. Tap Done.

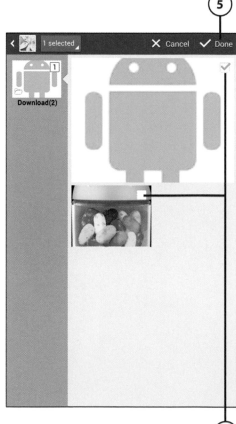

6. The Picture Frame widget appears on the Home screen's Setup screen so you can see how the Picture Frame will look on the screen. If more than one image appears in the widget, you see the slideshow of photos. You can move the widget around on the screen and you can resize the widget by tapping, holding, and dragging one of the four resizing handles on the sides of the widget box.

7. Tap the Back touch button.

8. The Picture Frame widget appears in your desired location on the Home screen.

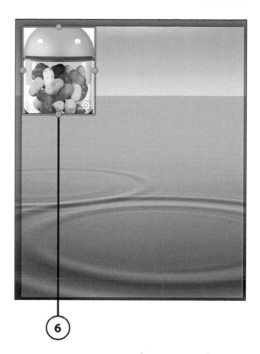

How Do I Change the Picture Frame Settings?

You can change the Picture Frame widget settings by tapping the gear icon at the lower-right corner of the widget. In the Picture Frame screen you can change the pictures you view, the layout of the pictures (for example, you can have one picture appear on top of another within the widget), and change the interval between slides.

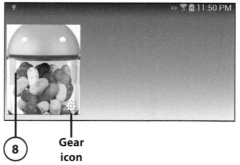

Gear icon

Access Web Bookmarks Quickly Using S Bookmarks

The S Bookmarks widget enables you to store bookmarks on your Galaxy Tab 3 or use the bookmarks stored with your Gmail account. After you set up the S Bookmarks widget, you can browse for bookmarks directly within the widget and open the bookmarked website in the Internet or Chrome app.

1. After you add the S Bookmarks widget to your desired Home page, tap the account that contains the bookmarks within the Internet window.

2. The S Bookmarks widget appears on the Home screen's Setup screen so you can see how the widget will look on the screen. You can move the widget around on the screen and you can resize the widget by tapping, holding, and dragging one of the four resizing handles on the sides of the widget box. For this example I resized the widget so it takes up the left side of the Home screen.

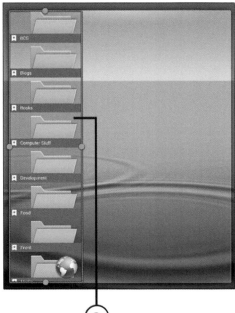

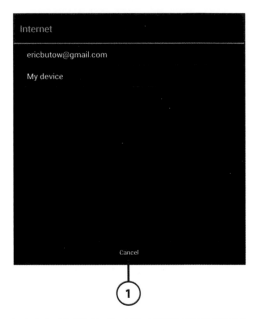

3. Tap the Back touch button.

4. Swipe your finger up and down within the widget to view all the folders that contain your bookmarks.

5. Tap the folder that contains the bookmarked website you want to view.

6. Swipe your finger up and down within the widget to view all the bookmarks (and any subfolders) contained with the folder. Go back to the previous folder by tapping the folder name at the top of the folder list.

7. Tap the bookmark that contains the website you want to view.

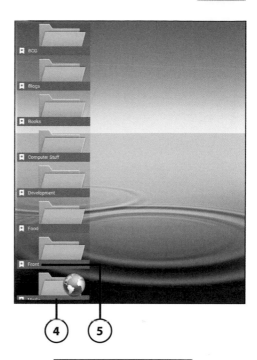

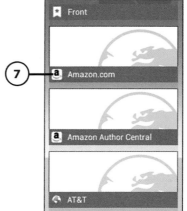

8. If you see the Complete Action Using window, tap the browser app icon to view the website within that browser app.

9. Tap the Always button to open websites from the widget using the selected browser app. If you want the app to ask you to select your browser app each time you open a bookmarked website, tap the Just Once button.

10. The website appears in your desired browser app.

11. Tap the Back touch button to return to the Home screen that contains the S Bookmarks app.

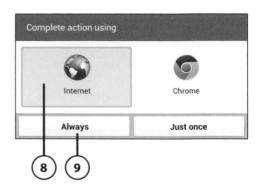

See Your Calendar at a Glance Using S Planner

There are two S Planner widgets: The Mini Today widget that shows you the appointments you have for the current day and the Month widget that shows all your events for the current month.

S Planner (Mini Today) Widget

You can view events on dates other than the current date and you can also add an event for the current date within the Mini Today widget.

1. After you add the widget to your desired Home screen, the widget appears at your desired location on that Home screen.

2. Tap the left arrow icon to see events on the previous day.

3. Tap the right arrow icon to see events on the following day.

4. If you're viewing events on a day other than the current day, return to appointments on the current day by tapping Today.

5. Tap the plus icon to add a new event.

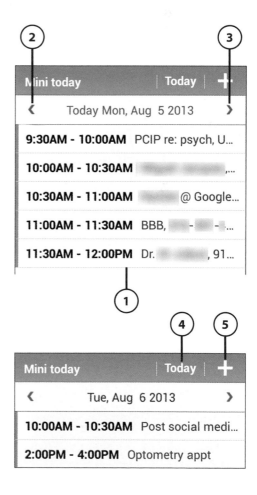

6. The S Planner screen opens so you can add a new event to your calendar. Read Chapter 9, "Using Productivity Apps to Simplify Your Life," to see how to add an event to your calendar Tap Save after you've entered the details of your appointment.

7. The new appointment appears in the Mini Today widget.

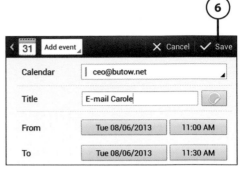

S Planner (Month) Widget

You can view events for the current month stored in S Planner by adding the Month widget to a Home screen.

1. After you add the widget to your desired Home screen, the widget appears at your desired location on that Home screen. The current date is highlighted in blue and the date is circled.

2. Tap the left arrow icon to see events for the previous month. The three-letter abbreviation for the previous month appears to the right of the icon. In this example, July is the previous month and it has the abbreviation Jul.

3. Tap the right arrow icon to see events for the following month.

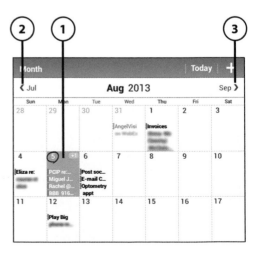

The three-letter abbreviation for the following month appears to the left of the icon. In this example, September is the next month and it has the abbreviation Sep.

4. Tap another date to highlight that date and also to add an event for that date.

5. If you're viewing events on a day other than the current day, highlight the current day by tapping Today.

6. Add a new event by tapping the plus icon.

7. The S Planner screen opens so you can add a new event to your calendar. Read Chapter 9 for details about how to add an event. Tap Save.

8. The new appointment appears in the Month widget.

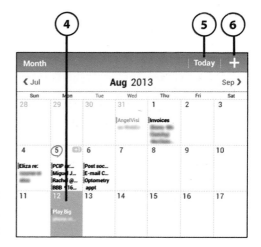

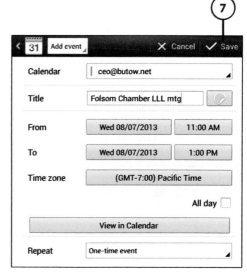

Tell Your Story in Story Album

The Story Album widget enables you to access the Story Album app and create digital picture albums that you can view and access directly from the widget on a Home screen. You can use the Story Album app to publish your album as hard copy photo books to give to family and friends.

1. After you add the widget to your desired Home screen, the widget appears at your desired location on that Home screen.

2. Start setting up Story Album by tapping in the widget.

3. Tap Next in the Welcome to Story Album screen.

4. Tap Start to Continue the setup process.

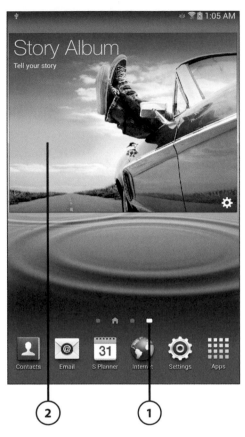

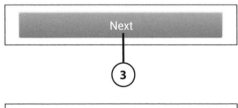

Next

Your digital picture albums can be published as hard copy photo books. Your treasured memories will always be with you.

Previous   Start

5. You can create an album from the Gallery app or search for images by tags, which are descriptions of the image contained within the image file. Tap From Gallery.

6. Tap the folder that contains the images you want to include in your Story Album.

7. Select the image to add to the Picture Frame widget by tapping the check box at the upper-right corner of the image tile.

8. Tap Done.

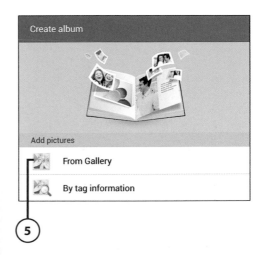

Create album

Add pictures

From Gallery

By tag information

5

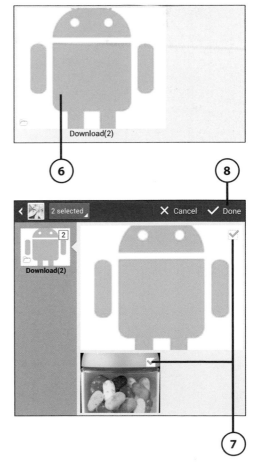

Download(2)

6

8

2 selected   X Cancel ✓ Done

Download(2)

7

9. Change the title of your album by tapping in the Title field and typing the new album name.

10. The default theme for your album is Grid, but you can change this by tapping Theme and then selecting the theme in the Select Theme screen.

11. Change the album cover image by tapping Cover Image and then selecting the image within the album that you want to use as the cover image in the Select Cover screen.

12. Tap Create Album.

13. View images in the album by tapping the album cover image.

14. Press the Home button. Parts of the images appear as a slideshow within the widget.

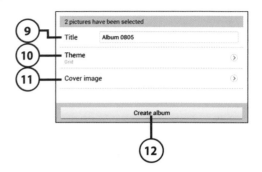

How Do I Change the Story Album Settings?

You can change the story album that the widget displays by tapping the gear icon at the lower-right corner of the widget. Within the Story Album screen, you can change the album as well as the interval between images in the album.

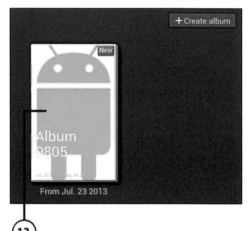

Gear icon

Get Travel Tips in S Travel

If you're going on a trip sometime soon with your Galaxy Tab 3, you can view travel information at a glance from a Home screen using the S Travel widget. You can view worldwide travel information or information for a specific city such as local landmarks you can visit during your stay.

1. After you add the widget to your desired Home screen, the widget appears at your desired location on that Home screen.

2. Start setting up S Travel by tapping in the widget.

3. The S Travel window informs you that the widget will provide you with worldwide travel information. If you don't want to see this window every time you tap the widget, tap the Do Not Show Again check box.

4. Tap OK.

5. In the Select City to Display screen, the Recommended Destination button is selected by default so you see popular destinations around the world within the widget. Tap Select City to choose the city for which you want to get travel information.

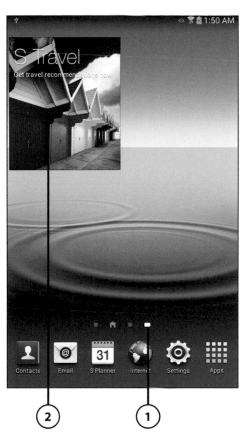

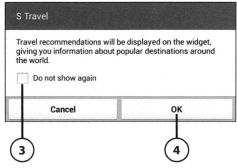

6. Type the city to which you want to travel within the Search for Cities field. As you type, suggestions for the city that may match what you're typing appear in the drop-down list underneath the field.

7. When you find the city you want, tap the city in the drop-down list. The map changes and the pointer appears over the selected city on the map.

8. Tap Done.

9. Tap the Back touch button. A slideshow of attractions in your destination city appears within the widget. Each attraction also includes positive comments about it.

10. You can save the attraction to your travel itinerary in the built-in TripAdvisor app by tapping the Favorites icon.

11. Change your destination city or view popular destinations around the world by tapping the Settings icon. The Select City to Display screen appears so you can change the destination as you did earlier.

12. Refresh the attractions slideshow in the widget by tapping the Refresh icon.

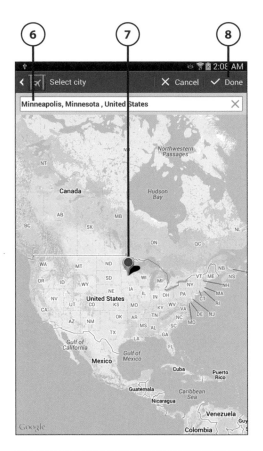

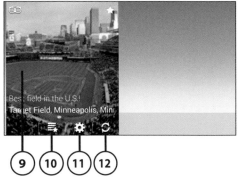

Store and
search all
your contacts

Track your
appointments
and events

Monitor the
weather, news, and
stocks from one
convenient location

In this chapter, you find out how to organize your daily schedule, news, and information. You also see how to add and search contacts and calendar events. Topics in this chapter include:

→ Choosing a weather forecast for your briefing
→ Tracking stocks
→ Selecting your news settings
→ Checking and adding to your personal schedule
→ Setting up contacts accounts
→ Managing contacts
→ Using contacts
→ Creating calendar events
→ Using calendar views

Using Productivity Apps to Simplify Your Life

Your Galaxy Tab 3 is highly capable of helping you organize your busy life. The preinstalled Contacts and Calendar widgets help you improve your daily efficiency by enabling you to manage personal contacts and schedule important appointments. You can also download free productivity apps from the Google Play Store to get the latest weather forecast, learn what's happening on the stock market, and view the latest news stories. This chapter takes a close look at what these productivity apps, as well as the Contacts and Calendar widgets, can do for you.

Staying Up to Date

If you want to stay up to date with news, weather, and stock information, there are several well-reviewed free apps available in the Google Play Store.

- AccuWeather, which is an app that enables you to get up-to-the-minute weather conditions and forecasts for your area.

- The Stock Alert Tablet Edition app enables you to view all sorts of information about stocks.

- If you're looking for news, search for News360 for Tablets.

This section gives you a brief look at these three apps so you can get the information you're looking for on your Galaxy Tab 3. Start by downloading the apps. (You can find out how to download apps in Chapter 16, "Finding and Managing Apps.") You can also explore the Google Play Store to see what other apps might meet your needs.

Choose a Weather Forecast

Follow these steps to display the forecast for a specific city in AccuWeather:

1. On the Home screen, tap Play Store.

2. Tap the Search icon.

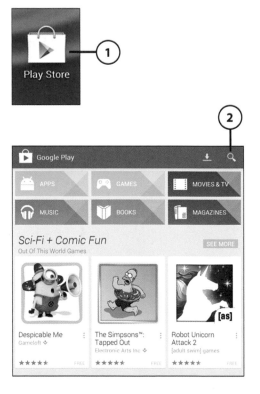

3. Start typing AccuWeather in the Address field.

4. Tap AccuWeather in the search list.

5. Tap AccuWeather in the Apps page.

6. Tap Install.

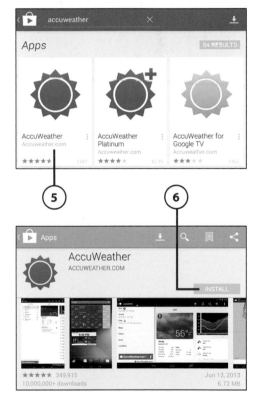

7. Tap Accept.

8. After the Galaxy Tab 3 downloads and installs the app, tap Open. Tap I Agree on the Terms of Use page.

9. Tap Let's Go! on the What's New screen.

10. Tap No Thanks on the Quick Setup screen.

11. Tap My Current Location in the Choose a Location screen.

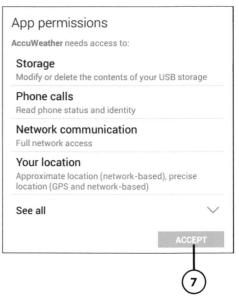

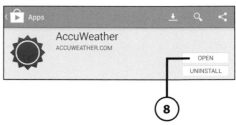

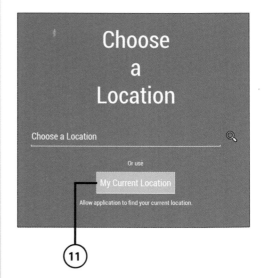

12. The current conditions appear on the screen.

13. Swipe from right to left to view the 15-day forecast in the Daily column. Within the list of forecast dates and temperatures, you can scroll down the days to see the forecasted conditions for the next 15 days.

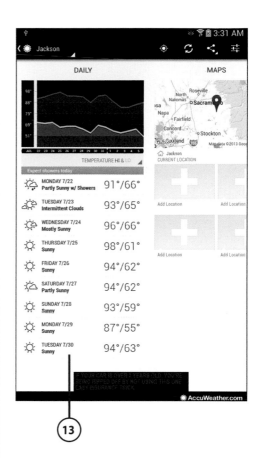

Adding Additional Forecasts

You can add additional forecasts by tapping your current location at the left side of the menu bar, which is located at the top of the screen. In the drop-down menu that appears, tap Add Location. In the Locations column, type a new city and then tap the Search button on the keyboard. You can navigate among the multiple forecasts by tapping the location at the left side of the menu bar and then selecting the location from the drop-down menu.

Updating Forecasts and Other Settings

By default, you must manually refresh the weather forecast by tapping the Refresh icon at the right side of the menu bar. You can further customize your forecasts by tapping the Settings icon that appears at the far right of the menu bar. For example, you can change the wind speed units (such as km/h) and time format.

Track Stocks

You can configure the Stock Alert Tablet app so that you can monitor a desired stock for a company.

1. Tap Play Store on the Home screen.

2. Tap the Search icon.

3. Type Stock Alert in the Search field.

4. Tap Stock Alert in the list.

5. Tap Stock Alert Tablet Edition on the Apps screen.

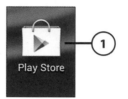

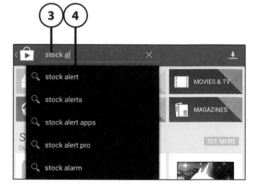

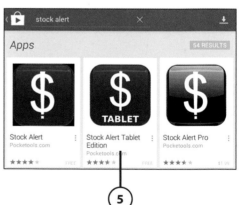

6. Tap Install.

7. Tap Accept. The Galaxy Tab 3 downloads and installs the Stock Alert Tablet Edition app automatically.

8. After the Galaxy Tab 3 downloads and installs the app, tap Open.

9. If this is your first time starting Stock Alert Tablet, tap Accept to accept the End User agreement.

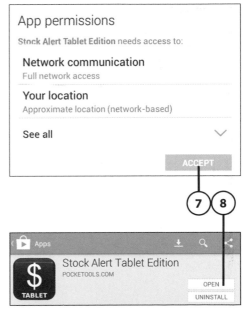

10. Tap the Add Stock icon to add a stock.

11. Type the name of the company with the stock that you want to track. You can also type the stock ticker name.

12. Tap Search to view a list of results for the stock.

13. Scroll down the stock list in the window if necessary. Tap the name of the stock that you just added to view the stock summary.

Adding Additional Stocks

You can add an additional stock by tapping the Add Stock icon, typing in a new stock ticker in the ticker box directly underneath the Search box, and then tapping Add. You can navigate between multiple stocks by scrolling up and down your list of stocks in the left column and then tapping the stock you want to view.

Refreshing Stocks

By default, your stock information must be manually refreshed by tapping the Refresh Rates icon above the list of stocks in the left column on the screen.

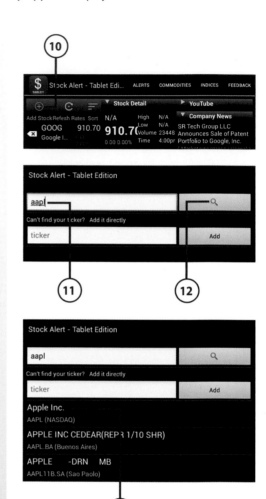

Select Your News Settings

You can browse the latest world, national, and local news stories by customizing your news settings in News360. However, before you can do so you need to create a News360 account.

1. Tap Play Store on the Home screen.

2. Tap the Search icon.

3. Type News360 in the Search field.

4. Tap News360 in the list.

5. Tap News360 on the Apps screen.

6. Tap Install.

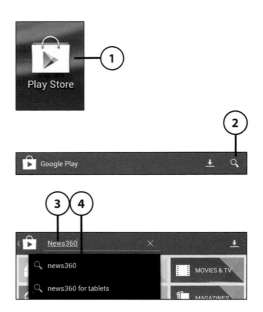

7. Tap Accept. The Galaxy Tab 3 downloads and installs the News360 for Tablets app automatically.

8. After the Galaxy Tab 3 downloads and installs the app, tap Open. On the launch page of the app, tap Sign In to sign in with an existing social networking account.

9. Choose how you want to authenticate with News360 by tapping the appropriate social networking icon. You can use your Facebook, Twitter, Google+, or email account information. This example uses a connection through a Facebook account.

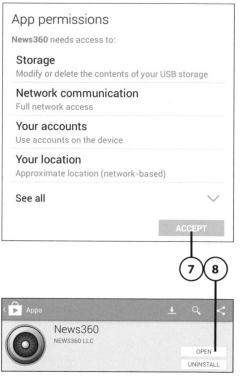

10. In the Facebook screen, type your email account and password, and then tap Log In.

11. Tap OK to give News360 access to your public profile and friend list on Facebook.

12. The opening screen shows you some important features of the News360 screen and how to use the app. Tap Got It, Continue. After you review the information on the screen, tap Start Using News360.

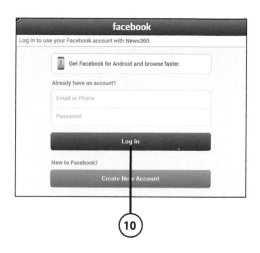

Learn About Important Features

In the opening screen, you can learn about important features including how to save stories to the Galaxy Tab 3, mark stories as interesting, and sync news stories on other devices and the Web.

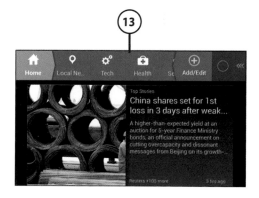

13. Above the default list of stories on the home page, the list of your interest categories appears in the category bar. Swipe left and right within the bar to view all categories in the list. Tap one of the categories to make stories within that category display under the category bar. If there are no stories in the category, News360 invites you to return later.

14. Swipe from right to left in the category bar and then tap Top Stories.

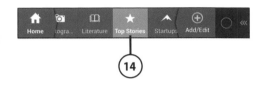

15. The list of top stories appears. You can scroll up and down the list and tap a story title to read it.

Viewing Subcategories

If a category has subcategories underneath it, then those subcategories appear in the category bar. The category appears at the left side of the bar (to the right of the Back icon) and you'll see subcategories to the right of that category. For example, in the Science category there are subcategories that include Space, Biology, and Math. Tap the Back icon to view the main categories again.

16. Options for filtering and customizing your news are located at the upper-right corner of the screen. Tap the arrow icon at the upper-right corner of the screen and then tap the Search icon to search for articles or topics.

17. Tap the Add/Edit icon to open the settings page.

18. Remove one of your existing categories by tapping the X button to the upper left of the category icon or by tapping a gray topic tile that has a green check mark in the upper-right corner of the tile.

19. Add a new section by tapping New Section.

20. Type the category name in the Enter Name box.

21. Hide the keyboard by tapping the Back touch button below the screen.

22. In the Choose Custom Icon section, swipe to the left and right to view all the icons and then tap the icon tile that you want to associate with the category name.

23. Tap Done.

24. Swipe back and forth to view a list of categories you can add to the section, and then tap the category tile you want to add. After you add the category tile, a green check mark appears in the upper-right corner of the tile.

25. After you add all the categories you want to add to the section, tap Done.

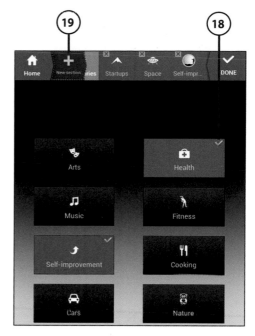

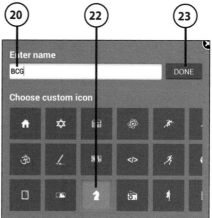

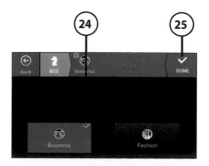

26. Your new section with the category (or categories) you added appears in the category bar, although you might need to swipe to the left within the bar to see it.

26

HOW DO I REARRANGE MY CATEGORIES IN THE CATEGORY BAR?

>>>Go Further

If you want to rearrange categories in the category bar, tap the Add/Edit icon in the bar. In the Add/Edit page, tap the category name at the top of the list, such as My Interests. Next tap and hold your finger on the category name you want to move. Drag the category name to the left or right and then release your finger when the category is in your desired location in the menu.

As you move the icon, you'll see where your icon will appear and other icons will move aside to make room for your icon. Release your finger to place the icon in that location. If you want to move your selected icon to a location in the bar that's currently not visible, move the icon to the right side of the bar. Next, swipe to the left within the bar to view the remaining icons in the bar, and then move your selected icon to the right until the icon is where you want it.

27. Tap the left arrow at the upper-right corner of the screen and then tap the Profile icon.

27

28. In the left side of the screen, swipe up and down to view your account information and sign out of News360, view social networking and app accounts to which you're connected, and to change application settings. These settings include showing or hiding high-quality images when you're connected to the Internet using a 3G connection and to show or hide pop-up messages when you earn stars. You learn more about stars starting in Step 32.

29. On the right side of the screen, swipe up and down to disconnect from your connected service (such as Facebook), change your application settings, and get more information about News360.

30. Return to the News360 home page by tapping Home.

31. Tap the Reading Stats icon.

32. The Your Reading Stats page shows you how many stars you've collected as you've been reading stories. Every time you read a story you receive a star. When you receive 20 stars, News360 begins to personalize the stories you see on the home page so they're in the categories you prefer.

33. Return to the home page by tapping Home.

It's Not All Good

REFRESHING NEWS STORIES

By default, News360 refreshes news stories when the app finds new stories to post in your headlines list. If you want to refresh your headlines list manually, tap the category name in the category bar. After a second or two, updated stories appear in tiles on the screen.

Managing Contacts

The Contacts widget enables you to manage all the important information you receive from colleagues, friends, and prospective business associates. Think of your Galaxy Tab 3 as a virtual filing cabinet or Rolodex where you can store contact information such as names, addresses, emails, and notes. If you collect contacts with other social networking services, you can also configure Contacts to sync information between accounts.

Set Up Contacts Accounts

The Galaxy Tab 3 can synchronize its contacts information with multiple accounts, such as Google, Corporate Exchange, other email providers, and sites such as Facebook and Google+. Information on your Galaxy Tab 3 is updated when you make changes to information in your accounts. Setting up a contacts account is quite easy.

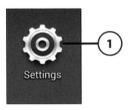

1. Tap Settings on the Home screen.

2. Scroll down the Settings list and then tap Add Account.

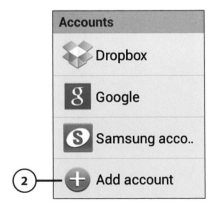

3. Tap an account that you would like to set up.

4. Follow the prompts to set up each account that you would like to add. The accounts you add appear in the Accounts area within the Settings list.

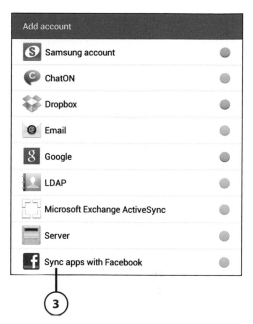

Add account

Samsung account

ChatON

Dropbox

@ Email

Google

LDAP

Microsoft Exchange ActiveSync

Server

Sync apps with Facebook

3

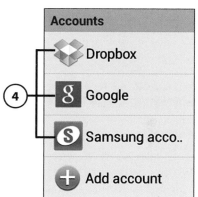

Accounts

Dropbox

4 Google

Samsung acco..

+ Add account

Add Contacts

Using the Contacts widget, you can store contact information for family, friends, and colleagues for quick access and to send messages.

1. Tap Contacts on the Home screen.

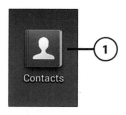

Contacts

1

2. A list of all contacts appears. Your own contact information appears listed by default.

3. Tap the New button at the upper-right corner of the screen to open the Create Contact form window.

4. Tap Device to change the account for which you want to add a contact. For example, you can add a contact in your Google account.

5. In the Attention window that appears, tap OK to close it and ensure that you will not see the message about sync being unavailable for contacts you add to your device.

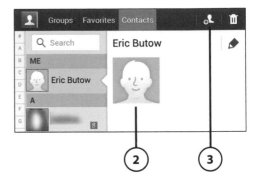

Why Can't I Sync Contacts I Add to the Tab 3?

The Galaxy Tab 3 can't sync contacts you add to the device itself to any other device to which you connect the Tab 3. If you want to sync to other devices you can add the contact to your online contact database stored in your Samsung, Google, or Microsoft Exchange ActiveSync account.

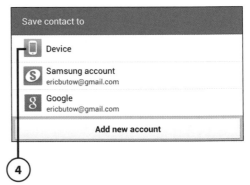

6. Type the first and last name in the Name field.

7. If you want to add the first and last name in different fields, tap the arrow icon located to the right of the Name field to add a Name Prefix, First Name, Middle Name, Last Name, and Name Suffix to the contact. There is no need to use the Shift key on the keyboard to capitalize the name because the Galaxy Tab 3 does this automatically.

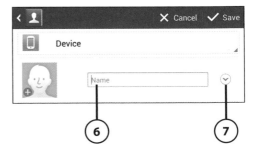

Don't Worry About Formatting

You don't need to type parentheses or dashes for the phone numbers you enter. The Galaxy Tab 3 formats the number for you.

8. Tap the labels within fields to reveal a pop-up menu with other labels to choose from. For example, tap Mobile to the left of the phone number to open the pop-up menu so you can add other phone numbers such as the person's home phone number.

9. Tap the plus icon in the Phone field to add an additional field, or tap the minus icon to remove a field.

10. Add information in the Email section as you did in the Phone section.

11. Add another field to the contact by tapping Add Another Field. You can add the user's phonetic name, organization, instant messaging address, physical address, any notes about the user, the user's nickname, website, Internet phone number, events related to the contact, and the contact's relationship to you.

12. Tap Events to add events related to the contact, such as the person's birthday.

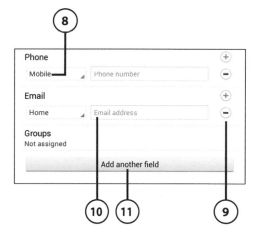

13. Tap the Birthday label to choose the type of event you want to add.

Assigning Contacts to Groups

You can assign a contact to one of six groups (Business, Co-Workers, Family, Friends, My Contacts, or Starred in Android) by tapping the Groups field located toward the bottom of the New Contact sheet and then tapping a group.

14. Add another field to the form by tapping Add Another Field and tapping the field type you want to add.

15. Tap Save to complete the new contact.

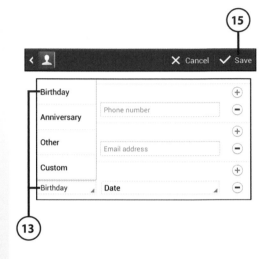

UPDATING A CONTACT AND DISPLAYING CONTACTS

>>>Go Further

You can update a contact by first tapping an existing contact in the Contacts list and then tapping the Edit icon located at the upper right of the screen next to the New icon. The contact sheet opens so that you can edit or add information.

You can control how your contacts are listed by setting the sorting and display preferences. After you launch the Contacts widget, you can tap the Settings icon located at the upper-right corner of the screen, tap Settings, and then tap Display contacts by. The Display Options menu enables you to list by First Name (which is the default setting) or by Last Name First.

Search for Contacts

Your list of contacts is sure to grow the longer you have your Galaxy Tab 3. So how do you search your large list of contacts for a specific contact?

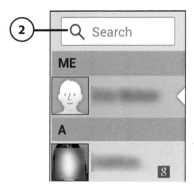

1. Tap Contacts on the Home screen.

2. Tap the Search field and use the keyboard to type the name of the contact you are looking for. As soon as you begin to type, the screen displays the contact that most closely reflects what you've typed into the field. Continue typing until you have narrowed the search.

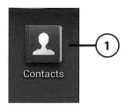

3. View the contact in its entirety by tapping the Back touch button to close the keyboard.

4. Tap the X located in the Search field to clear the Search field of your term. The contact that appears from your search remains visible in the Contacts screen.

Join Contacts

When you synchronize the contacts on your Galaxy Tab 3 with multiple accounts, such as Facebook, Twitter, and Google, you can have varying numbers and address information for a single contact. You can see all the contact's numbers and addresses in a single contact entry by joining contacts. Joining contacts can help you keep your contact information up to date.

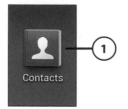

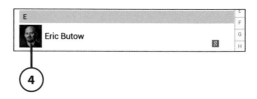

1. Tap Contacts on the Home screen. Your contact information appears on the screen.

2. Scroll down the contact list until you find the contact to which you want to join another contact. Tap and hold your finger on the contact name in the list until a pop-up menu appears.

3. Tap Join Contact in the menu.

4. In the Join Contact window, scroll down the list until you see the name of the contact you want to join to the contact you selected in Step 2. The contacts are now joined and the information for both entries in each account has merged.

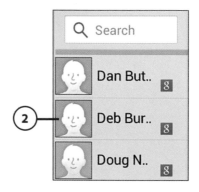

How Do I Unjoin Contacts?

Unjoin contacts by tapping the contact that has the joined contacts attached to it. For example, if Contact A is joined to Contact B, tap Contact A's name in the list. Then tap the Menu touch button below the screen. In the menu, tap Separate Contact. In the Separate Contact window, tap the minus sign next to Contact B. Tap OK to separate the link. Contact B's information is no longer in the record for Contact A.

Use Contacts

After you have entered a contact in your Galaxy Tab 3, you can utilize a few functions and displays directly from the Contacts page. Start by opening a contact's record.

1. Tap the star icon to the left of the contact name to set that contact as a favorite.

2. Tap the Groups tab to view the list of contacts you have assigned to a group.

3. Tap the Favorites tab to view the list of contacts you have designated as favorites.

4. Tap the Contacts tab, and then press and hold your finger on a contact's name in the contact list.

5. Tap Share Namecard Via.

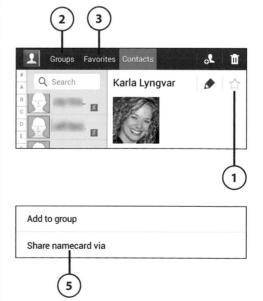

6. In the Share Namecard Via window, share a namecard via Bluetooth, the ChatON messaging service, email, Gmail, or Wi-Fi Direct. Think of a namecard as an electronic business card.

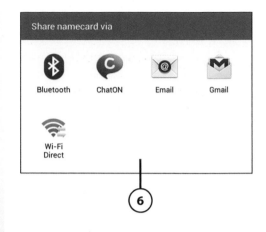

Managing Contacts

After a contact has been entered into your Galaxy Tab 3, you can manage many of the features of a contact by pressing your finger to a it and holding. Options include Join Contact, Add to Favorites, Add to Group, Share Namecard Via, and Print Namecard.

7. Compose a new email to your contact by scrolling down the Contact screen until you reach the Email section and then tap the email icon to the right of the contact's email address.

Managing Your Busy Schedule

The S Planner app enables you to manage all your appointments and events from one convenient location. Calendar enables you to view a busy schedule in multiple views such as Day, Week, Month, and List. You can also instruct Calendar to send you a little reminder, in the form of an alert, before an event to help ensure that you never miss a meeting and are always on time.

Create Calendar Events

Your Galaxy Tab 3 was designed for you to be mobile while still enabling you to manage the important stuff, such as doctor appointments, business meetings, and anniversaries. The S Planner enables you to add important event dates to calendars to help ensure that you do not overlook them.

1. Tap Apps on the Home screen.

2. Swipe the screen from right to left to move to the second page on the Apps screen. Tap S Planner.

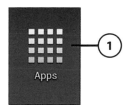

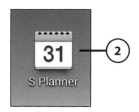

3. By default, the calendar opens to the Year view. Tap the Month tab to open the current month. The current date displays a blue circle around the date.

4. Tap the date for which you want to add an event. The date becomes highlighted.

5. Tap the + button at the top-right corner of the screen. Note that if you see the New Event window informing you that the calendar cannot sync with Samsung Kies, tap the Do Not Show Again check box and then tap Done.

6. The Title field is selected by default. Type a title for the event in the field.

7. Tap the date and time buttons in the From field to enter the start date and time of the event. You can also use the controls in the Set Date window to designate an event for a future date and not just the date you specified in Step 4. When you tap the Date button, a calendar opens, enabling you to select a future date.

8. Tap the controls to enter the start time for the event.

9. Tap Set.

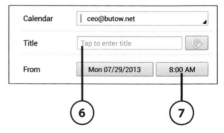

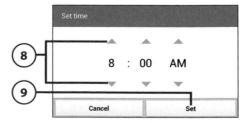

10. Tap the Date tab in the To field to bring up the controls and set the date for the event as you did when you set the date in the From field.

11. Tap the Time tab in the To field to bring up the controls. Adjust the end time for the event in the same manner as setting the begin time.

12. Tap the Time Zone button to change the time zone for the event.

13. Tap the All Day check box if the event will happen all day.

14. Tap Reminder to choose an alarm time for the event. You can choose the time you want the reminder to appear as a notification in the Notification bar or you can send the notification to your email account. Tap the plus button at the right of the Reminder field to add another notification that will appear at a different time and/or delivered in a different manner.

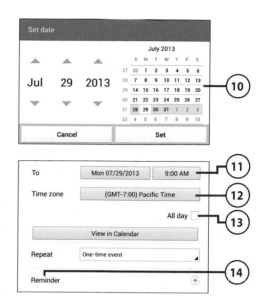

How Do I View the Reminder in the Status Bar?

When you receive a reminder, you get an audio reminder and also see a reminder icon at the left side of the Status bar. Tap and hold your finger on the top edge of the screen and swipe down to open the Quick Settings and Notifications screen. The reminder displays at the bottom of the Notifications area.

15. Tap Repeat if you need to set a repeating cycle for the event. Scroll down to see more options you can set.

16. Tap the Location field to add a location for the event. If you want to find the location in the Maps app, tap the Maps button to the right of the field. You find out more about using the Maps app in Chapter 15, "Using Maps, Navigation, Places, and Latitude."

17. Tap the Description field to type a description for the event.

18. Tap the Participants field to add names from your contacts.

19. Tap the Contact button to the right of the field if you want to select names from the Contacts app. In the pop-up window that appears, select one or more contacts by tapping the check box to the left of the contact name.

20. Tap the Show Me As field if you want others to see that you're available even during the event. Otherwise, the calendar shows you as busy and blocks out that time so anyone else who views your calendar sees that you're unavailable. Scroll down to set more options.

21. Tap the Privacy field and then tap Private in the menu. Otherwise, the event is public so anyone who sees your calendar can view the event.

22. Tap the plus icon to the right of the Images field if you want to add an image to the event. You

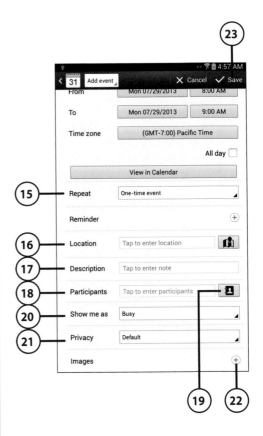

can then take a photo in the Camera app or you can select an image from the Gallery app. You find out how to take photos in Chapter 14, "Capturing and Managing Photos."

23. Tap Save to complete the event and save it to your calendar.

Use Calendar Views

There are six views in which you can view the contents of your calendar: Year, Day, Week, Month, List, and Task. This section examines each view.

Year View

The Year View shows the entire calendar year. At the bottom of the screen, the current year is highlighted. Tap one of the two previous years to the left or the two forthcoming years to the right of the current year to view a calendar for that year. When you change the year, your selected year appears highlighted in the center and links to the two previous years and two subsequent years appear on either side of the selected year.

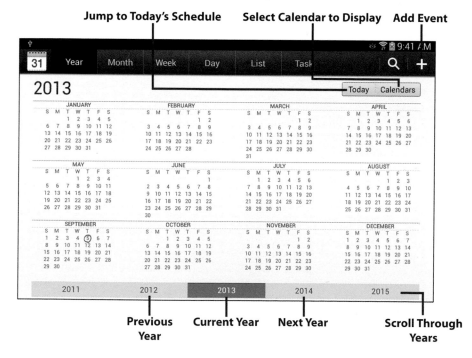

At the top of the screen, two buttons appear to the right of the year. Tap Today to highlight the current date in the calendar. Tap Calendars to select the calendars that appear on the screen from all accounts. These accounts include the calendars stored within the app and all web service accounts connected to your system, such as your Google account.

Day View

The Day view is composed of a list of events blocked for each half hour, with a section at the bottom that enables you to scroll through days and jump to the next or previous month.

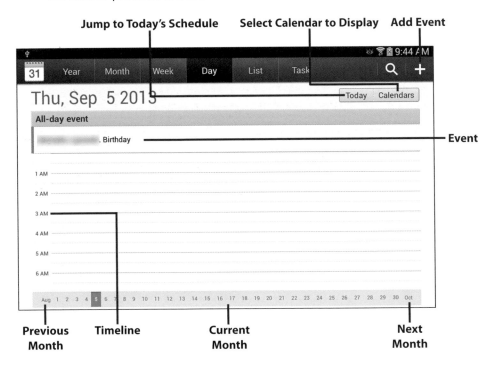

You can press your finger to the list and flick up or down to scroll through the list. All events scheduled with duration of All Day are located at the very top of the list.

Two buttons appear to the right of the date. Tap Today to open the calendar for the current date. Tap Calendars to select the calendars that appear on the screen from all accounts. These accounts include the calendars stored within the app and all web service accounts connected to your system, such as your Gmail account.

The timeline located at the bottom of the screen enables you to scroll or tap forward or backward through days on the calendar. You can also press your finger to the list and swipe left or right to move backward or forward through the schedule in daily increments. Tap the arrows located at each end of the timeline to jump to the previous or next month. The Today button, located in the upper right, enables you to return to the current day's schedule no matter where you are in the calendar.

You can tap an event in the list to view notes, edit the entry, delete the event, or send it via Bluetooth, messaging, the Dropbox online file storage service, email, or Wi-Fi.

Week View

The week view is arranged into seven day parts. The timeline located at the bottom enables you to scroll or tap forward or backward one week at a time, and month abbreviations located at each end let you jump to the previous or next month, such as Sep and Nov if you're looking at a week in October.

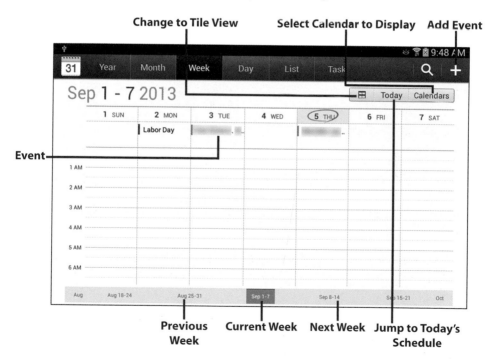

Three buttons appear to the right of the current week at the top of the screen. Tap the Tile button to change the presentation of days into a tile for each day. Tap Today to highlight the current date. Tap Calendars to select the calendars that appear on the screen from all accounts. These accounts include the calendars stored within the app and all web service accounts connected to your system, such as your Google account.

Each event for that week is found in its respective scheduled day block. You can tap an event for any date to view notes, edit the entry, delete the event, or send it via Bluetooth, messaging, the Dropbox online file storage service, email, or Wi-Fi.

Month View

The Month view provides a broad view of events for a given month. Month view is composed of two sections: the monthly calendar and the day's event schedule.

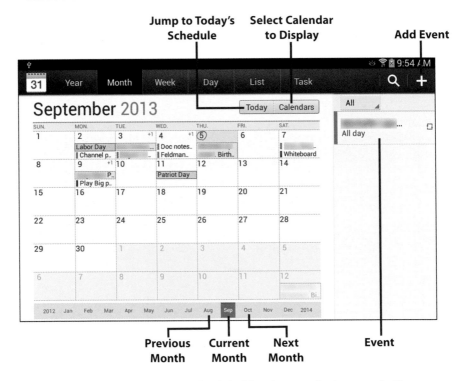

Each section lists the events scheduled for that particular month. The current day block you are viewing is highlighted within the calendar section. Any event designated as an All Day Event is highlighted in the day block of the Calendar view.

Two buttons appear to the right of the month at the top of the screen. Tap Today to highlight the current date in the calendar. Tap Calendars to select the calendars that appear on the screen from all accounts. These accounts include the calendars stored within the app and all web service accounts connected to your system, such as your Gmail account.

The timeline located at the bottom of the screen becomes a monthly timeline in which you can scroll or tap a new month to view. The years located at each end of the timeline enable you to jump to the corresponding month of the previous or next year.

List View

The List view provides a comprehensive view of all scheduled events for an entire year in one list. You can flick the screen upward or downward to view the entire list or tap the appropriate year located at the bottom to jump to a previous year's event schedule or a subsequent year's.

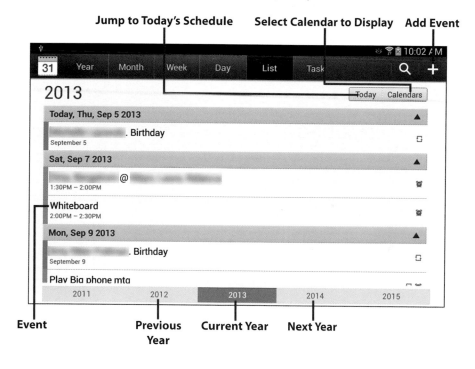

You can tap an event to view notes, edit the entry, delete the event, or send it via Bluetooth, messaging, the Dropbox online file storage service, email, or Wi-Fi.

Task View

The Task View contains the current monthly task and the list of tasks on the right side of the screen. If you don't have any tasks, tap the Tap to add tasks icon in the center of the screen.

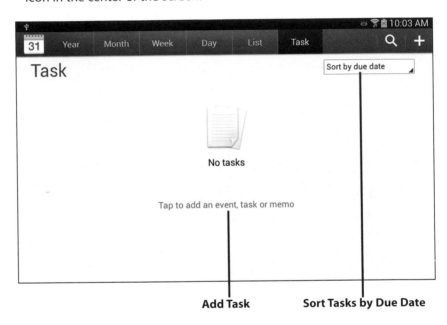

Add Task   **Sort Tasks by Due Date**

1. Tap the Task field and select a person in the menu if you're assigning the task to someone else who also uses S Planner on your Galaxy Tab 3.

2. The Title field is selected by default. Type a title for the event in the field.

3. Tap the date button in the Due Date field to enter the due date for the task. When you tap the date button, a calendar opens in the Set Date window, enabling you to select a due date.

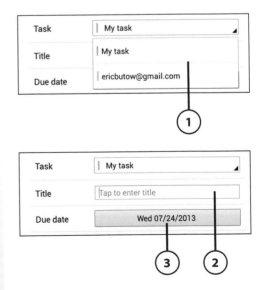

4. Tap the controls to enter the due date for the event.

5. Tap Set.

6. Tap the No Due Date check box if there is no due date.

7. Tap the right arrow button to the right of the Reminder field to open the Reminder window and set a reminder type. You can set a reminder on the due date or set a customized reminder, which is on a date of your choosing.

8. Tap the Priority field to change the priority level in the menu to High, Medium, or Low. The default priority is Medium.

9. Tap the Description field to type a description for the event.

10. If you want to add an image along with the text, tap the plus icon to the right of the Images field. You can then take a photo in the Camera app or you can select an image from the Gallery app. You find out how to take photos in Chapter 13.

11. Tap Save to complete the task and save it to your calendar. The task appears in the Task screen.

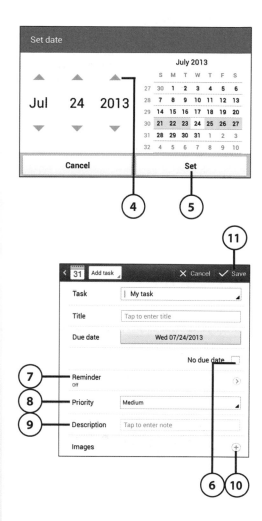

Connect to the cloud
with the Dropbox app

Connect to other devices
using Wi-Fi Connect

The Galaxy Tab 3 is a great tool for viewing web pages, whether you're at home or you're on the go. No matter which Galaxy Tab 3 model you use, the screen is much larger than a mobile phone so you can see more on the Galaxy Tab 3's screen. Because you can touch the screen, you can interact with web content in ways that a computer typically cannot. This chapter covers the following:

→ Connecting using Wi-Fi Connect

→ Printing wirelessly

→ Using the Dropbox app

→ Finding other cloud services

→ Sharing music and video

Connecting to Devices and the Cloud

Connecting Using Wi-Fi Direct

If you need to wirelessly transfer data to or connect with another device such as your smartphone, you don't need to buy a cable or even a wireless router to connect your Galaxy Tab 3 to another device. You can use the Tab 3 Wi-Fi Direct feature to connect to another device that also has Wi-Fi Direct enabled.

Set Up Wi-Fi Direct

1. Tap Settings on the Home screen.

2. Tap the Wi-Fi option in the menu on the left side of the screen if the option isn't selected already.

3. Tap Wi-Fi Direct.

4. The name of your Galaxy Tab 3 appears in the My Device Name section of the Wi-Fi Direct setting options area.

5. The Tab 3 searches for available devices available near you and displays those devices in the Available Devices section.

6. Tap Multi-Connect if you want to show only those devices that can connect to multiple devices through a Wi-Fi Direct connection, such as a wireless printer.

7. Tap the check box next to the device you want to connect to, or tap Select All to connect all devices.

8. Tap Done when you're finished adding devices.

How Do I Know I'm Connected to a Device Through Wi-Fi Connect?

If you're not sure you're connected to another device through Wi-Fi Connect, look in the Status Bar at the top of the screen. The Wi-Fi Connect icon appears to the left of the Wi-Fi icon at the right side of the bar.

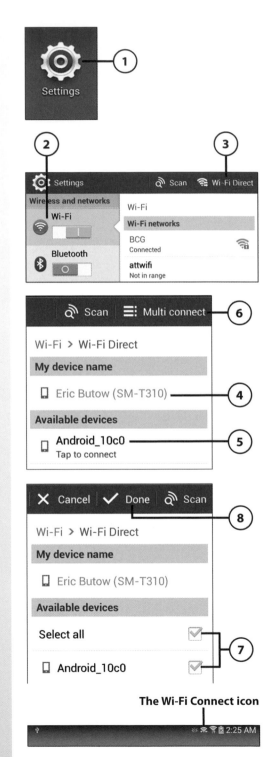

The Wi-Fi Connect icon

>>>Go Further

TROUBLESHOOTING CONNECTION ISSUES

If the Galaxy Tab 3 can't find your Wi-Fi Direct device, check the other device's Wi-Fi connection and ensure the other device offers Wi-Fi Direct. In the Tab 3 Settings screen, try connecting to your Wi-Fi Direct device again by tapping Scan at the right side of the menu bar.

You should also check the Wi-Fi Alliance website to learn if your device is Wi-Fi Direct enabled. The Wi-Fi Alliance is a non-profit group founded in 1999 that was formed to grow Wi-Fi acceptance in the marketplace, support industry standards, and provide a forum so Wi-Fi companies can collaborate and improve Wi-Fi technologies. You can begin searching for products that include Wi-Fi Direct functionality by opening the Internet app and then accessing the Certified Products page at http://certifications.wi-fi.org/search_products.php?advanced=1&en.

Printing Wirelessly

It's easy to print a file such as a word processing document or spreadsheet from your Galaxy Tab 3. You don't need any cables, and you don't need to transfer your files to another computer, either. However, there are some limitations to the printing functionality built into the Tab 3, but you can download apps and use web-based services to get around those limits.

Connect a Wi-Fi Printer

Your Tab 3 automatically scans for wireless printers that are available through a Wi-Fi connection. Note that you might have to enable a Wi-Fi connection on the printer as well. For this example, I use my Hewlett-Packard (HP) Officejet Pro X576dw printer, which I refer to from here on out as the Officejet Pro. The Officejet Pro requires the user to enable HP Wireless Direct functionality on the printer before any device can see the printer.

1. Tap Settings on the Home screen.

2. Connect to the printer by tapping the printer name in the Wi-Fi Networks list.

3. Tap Connect.

4. The printer appears at the top of the Wi-Fi Networks list and displays the Connected status.

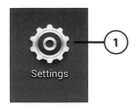

What if the Tab 3 Can't Find My Wireless Printer?

If the Galaxy Tab 3 doesn't recognize your wireless printer, you might need to bring your Tab 3 closer to the printer. You can scan for the printer again by tapping Scan in the Settings menu bar that appears at the top of the screen. When the wireless printer appears in the Wi-Fi list, connect to the printer by tapping the printer name.

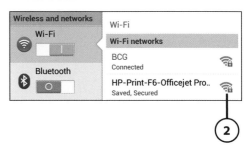

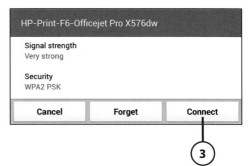

Connect a Bluetooth Printer

If you have a Bluetooth printer, you can also connect that printer to your Galaxy Tab 3 so you can print wirelessly.

1. Tap Settings on the Home screen.

2. Tap Bluetooth.

3. Swipe the slider button from left to right to turn on Bluetooth connectivity. The Tab 3 finds your printer.

4. Tap the printer name.

5. Type the printer PIN in the Bluetooth Pairing Request window using the keypad at the bottom of the screen. You will need to consult your printer documentation and/or the printer manufacturer's website to find the PIN.

6. Tap OK.

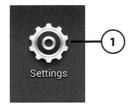

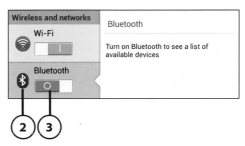

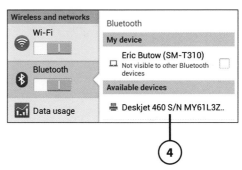

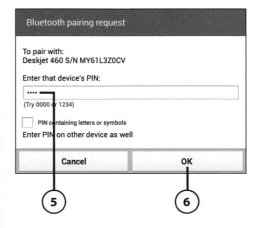

7. The paired Bluetooth printer appears in the Paired Devices section.

8. Tap the Settings icon to the right of the printer name to change the printer name and unpair, or disconnect, the printer from the Tab 3.

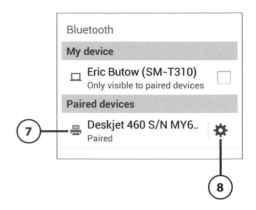

DOWNLOAD A PRINT APP

Samsung boasts that you can print directly from within an app on your Galaxy Tab 3 to any compatible printer without having to connect to a Wi-Fi or Bluetooth printer. Unfortunately, what Samsung doesn't tell you is that you can only print to Samsung's printers. You find this out when you try to print from an app for the first time and see a "You can only print to a Samsung printer" message. Fortunately, there are apps available from the Google Play Store so you can print to other printers.

For example, if you have a Hewlett-Packard printer as I'm using in this example, you can download the HP ePrint app. You can also search for your printer manufacturer in the Google Play Store to see if a printing app is available. There are also apps available from the Play Store for printing to a variety of devices such as PrinterShare Mobile Print, which is free.

If you find a printing app in the Google Play Store that doesn't work for you (or doesn't work at all), another option is to use Google's Cloud Print service. This service connects your printers to the Web so any web-enabled device, including the Tab 3, can access a printer connected to Cloud Print. As of this writing, Google Cloud Print is still in beta test status, so be aware that the service's performance might not match your expectations.

You can access the Google Cloud Print website in the Internet app at www.google.com/cloudprint/learn. After you open the site, you're invited to log in using your Gmail account. After you log in, you can add a printer that's connected to a laptop or PC, or you can add a Cloud Ready printer that is a printer that connects directly to the Web.

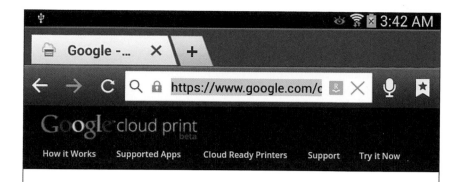

Google Cloud Print

Print anywhere, from any device.

Google Cloud Print is a new technology that connects your printers to the web. Using Google Cloud Print, you can make your home and work printers available to you and anyone you choose, from the applications you use every day. Google Cloud Print works on your phone, tablet, Chromebook, PC, and any other web-connected device you want to print from.

Try it now

Print Anywhere   Print Anything

Google Cloud Print works with all printers, but for the best printing experience we

Any type of application, on any web-connected device, can use Google Cloud Print.

The Google Cloud Print website

Sharing Files

A "cloud storage" service enables you to upload files onto its server computers. Cloud storage services make it easy for you to share large files with others, especially because the maximum file attachment sizes in email messages can vary depending on the email service you use. And downloading email messages with large file attachments can take a long time, anyway.

Use the Dropbox App

The Dropbox app came installed on your Galaxy Tab 3, and you might have set up your Dropbox account when you set up your Tab 3. You can give another Dropbox user access to one or more folders in your account so that other users can upload files to and download files from that folder. The Dropbox icon is available on the main Home screen and/or within the Apps screen.

Add Galaxy Tab 3 Images to Dropbox and Create an Album

1. Tap Dropbox on the Home screen.

2. Tap Start in the Welcome to Dropbox screen.

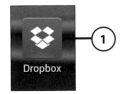

Your stuff, wherever you are

Dropbox lets you bring your photos, docs, and videos anywhere.

Start

3. Type your Dropbox email and password in the Email and Password fields.

4. Tap Sign In.

What if I Don't Have a Dropbox Account?

If you need a Dropbox account, tap New to Dropbox? and create a free account at the bottom of the Dropbox login page. The app takes you step by step through setting up your account.

5. Tap Turn On Camera Upload (which is what this example does) to automatically upload all the images stored on your Galaxy Tab 3 to Dropbox.

6. Tap Skip This if you don't want to upload your images to Dropbox.

7. Swipe up and down in the Photos page to view all the photos that were uploaded to Dropbox.

8. Tap the Select icon to add to put photos into an album.

9. Tap the photo(s) you want to add to the album. Selected photos contain a blue checkbox in the upper-right corner of the photo.

10. Tap Add to Album.

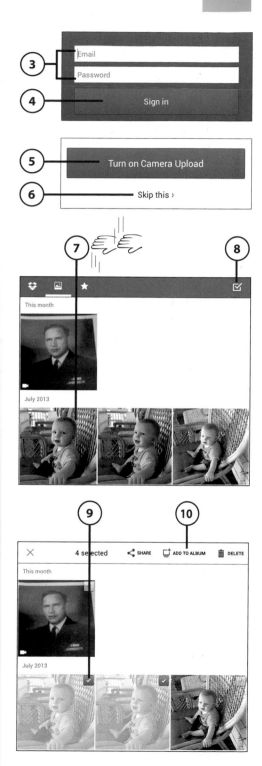

11. Type the name of your album in the Name Your Album field.

12. Tap Done in the keyboard. The completed album displays on the screen.

13. Tap Share Album to share a link to the album on your Dropbox account.

14. Tap the service or app you want to use to share the link.

15. For now, return to the album page by tapping the Back touch button.

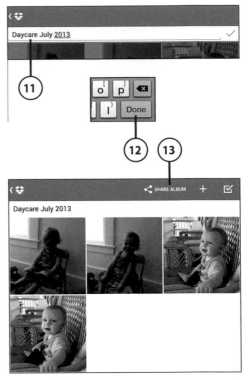

16. Go back to the Photos page by tapping the Dropbox icon.

17. View your list of albums by tapping Albums.

18. View photos in the album within the album page by tapping the album name in the list.

19. Go to the Dropbox home screen by tapping the Dropbox icon in the menu bar.

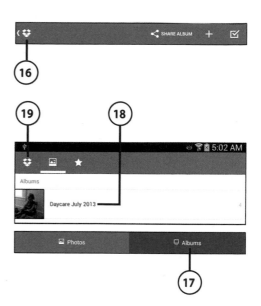

View and Share Files in Dropbox

The Dropbox home screen contains all the files and subfolders within the Dropbox folder.

1. View files within a folder by tapping the folder name in the list.

2. Swipe up and down in the screen to view all the files within the folder. When you find a file that you want to view, tap the file to view it. If the file is a photo or image file as in this example then the file opens within the built-in Dropbox image viewer.

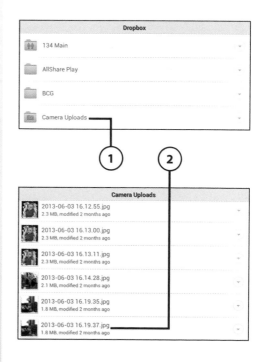

3. After a couple of seconds, the menu bar at the top of the image disappears so you can view the image in its entirety. Open the menu again by tapping on the image.

4. Tap the Trash icon to delete the image from Dropbox.

5. Tap the Share icon to share a link to the file.

6. Tap the service or app you want to use to share the link in the Share a Link to this File message as you did earlier in this chapter. For now, return to the image viewer screen by tapping the Back touch button.

7. Tap the Favorite icon to add the image file you're viewing to your Favorites folder and save the image file to your Tab 3 so you can access it when you don't have a Wi-Fi connection to your Dropbox account.

8. Tap the Menu icon so you can either open the file in another app (such as the image file) or export the file. You can export the file to an SD card, to a photo app, through a direct connection such as Bluetooth or Wi-Fi, in an email message, or on a social networking service in Google+ or your social networking sites within the Social Hub app.

9. Return to the folder page by tapping the Back touch button.

10. You can return to the main Dropbox folder by tapping Up to Dropbox at the top of the list or by tapping the Back touch button.

Access Menu Options

1. The Dropbox home screen icon appears by default and the icon contains a white line under it, which indicates that the home page is active.

2. Tap the Photos icon to view, add, and delete photos and albums in your Dropbox account.

3. Tap the Favorites icon to view all the files you marked as favorites in the Favorites screen.

4. Tap the Search icon to search for files in Dropbox. The Search icon appears only in the Dropbox home screen.

5. Type your search term(s) in the Search My Dropbox field.

6. Tap the Search button in the keyboard. Results display in the Search Dropbox screen.

7. Swipe up and down the screen to view all the files in the list. Tap on a file to view the contents on the screen.

8. Return to the Dropbox home screen by tapping the Back touch button.

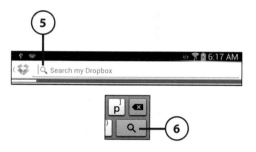

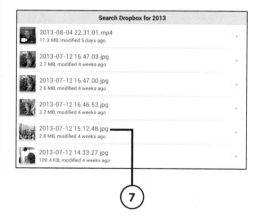

9. Open a menu with more options by tapping the Menu touch button.

10. Tap Upload Here so you can upload files to the current folder you're viewing.

11. Tap New Folder to add a new subfolder within the current folder.

12. Tap New Text File so you can type a new text file within the New Text File screen. This new text file will appear in the folder and is useful if you want another Dropbox user who has access to the folder to read important information.

13. Tap Sort to change the sort order. The default is alphabetical order, but you can change the order to list files from newest at the top of the list to oldest at the bottom.

14. Tap Refresh to refresh the list of files and/or subfolders.

15. Tap Help to get answers to your most common questions about Dropbox.

16. Tap Settings to get information about your account, change your account settings, and learn more about Dropbox.

17. Tap Unlink Device from Dropbox if you don't want to use Dropbox with your Tab 3 any longer but you still want to keep the Dropbox app.

18. Tap Turn Off Camera Upload to tell Dropbox not to upload anymore photos from the Tab 3.

19. Return to the Dropbox home screen by tapping the Dropbox icon in the menu bar.

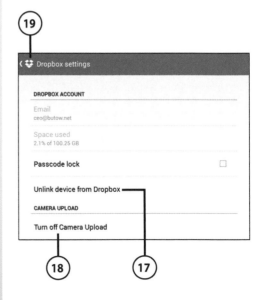

>>>Go Further

GET MORE DROPBOX SPACE

The most important feature on the Settings screen is the amount of space used in the Space used area. The default amount of space you receive is 3GB. When you run the Dropbox app for the first time you receive an email message inviting you to add 48GB to your total space so you have more than 51GB of space available for the next 12 months. After the 12-month period is over, you're asked to renew use of that space for a fee.

When you visit the Dropbox website (www.dropbox.com), you'll see different ways to add more space to your account—many of them free. For example, if you refer someone to Dropbox and that person signs up, you get 500MB of extra space per friend up to 16GB (that is, 32 friends). You can also purchase monthly plans starting at $9.99 per month for 100GB of space.

Find Other Cloud Services

If you prefer to use another cloud storage app other than Dropbox, you can shop the Google Play Store for other cloud storage apps that are optimized for the Android operating system.

1. Tap Play Store on the Home screen.

2. Tap Apps.

3. Tap the Search icon in the menu bar.

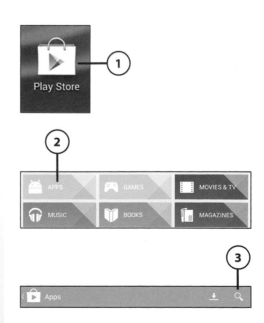

4. Type cloud storage in the Search Google Play field.

5. Tap the search button in the keyboard.

6. Swipe up and down within the list of apps in the search results screen. Tap a tile to view more information about the app. You'll learn more about shopping for apps in the Play Store in Chapter 16, "Finding and Managing Apps."

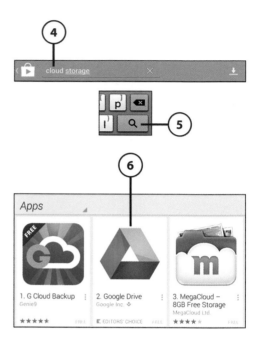

Sharing Music and Video

There are a number of ways you can share your music and video between different devices or between your computer and your Galaxy Tab 3. If you have a computer that runs Windows, you can connect the Tab 3 to your computer and copy files with Windows Media Player. You can also connect your Tab 3 to your Windows computer and tell Windows that your Tab 3 is a storage device. One other alternative is to connect your PC or Mac to your Tab 3 using Samsung's free Kies application.

Copy Files with Windows Media Player

When you connect your Galaxy Tab 3 to your PC with the data cable, you can choose how you want to connect and/or synchronize media files with your Tab 3. One option is to sync your computer and your Tab 3 with Windows Media Player.

1. Connect the data cable from the Tab 3 to the USB port on your computer.

2. In the AutoPlay window on your PC, click Sync Digital Media Files to This Device using Windows Media Player.

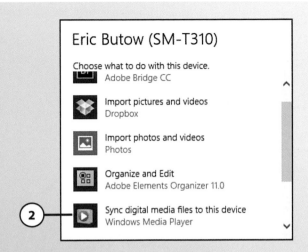

3. Windows Media Player opens and lists media items available for you to copy to the Tab.

4. Click and drag the song title(s) you want to copy to the Sync list.

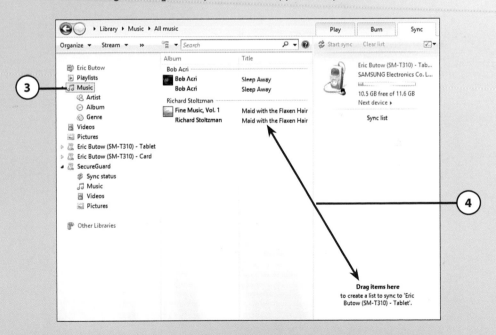

5. The list of music you select appears in the Sync list. All tracks in the albums are selected by default. You can deselect any songs that you do not want to copy by right-clicking the song and clicking Remove from List.

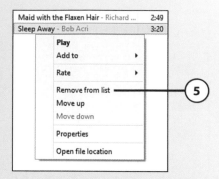

6. Tap Start Sync to begin copying the files from your PC to your Galaxy Tab.

7. After sync is complete, the music is available for playback when you tap the Music Player app on your Tab.

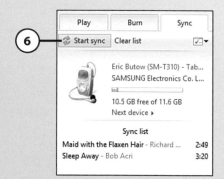

Connect as a Mass Storage Device

You can drag and drop files from a PC to your Galaxy Tab 3 by connecting as a removable disk. Follow these steps to transfer music from your PC to your Tab 3 using the Mass Storage USB mode.

1. Connect the data cable to the Tab 3 and the USB connector to the USB port on your computer.

2. In the AutoPlay window on your computer, click Open Device to View Files to drag and drop music files directly from your computer into a folder on your Tab 3.

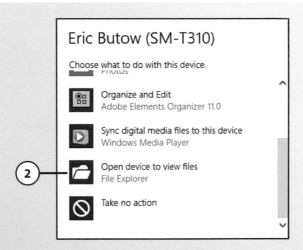

3. Your Tab 3 appears as a removable disk in the Computer section.

4. Display the home Tablet directory by double-clicking on the directory name.

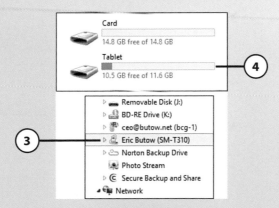

5. Locate the files that you want to transfer from your computer and then drag them to the Music folder on your Tab 3. The files are copied to your device.

6. After you have finished copying files to your Tab from your computer, remove the USB cable from the PC.

7. When you open the Music Player app on your Tab, the music you have transferred is available for playback.

>>>Go Further

CONNECTING TO A MAC

You need extra software to connect your Tab to a Mac. Android File Transfer is an application for Macs running OS X 10.5 or later that enables you to view and transfer files between your Mac and Galaxy Tab 3. This application works with Android devices running Android 3.0 or later. You can download Android File Transfer from www.android.com/filetransfer/.

Samsung Kies for PCs and Macs

The Samsung Kies application makes it easy for you to manage your music, movies, and photos between your computer and your Galaxy Tab 3. When you connect your Tab to your PC or Mac, Samsung Kies acts much like iTunes and Windows Media Player, enabling you to sync your content libraries.

PC and Mac Interfaces

The Multimedia Sync interface is slightly different in PC and Mac versions. You can perform these first few steps on either version, regardless of a few interface differences. The following steps are demonstrated on a PC.

1. After you have installed Samsung Kies onto your computer, connect your Tab to your PC or Mac. Close the AutoPlay window that pops up on your PC.

2. Launch Samsung Kies on your computer. Your Tab opens under the Connected devices list in the sidebar on the left side of the window.

3. If this is your first time using Samsung Kies, you need to populate the library with music located on your computer. Click Music under Library.

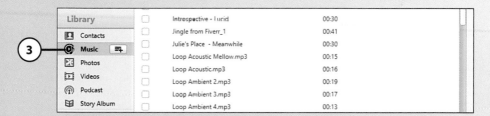

4. Select files by clicking the check boxes to the left of the titles.

5. Click the Transfer to Device button.

6. Click Internal Memory to copy the file(s) to internal storage on your Tab 3; click External Memory to copy the file(s) to the MicroSD card installed on the Tab 3.

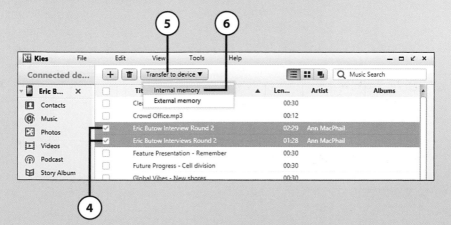

7. After Kies copies the file(s) to your Tab 3 successfully, a message appears in the status bar.

8. Click the Music folder under Connected Devices.

9. The copied files appear in your Music directory within Kies and on your Tab 3.

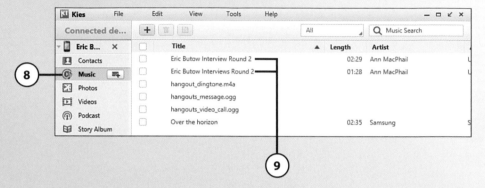

10. Click the Tab 3 name in the Connected Devices list.

11. Click the Sync tab.

12. Select the content that you want to sync to your Tab. As soon as you click the check box for a multimedia category, you are able to select all content for that category or select only specific content.

13. Click Sync. The content is synced to your Tab.

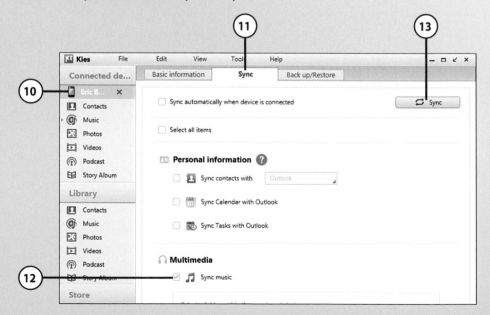

>>>Go Further

USAGE RESTRICTIONS

Some of the music In your Library is Digital Rights Management (DRM) protected, which means use of those files has been restricted. These music files
are from a time when music was not DRM free on iTunes. You won't be able
to transfer these songs without upgrading them for a fee. Visit the iTunes
Store for more information.

Use built-in apps on your Galaxy Tab 3 to enhance your productivity

The Galaxy Tab 3 is a great tool for viewing web pages, whether you're at home or you're on the go. No matter which Galaxy Tab 3 model you use, the screen is much larger than a mobile phone so you can see more on the Galaxy Tab 3's screen. Because you can touch the screen, you can interact with web content in ways that a computer typically cannot. This chapter covers the following:

→ Getting updates from Google Now
→ Using ChatON
→ Connecting to Google+
→ Creating documents and presentations with Polaris Office

11

Using Apps for Learning, Creating, and Sharing

Staying Up to Date with Google Now

Google Now is a new feature that monitors your activity on your Galaxy Tab 3 and shows you various features in various tiles, called cards, that Google Now thinks you'll be interested in based on your past activity. For example, you might see cards with your local weather, upcoming appointments, and current traffic conditions where you live.

Start Google Now for the First Time

You start Google Now by tapping on the Google Search box on the main Home screen.

After you tap the box the Google Now setup screen appears so you can set up and get more information about the app.

1. Tap Next.

2. Google Now gives you an example of how you can use the app to make your life a bit easier, such as getting estimated travel time information to your destination. Tap Next.

3. You can also get information about your upcoming flight. Tap Next.

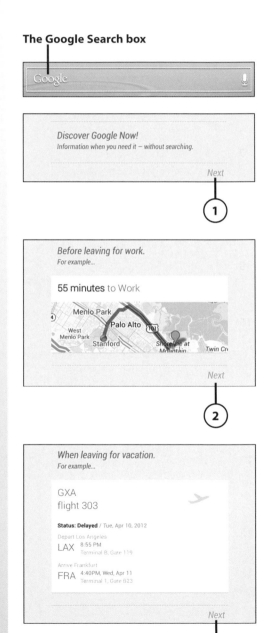

The Google Search box

4. Tap Learn More if you want more information.

5. Tap No, Maybe Later if you prefer to set up Google Now the next time you tap the Google Search box.

6. Tap Yes, I'm In to continue the setup process as described in the rest of this task. The opening Google Now screen displays.

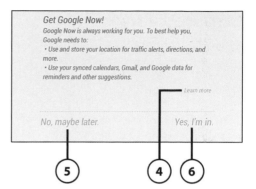

7. Search Google by tapping the Search field, typing your search term(s), and then tapping the Search button in the keyboard.

8. Tap Show Sample Cards to view sample cards.

9. Delete cards by tapping and holding on a card and then swiping to the left or right.

10. Tap Try It Now within the Set Reminders card if you want to try using reminders. You can have Google Now save and display your reminder by saying "remind me" and then stating what you want to be reminded about. Scroll down to see more options.

11. View the current weather information for your city or area by swiping from the bottom of the screen to the top.

12. View your next appointment in the bottom card.

13. Press the Home button to return to the Home screen.

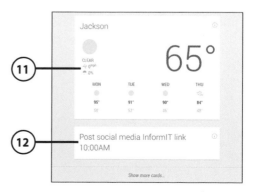

Use Google Now

After you finish setting up Google Now, you can access it by tapping the Google Search box on the primary Home screen. The Google Now screen looks a little different than when you set up the app for the first time.

1. Tap the Google Search box.

2. Type any search term(s) in the Search field. As you type, the first three search results display below the Search field.

3. Tap an item in the result list to open a search result.

4. If you search for a name and/or location, any search results in your Contacts database appears in the list of contacts. View more contact information by tapping the name of the contact. You can also search for more contacts by tapping Search Tablet.

5. View more search results by tapping the Search button in the keyboard.

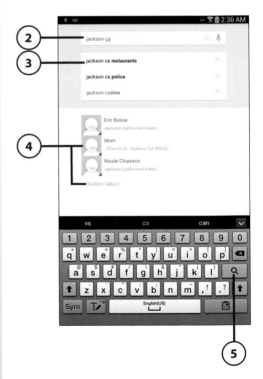

6. The Search results page appears on the screen. Swipe up and down the screen to view the entire list of results on the page.

7. Tap the Back touch button to return to the Google Now screen.

8. Even if you don't search for anything, Google Now remembers your last three searches on the Google search engine and displays them underneath the Search field.

9. Tap Show Sample Cards to view the types of cards that Google Now can add based on your usage of the Galaxy Tab 3.

10. Swipe up and down the page to view all the card types that may appear in Google Now. You can view an alphabetical list of all cards by tapping a card in the Other Cards section.

11. Tap Sample Card under a card's title to view an example of what you'll see in the card.

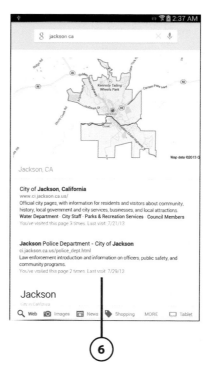

6

8

9

11

10

12. Close the window by tapping the Back touch button.

13. Tap Settings within each card's section to change the Google Now settings. The type of card for which you want to change settings determines the available options in the Setting screen. This example uses the Next Appointment card.

14. View the on/off settings for all the cards. By default, all cards are on. You can turn a card off so you won't see it in Google Now by sliding the On button to the left.

15. Deactivate Google Now by sliding the On button at the right side of the menu bar to the left and then tapping Turn Off in the Turn Off Google Now? window.

16. Return to the Sample Card screen by tapping the Google icon at the left side of the menu bar.

17. Return to the Google Now screen by tapping the Back touch button.

18. View other cards by swiping up and down in the screen. View more cards by tapping Show More Cards.

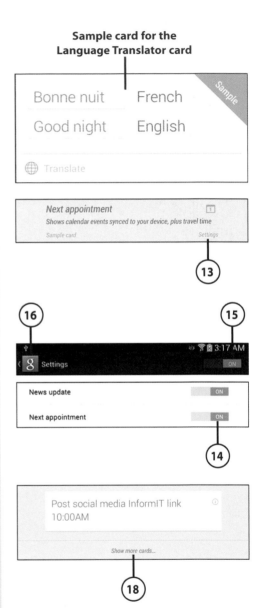

Sample card for the Language Translator card

Bonne nuit   French

Good night   English

Translate

Next appointment

Shows calendar events synced to your device, plus travel time

Sample card   Settings

13

16   **15**

Settings   ON   3:17 AM

News update   ON

Next appointment   ON

14

Post social media InformIT link
10:00AM

Show more cards...

18

19. More cards appear at the bottom of the screen. You can view more sample cards as you did earlier by tapping Show Sample Cards.

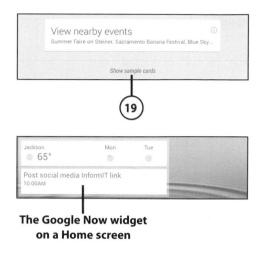

Can I Add a Widget for Google Now?

There is a Google Now widget contained on the Widgets screen covered in Chapter 5, "Adding Widgets to Your Home Screens." After you add the widget to your desired Home screen, the widget appears and displays the current weather conditions for your location. Open the Google Now app by tapping on the widget.

The Google Now widget on a Home screen

Using ChatON

Samsung's ChatON service is an instant messaging app for the web and mobile platforms that's preinstalled on your Galaxy Tab 3. Instant messaging, better known by its acronym IM, is a category of apps that enable you to chat with one or more people in real time by typing text messages and/or using your webcam to talk with each other. Some IM apps are available on the Web only, such as Google+ Hangouts. Others are proprietary apps such as Microsoft's Skype and Samsung's ChatON.

1. Tap ChatON on the Home screen.

2. Tap Next to have the ChatON app check to see if you're logged into your Samsung account.

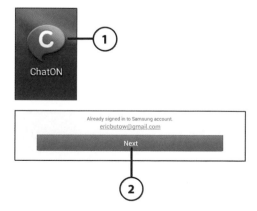

Its Not All Good

WHAT IF I DON'T HAVE A SAMSUNG ACCOUNT OR I'M NOT LOGGED INTO MY SAMSUNG ACCOUNT?

If you didn't log into or set up a Samsung account when you set up your Galaxy Tab 3, you can't set up ChatON. You will have to close the ChatON app, open the Internet or Chrome app, get an account at www.samsung.com, add a new account by tapping Add Accounts, and then tapping Samsung Account in the Add Account window. Your Samsung account appears in the list of accounts after you add the account.

If you aren't logged into your Samsung account, open the Quick Settings and Notification screen and then tap the Samsung notification in the Status window. After you sign into your Samsung account successfully, tap the Next button in the ChatON opening screen again.

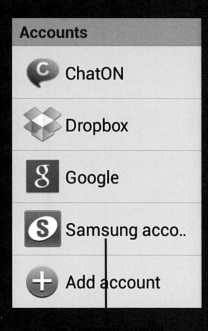

3. The ChatON window opens with the Buddies tab open. If you don't have any buddies then the buddies list shows only your name.

4. Tap the Add Contact button to add a buddy.

5. Tap Search by ID.

6. Tap in the Email field, type the email address of the person you want to add as your buddy, and then tap the Search button in the keyboard.

7. Tap the Add button to add a buddy from the Results list. After a second or two, a pop-up box appears at the bottom of the screen that informs you the app has added the contact. After a few seconds, that pop-up box disappears.

8. Tap the arrow at the left side of the menu bar to go back to the main ChatON screen.

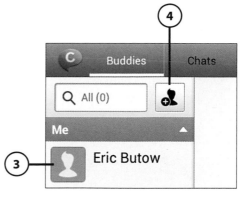

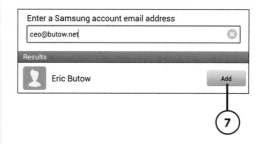

9. Tap the name of your new buddy in the New Buddies list.

10. Tap the Chat button in the contact information that displays on the right side of the screen.

11. Tap in the Enter Message field and type your message.

12. Tap the Send button.

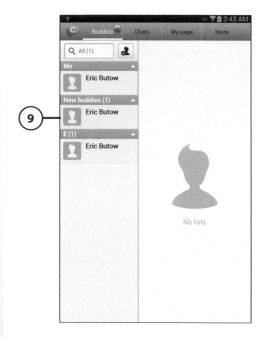

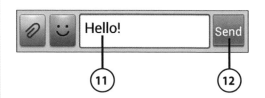

13. Your message appears in the Chat area. Any responses appear below your initial message.

14. Type a response in the Enter Message field.

15. The app saves your chats and displays them in the Chats list. You can view past chats at a later time by tapping Chats in the menu bar and then tapping the chat you want to view in the list. The entire chat appears in the Chat area.

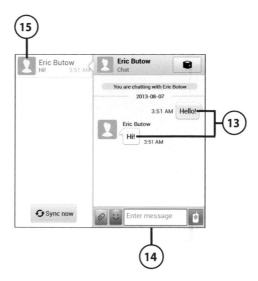

Connecting to Google+

The Google+ social networking website is the sixth most popular such website in the world with an estimated 65 million monthly visitors as of August 2013 (www.ebizmba.com/articles/social-networking-websites). It might come as no surprise that Google is pushing its social networking service by preinstalling its Google+ apps on the Android operating system, and the same is true for Jelly Bean on the Galaxy Tab 3.

Set Up Google+

1. Tap Apps on the Home screen.

2. Tap Google+.

What if I Don't Have a Google+ Account?

This book doesn't discuss creating a new Google+ account. You can learn more about the different types of accounts you can create and how to create an account by visiting the Google Plus website at https://plus.google.com.

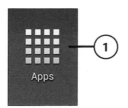

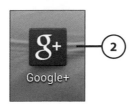

3. When you start the Google+ app, it will log you in automatically using your Google account name and password. If you have more than one Google+ account, the Choose Account screen appears so you can tap the button to the right of the account name with which you want to log in.

4. Tap Next.

5. The Your Contacts screen asks if you want to keep your address book up to date by adding your Google+ connections to your Android contacts. This screen also asks if you want Google to make suggestions about adding new Google+ connections based on who you communicate with most often on your Galaxy Tab 3. The check boxes for these two options are checked by default, which means Google+ enables both of these options. You can disable one or both options by tapping the check box to the left of the option name.

6. Tap Next.

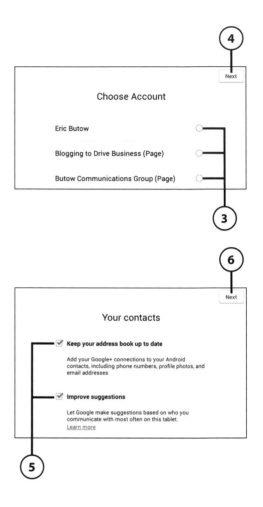

7. The Back Up Your Photos screen appears so you can back up the photos on your Galaxy Tab 3 to a private account on Google+. You can't share this private account with anyone else, and no other Google+ user can see these photos except you. The Over Wi-Fi Only option is checked and highlighted by default.

8. Tap Not Now if you don't want to back up the photos on your Galaxy Tab 3 to your Google+ account.

9. By default, you will also back up any existing photos and videos stored on your Galaxy Tab 3. If you don't want to do this, tap the check box to clear it.

10. Tap Done.

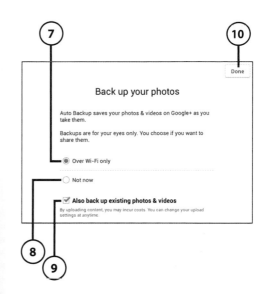

Use Google+

After you set up Google+, the main Google+ screen appears and the latest message from one of your Google+ friends appears at the top of the screen.

1. The gray menu bar appears at the top of the screen so you can access menus, change the updates you view, refresh the screen, and also see how many updates you have.

2. The latest updates appear as tiles on the screen. Swipe up and down the screen to read more updates.

3. The black message bar contains four icons so you can share a

photo you took on your Galaxy Tab 3, send your current location to your Google+ friends, send a message to your friends about your current mood, or write and post a message to your contacts.

4. Tap a tile to open the post on the entire screen.

5. Tap the Add a Comment field and use the keyboard to type your message to comment on the post.

6. Tap the Send icon.

7. Tap the Google+ icon to return to the Google+ home screen.

8. Tap the Google+ icon to open the side menu that shows a variety of options for accessing different parts of Google+.

9. Scroll up and down the list to view all of the options. For example, if you want to create a Google+ Hangout that enables you to set up a video chat with several other users, tap Hangouts in the list to open the Hangouts screen.

10. Tap Home to return to the Home screen.

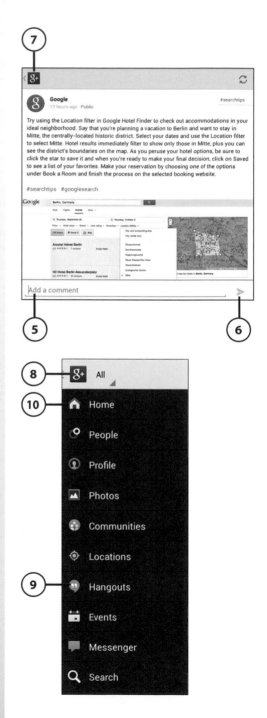

11. By default, you view posts from all of your "circles", which are groups of your Google+ friends that you can modify. View members of only one circle—for example, only people in the Family category—by tapping All to see the menu of circle categories.

12. Tap the circle that contains users whose posts you want to view. After you tap the circle, the screen refreshes and displays the latest posts from Google+ users in that circle.

13. Tap the Refresh icon to refresh the posts on the screen. The icon is blue if there are new posts for you to read.

14. View new and recent notifications in the Notifications list by tapping the Notifications icon. The number of new notifications you have received, such as a new post in a group, appears next to the Notification icon as an orange box with the number of new messages inside it. If there are no new messages, no box appears.

15. New notifications appear at the top of the list. If you see a notification you want to view on the screen then tap it in the list.

16. Close the Notifications list by tapping the Back touch button.

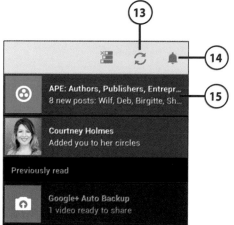

Write a Post

You can write a new post at any time to transmit to circles of friends that you want to receive the message.

1. Write on the Google+ home screen.

2. Type your message in the Text field.

3. Close the keyboard by tapping the Back touch button.

4. Tap the down arrow icon to the right of the list of circles to specify one or more circles with which you will share your post. Otherwise, your message will be sent to all your circles as well as to everyone in the Public circle—that is, all Google+ users.

5. Tap the circle(s) that will view your post from the list. You can also tap Or Pick People and Circles in the menu to open the Share With screen and pick your circles or specific contact name from the list.

6. Tap the Location field if you want to share your location of your post with your viewers.

7. Select your location from the Share Your Location screen. After you select your location, you might see a window reminding you how to delete your location. If you do, tap OK.

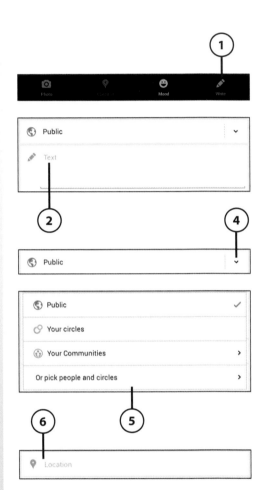

8. The location name you selected appears in the Write Post screen.

9. Tap Share when you're finished writing your post. After a second or two the main Google+ screen appears and your post appears as a tile on the screen.

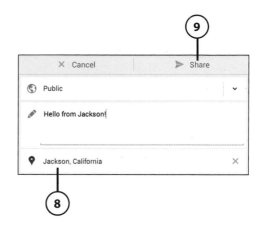

Creating Documents and Presentations with Polaris Office

Polaris Office is a productivity app from Infraware that's preinstalled on your Galaxy Tab 3 so you can work on your favorite Word, Excel, and PowerPoint files right on your Tab 3. You can send files to yourself and others by email or an online file-sharing service such as Dropbox. You can also print your documents and convert the files to Adobe PDF (Portable Document Format) files so others with a PDF reader app, such as the free Adobe Reader, can view documents exactly as you formatted them. What's more, you can open and read PDF files directly within the Polaris Office app.

Start Polaris Office for the First Time

1. Tap Apps on the Home screen.

2. Go to the second page of the Apps screen by swiping from right to left on the screen.

3. Tap Polaris Office.

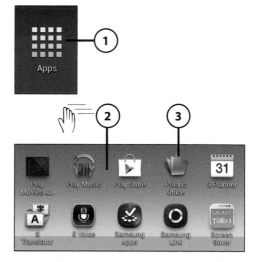

4. When you start the app for the first time, a registration screen appears so you can register the app with Infraware. Tap the Skip button if you don't want to register. You will receive a registration notice every time you start the app until you register, but you can turn off the registration notice for seven days by tapping the Do Not Remind Me for 7 Days check box.

5. Tap the Register button to register the program. Within a few seconds, the app registers itself and displays the Polaris Office home screen.

6. Tap a guide icon to read about how to edit Excel spreadsheets, PowerPoint presentations, and Word files.

7. Tap Browser.

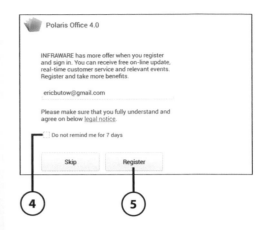

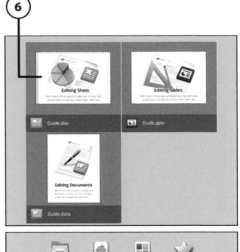

Icons for accessing files on your Tab 3 or an online file-sharing service

8. Scroll up and down the folder in the tree, tap the folder name within the tree, and then tap the file you want to open in the list on the right side. If there are subfolders underneath a folder, then the subfolders appear underneath the parent folder in the tree when you tap the parent folder name.

9. Tap the star icon if you find a file that you want to tag as a favorite for quick retrieval later. The star changes from gray to gold to signify that the file is a favorite. Read more about how to access your favorite files later in the "Mark and View Your Favorite Files" section later in this chapter.

10. Tap the arrow in the menu bar to return to the Recent Documents screen.

Subfolders

Access Files from a Cloud Service

1. Tap Clouds in the Polaris Office home screen to access an online file-sharing service, including Box, Dropbox, or Google Docs.

2. Tap the service you use in the menu. After you tap a service, you might be asked to install the app specifically designed for use with Polaris Office. This example uses Dropbox.

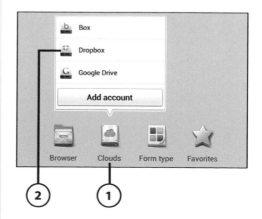

3. If you don't allow apps from locations other than the Google Play Store to install on your Tab 3, a window appears informing you of this; tap Settings.

4. Tap Unknown sources in the Settings screen, Security page.

5. Tap OK in the Unknown Sources window.

6. Return to the Polaris Office home screen by tapping the Back touch button.

7. Tap Clouds and then tap Dropbox.

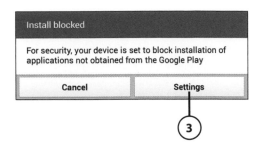

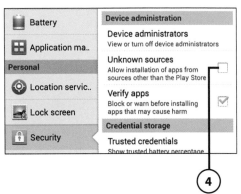

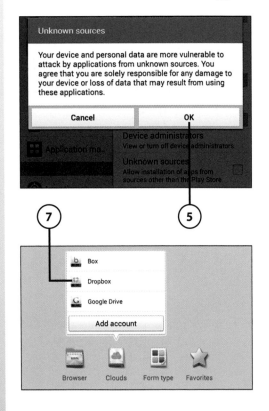

8. Install Dropbox for use with Polaris Office by tapping Install.

9. Tap Accept to continue installing Dropbox.

10. Tap Done when the app is installed.

11. Tap Clouds and then tap your Dropbox user ID in the list.

12. Folders within your Dropbox folder appear at the right side of the Browser screen so you can open the file you want within the appropriate folder or subfolder.

13. Return to the Polaris Office home screen by tapping the Back touch button.

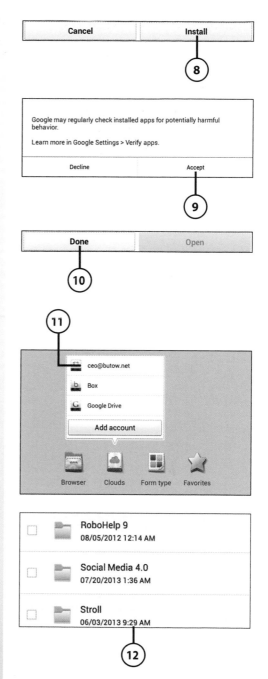

View Files by Document Type

1. Tap the Form Type icon in the Polaris Office home screen if you want to view documents by document type on your Galaxy Tab 3 and any registered online file-sharing services.

2. The Form type screen appears with a list of all Word documents Polaris Office has found on the left side of the screen.

3. Tap Documents in the menu bar.

4. Select from one of the five file types: Documents (Word documents), Sheet (Excel spreadsheets), Slide (PowerPoint presentations), Text (text files), or PDF (PDF files).

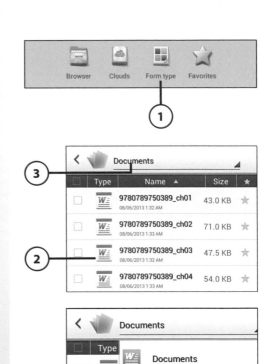

5. The list of files appears in alphabetical order on the left side of the screen.

6. You see thumbnail images of recently opened files in the Recent Files area on the right side of the screen.

7. Each file in the list contains the filename, the date and time the document was last updated, and the size of the file. You can swipe up and down the list to view all the files in the list. When you find a file you want to open, tap the filename.

8. Tap the check box to the left of one or more filenames to send the files to someone else.

9. Tap Send.

10. Tap the service or app you want to use to send the files. This example uses a Wi-Fi Direct connection that you can read about in Chapter 10, "Connecting to the Cloud."

11. Select the device to which you want to connect by tapping the device in the Connected Devices section.

12. Tap Done.

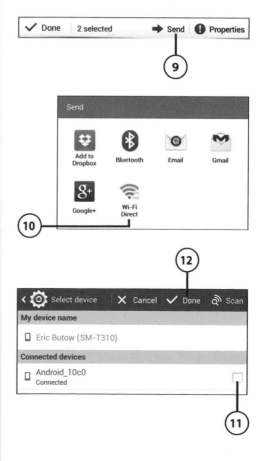

13. You see an upload completion icon in the Status Bar after the Tab 3 uploads the files to another device. In addition, a pop-up window appears at the bottom of the screen that informs you that the files were uploaded to the other device successfully.

14. You might also see a warning icon in the Status Bar; when you open the Quick Settings and Notifications screen you'll see the warning to disable Wi-Fi Direct after you use it to conserve battery life.

Mark and View Your Favorite Files

If you set any files as favorites, you can view them by tapping the Favorites icon.

1. Tap Browser in the Polaris Office home screen.

2. Open the folder that contains the file you want to add as a favorite.

3. Add the file as a favorite by tapping the star icon to the right of the filename.

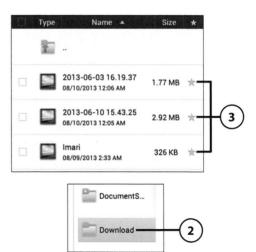

4. The star turns gold, which signifies that the file is now one of your favorites.

5. Return to the Polaris Office home screen by tapping the left arrow button at the left side of the menu bar.

6. Tap Favorites to view your favorite file. The list of favorite files displays on the left side of the screen.

7. Tap a file to view it in the associated app.

8. Send a file by tapping the check box to the left of the file(s) you want to send and then tap Send.

9. Tap the service or app you want to use to send the files as you did in the previous section, "View Files by Document Type."

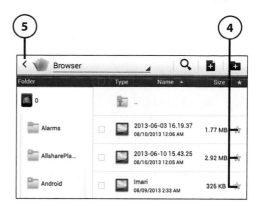

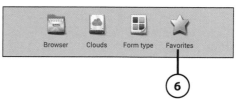

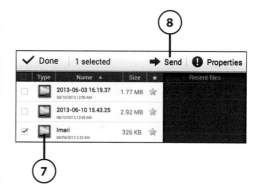

10. Tap the star to the right of a filename to remove the file from your favorites list. The star turns gray, which signifies the file is no longer a favorite. The next time you open the Favorites screen you won't see the file in the list.

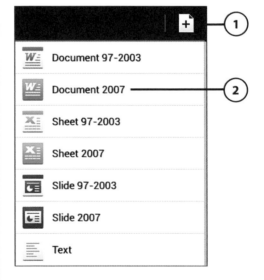

Create a New Document

Polaris Office makes it easy for you to create a new document, spreadsheet, slideshow, or text file. This example describes how to create a Document 2007 file, which is a file in Microsoft Word 2007 or later format.

1. Tap the New Document icon on the Polaris Office home screen.

2. Tap Document 2007.

3. Tap one of the six template thumbnail images that you want to apply to your document: A blank sheet of paper (no formatting), a formal letter, a manual, a fax cover sheet (called an official document), a report, or a résumé.

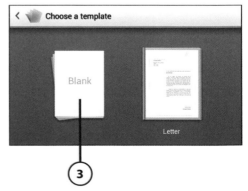

4. The new document appears on the screen with the keyboard at the bottom of the screen. As you type, your text appears in the default document font.

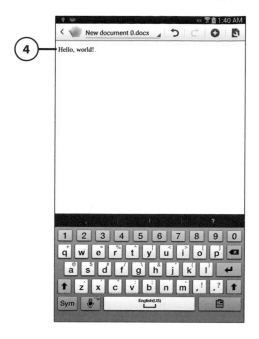

What Appears on the Screen When I Choose Another Template?

When you open a template that isn't blank, the new document opens with the template layout and dummy text. You can replace this dummy text, such as the name of the letter recipient, with the actual recipient's name.

5. Tap the arrow Icon on the menu bar to go back to the Polaris Office home screen. If you haven't saved the document, a Close window appears that asks if you want to save changes. If you want to return to editing the document, tap Cancel in the window.

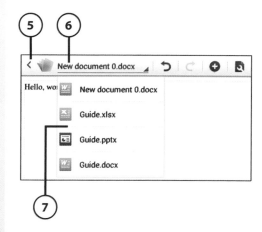

6. The default document title name shows New Document 0, which is the default name of the document.

7. Tap the filename to open a drop-down menu and view a list of documents you viewed recently. Tap the document name to open it.

8. Close the menu by tapping the Back touch button.

9. Tap Undo to reverse the previous action, such as deleting a word.

10. Tap Redo to reapply the previous action you previously undid. For example, if you tapped the Undo icon after deleting a word, tap the Redo icon to delete the affected word again.

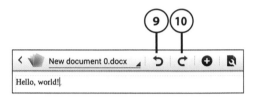

11. Tap the Add Object icon to select an object to add to your document within the drop-down menu. Objects include a saved image, a photo taken with the Camera app, and a table.

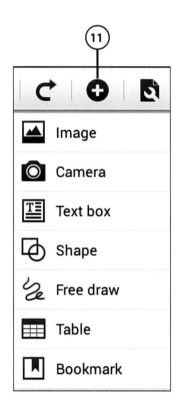

12. Tap the Format icon to change the font size, style, and color, change the appearance and alignment of the selected paragraph, and apply a text style to a selected area of text. For example, you can apply the Title style to a word you want as the document title.

13. Open the Tools menu by tapping the Menu touch button.

14. Tap Save to save the document with its current name in your chosen folder or subfolder.

15. Tap the Save As icon to save the document with a new name.

16. Swipe down the menu to view all the tools options, including the ability to export the document to a PDF file, find and replace text, and print your document if you're connected to a printer via a Bluetooth or Wi-Fi connection.

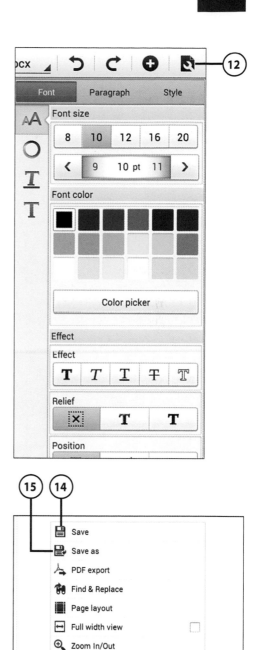

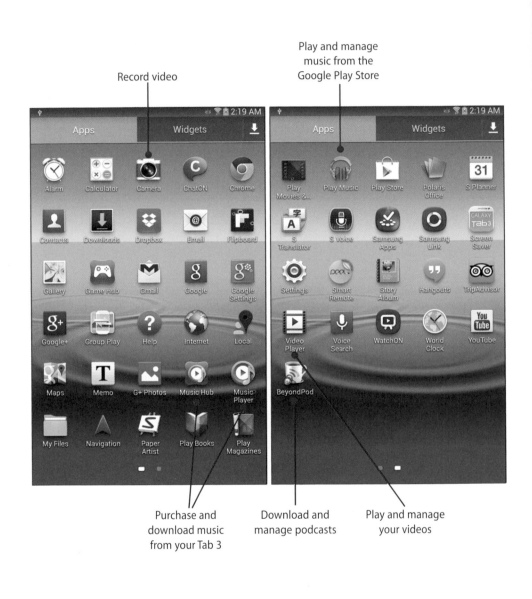

Record video

Play and manage
music from the
Google Play Store

Purchase and
download music
from your Tab 3

Download and
manage podcasts

Play and manage
your videos

In this chapter, you find out how to get the most out of the media and entertainment capabilities of the Galaxy Tab. Topics in this chapter include the following:

→ Purchasing music, movies, and TV shows
→ Playing videos
→ Recording video
→ Adding a podcast app
→ Playing songs
→ Creating your own playlists
→ Viewing YouTube videos

Playing Music and Video

Your Galaxy Tab 3 is a digital media player packed with entertainment possibilities as well as a camcorder capable of recording 1080p HD video. You can play music, movies, TV shows, podcasts, audiobooks, and videos; read eBooks; view photos; and access YouTube. Your Tab 3 is preloaded with a variety of apps for purchasing and downloading media.

Downloading Movies and TV Shows

The Google Play Store makes it easy for you to browse, purchase, and download the latest music, movies, and popular TV shows to your Galaxy Tab 3. If you want to find movies and television shows within the Google Play Store more quickly than shopping in the Play Store itself, try using the preinstalled Play Movies & TV app.

The Play Movies & TV app enables you to shop for movies and television shows, pay for a movie or show if necessary, download the movie or show, and then watch the movie or show within the app. In this example, you find out how to download a free television featurette.

Download a TV Show

1. Tap Apps on the Home screen.

2. Move to the second page in the Apps screen by swiping from right to left on the screen.

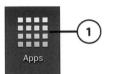

3. Tap Play Movies & TV.

4. Tap Shop in the menu. The Movies page displays.

5. Tap TV to view TV shows.

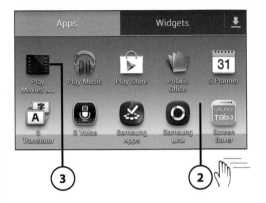

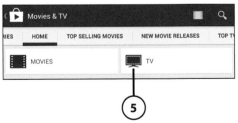

6. Swipe down the TV page until you see the Free Featurettes section. Tap See More.

7. Swipe down the page until you see the tile that contains the featurette you want to download and then tap the tile.

8. In the middle of the page, information about the selected featurette appears below the title, including an image, summary, and reviews from other Play Store users who have watched the video. Swipe down the page to read more reviews.

9. Tap Free to the right of the featurette title.

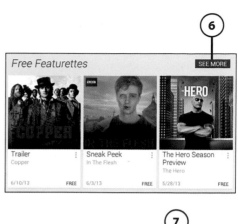

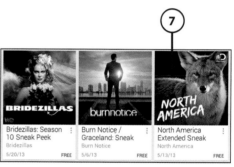

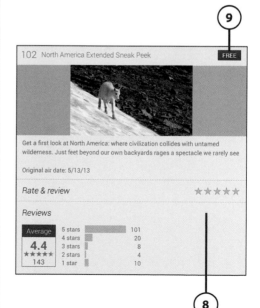

10. The Buy window shows you the credit card that you have on file with Google Play, which you need in order to buy a movie or TV show (even free ones) from the Play Store. If you don't have a card on file, Google Play will take you through the steps to register your credit card.

11. Tap Buy. After a second or two, the Payment Successful window displays. The window closes after a few seconds and the listing reappears with the Added indicator to the right of the featurette title.

12. Play the video in horizontal screen orientation by tapping Play.

13. When you finish viewing the featurette, tap the Back button. View the featurette again by tapping the tile.

14. Return to the My TV Shows screen by tapping the Movies & TV icon in the menu bar.

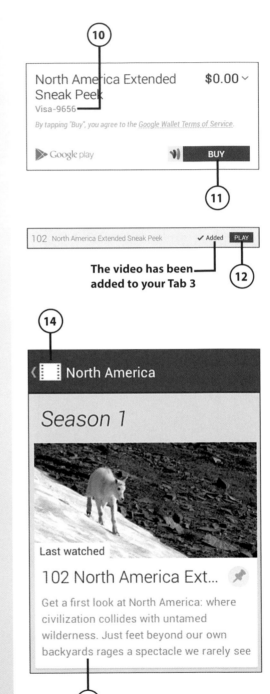

The video has been added to your Tab 3

Play the TV Show

The TV show you downloaded appears within the My TV Shows section so you can play it whenever you want.

1. On the Movies & TV app home screen, open the menu by tapping the Movies & TV icon in the menu bar. (Skip this step if the menu is open already.)

2. Tap My TV Shows. The shows you downloaded appear in each section; the most recent videos you downloaded appear at the top of the screen.

3. Tap a tile to play a video.

4. Tap See More to view more information about each video in the section.

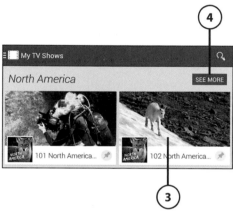

Shop for a Movie

1. On the Movies & TV app home screen, open the menu by tapping the Movies & TV icon in the menu bar. (Skip this step if the menu is open already.)

2. Tap Shop.

3. Tap Movies.

4. Tap Categories.

5. Tap the category you're interested in.

6. Swipe up and down in the page to view all the Top Selling movies in the category you selected. You can view new releases in the category by tapping New Releases.

7. Tap the tile with the movie you want more information about.

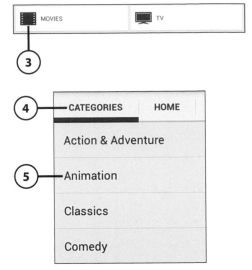

8. The name of the movie, the category, and buttons to either rent or buy the movie at the stated price appear at the top of the screen.

9. Swipe up and down the information area to view the video trailer; rate and review the movie; view user reviews; read the synopsis, cast, and credits; and get rental period information. In this example, the rental period for *Monsters, Inc.* specifies that you must start watching the movie within 30 days of purchase and you can continue to watch the movie for up to 72 hours after you start watching it.

10. Tap the Buy From button to purchase the movie and download it to your Galaxy Tab 3 so that you can watch it whenever you want.

11. If your Tab 3 supports HD format, you can buy the HD version of the movie for a higher price. The Galaxy Tab 3 7.0 as well as the 8.0 used in this example does not support HD playback, but you can purchase HD format movies on the Tab 3 10.1.

12. Tap Buy SD.

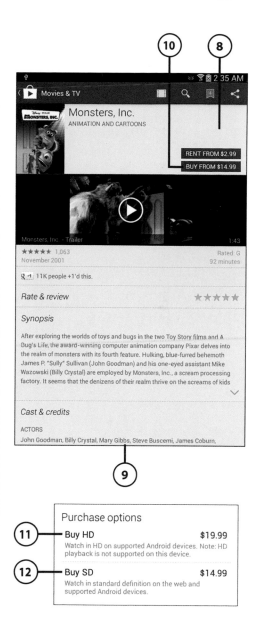

13. The Buy window shows you the credit card that you have on file with Google Play, which you need in order to buy a movie or TV show (even free ones) from the Play Store. If you don't have a card on file, Google Play will take you through the steps to register your credit card.

14. Buy the movie by tapping Buy. Google Play charges the card you have on file and downloads the movie to your Tab 3 so you can view the movie.

Playing Videos

There are two ways to view movies, TV shows, and other videos on your Galaxy Tab 3. One is to watch in the Play Movies & TV app. The other is the Video app that makes it easy for you to browse and play your downloaded and recorded videos.

Play Movies and TV Shows in the Play Movies & TV App

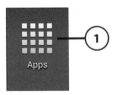

1. Tap Apps on the Home screen.

2. Move to the second page in the Apps screen by swiping from right to left on the screen.

3. Tap Play Movies & TV.

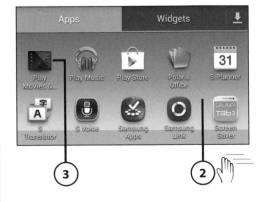

4. Tap Watch Now in the menu.

5. Swipe up and down in the Watch Now screen to view movies and TV shows you downloaded as well as get recommendations for movies and TV shows from Google Play.

6. Open and watch the video by tapping the movie or TV episode tile.

Play Videos in the Video Player App

1. Tap Apps on the Home screen.

2. Move to the second page in the Apps screen by swiping from right to left on the screen.

3. Tap Video Player.

4. By default the Video Player screen displays videos in Thumbnails view. That is, the video plays in a small area of the screen.

5. Change the screen view by tapping Thumbnails in the menu bar. You can view videos by List (a list of video files on your Tab 3), Folders (a list of files and folders), and videos on nearby devices.

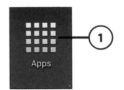

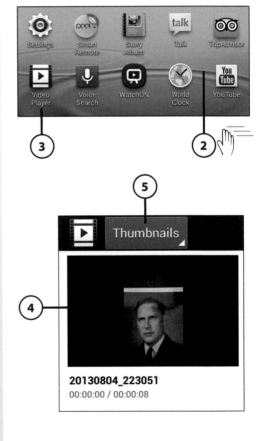

20130804_223051
00:00:00 / 00:00:08

6. View your video files and the folder that contains those files by tapping Folders.

7. Tap a video in the list to begin playing it.

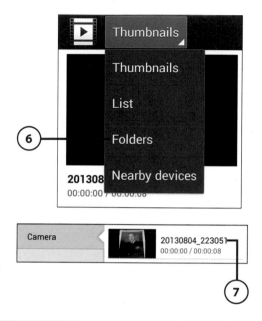

OTHER VIDEO OPTIONS

Tap the Menu touch button to choose how videos are listed, shared, and deleted or to customize playback options. The List By options enable you to arrange a video library by Name, Date, Size, and Type. The Share Via option enables you to upload videos to YouTube, Google+, AllShare, Bluetooth, Wi-Fi Direct, Dropbox, and even Gmail. You use the Delete option to select one or more videos and then delete them. The Video Editor option enables you edit the video in the Video Editor app that isn't installed on the Galaxy Tab 3 by default and so is not covered in this chapter. The Auto Play Next feature is set to Off by default, but you can configure your Tab 3 to automatically begin playing the next video in the list after the current video ends. You also can touch and hold your finger on a video in the list to reveal contextual menu options, such as Share Via, Delete, and Details.

8. After the video has started, tap in the middle of the screen to bring up the playback controls.

9. Adjust the volume of the video by tapping on the Volume icon and then sliding your finger on the Volume slider.

10. Tap the AllShare icon to select the device with which you want to share the video through the AllShare Play service.

11. Tap the Screen View icon to change the display mode to full screen or to return to the normal view.

12. Tap the Minimize icon to view the video in a small window on the screen. Tap once in the window to pause the video and tap twice to open the video in the previous view (that is, full screen or normal view).

13. Tap the Dolby icon to set the sound quality to Movie, Music, or Voice.

14. Drag your finger across the Movie Timeline to advance through the video or jump to a new location. You can also tap the timeline in a new location to jump to that location.

15. The Play button, located in the Playback controls, turns into a Pause button as the video plays. Tap the Pause button to pause the video.

16. Tap the Rewind or Fast Forward buttons to move to the beginning or end of the video, respectively.

17. Tap the Menu touch button.

18. Tap Share Via to share the video using ChatON, Dropbox, Google+, Bluetooth, Wi-Fi Direct, YouTube, Picasa, Gmail, or Email.

19. Tap to view each slide within the video.

20. Tap to edit the beginning and end of a video by performing a trim or to edit the video in the Video Editor app.

21. Tap to share the video with other devices via Bluetooth.

22. Tap to set the app to automatically turn off video after playing a certain amount of time. Options include After Playing, After 15 min, After 30 min, After 1 hour, After 1 hour 30 min, or After 2 hours.

23. Tap to connect to nearby devices. You learn how to use Bluetooth devices with your Galaxy Tab 3 in the "Pairing Bluetooth Devices" section of Chapter 17, "Adding New Hardware."

24. Tap to configure play speed, subtitles, and auto play settings.

25. Tap to view details of the video such as Name, Size, Resolution, Duration, Format, and Date Modified.

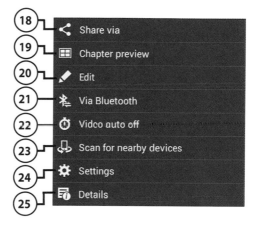

Viewing YouTube Videos

The high-resolution screen of the Galaxy Tab 3, along with its portability and built-in video camera, makes it great for viewing and sharing videos online. The preinstalled YouTube widget gives you the capability to browse and view videos posted by users from around the world. You can also upload videos as soon as you shoot them with your Tab 3.

1. Tap Apps on the Home screen.

2. Move to the second page in the Apps screen by swiping from right to left on the screen.

3. Tap YouTube.

4. Close the opening message by tapping OK.

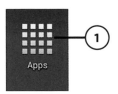

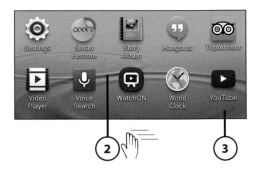

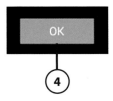

5. A list of your channels appears on the left side of the screen and a list of featured videos appears on the right side.

6. Tap Browse Channels to view channels YouTube recommends for you.

7. View channels by swiping up and down the screen. You can see videos and more information about the artist channel by tapping the channel tile.

8. Return to the YouTube home screen by tapping the YouTube icon in the menu bar.

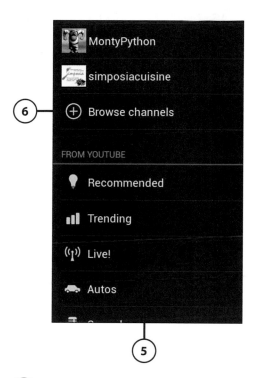

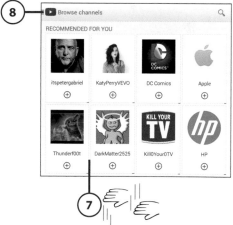

9. Tap the Search icon to search for a YouTube video.

10. Type the search terms in the Search YouTube field.

11. When you're finished typing, tap the Search button in the keyboard. The results appear on a separate Search page.

12. Hold your finger on the right side of the screen and swipe to the left to view all videos in your selected channel.

13. View videos within a channel by tapping the channel name in the Channels list.

14. Tap a video tile to play the video on the screen.

15. Tap the Bookmark icon to bookmark a video, add to Favorites, and create a new playlist.

16. Tap the Share icon to share a link to the current video via Wi-Fi Direct, ChatON, Google+, Google Hangouts, Bluetooth, Dropbox, Flipboard, a memo, Gmail, or email.

Other Sharing Options

Other sharing options might appear in this list if you have downloaded apps that allow for additional sharing features, such as BeyondPod.

17. Tap to turn closed captioning and HD playback on and off.

18. Tap the Menu touch button so you can change YouTube settings, send feedback to the app developer, and get help with the YouTube app.

19. Tap to pause and play the current video.

20. Drag the button in the timeline slider to move through the current video.

21. The video description appears below the video.

22. Tap to visit the channel of the user who posted this video.

23. Swipe up and down in the page to read more about the artists, view similar videos and artists, read comments about this video from other users, and create a response of your own.

24. Return to the YouTube home screen by tapping the Back button twice.

Recording Video

Your Galaxy Tab 3 is capable of recording 1080p HD video with its main 3-megapixel camera located on the rear of the device. The Galaxy Tab 3 is also equipped with some very helpful features commonly found on dedicated camcorders, including white balance, a video light, manual exposure, and effects.

1. Tap Camera on the Home screen. The Camera app opens in horizontal screen orientation.

2. If an SD card is inserted on your Tab 3, change the storage location to the SD card by tapping OK.

3. Tap the Video button to switch to video mode.

4. Pause recording by tapping the Pause button. After you tap the Pause button, the button changes and shows a red circle in the center. Resume recording by tapping the button with the red circle in the center.

5. Stop recording by tapping the Stop button.

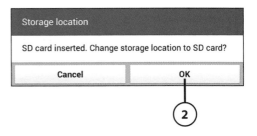

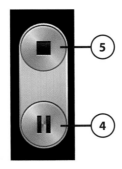

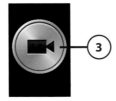

Options Under Settings

Some of the settings located under the Settings icon are the same setting represented as separate icons in the Camera interface. For example, the Effect option in the Settings menu includes the same options you find if you tap of the magic wand icon. The next few steps cover settings options that are unique to the Settings menu. Anything omitted in the Settings menu is covered under its respective icon on the interface.

Order of Menu Options Differs

If you are using the Tab 3 7.0, it is important to note that the order within the Settings menu is slightly different.

6. Tap the Menu touch button to customize Camera settings.

7. Tap Edit Quick Settings to customize the first five shortcuts to camera settings in the settings menu: Focus Mode, Timer, Voice Control, Recording Mode, and Share.

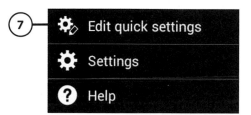

8. You can swap out these settings with others that appear when you tap Edit Quick Settings. Just drag a new setting on top of an old one to replace it.

9. Close the Edit Quick Settings window by tapping the Back touch button.

10. Tap the Menu touch button.

11. Tap Settings.

12. Tap the Video icon.

13. Tap Video Size to set a size for the images you capture.

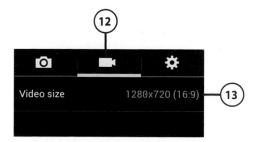

14. Tap the Settings icon.

15. Tap to choose an automatic white balance for the camera. The white balance features help accurately reproduce colors when you are recording in various lighting situations so that neutral colors, such as white and gray, are truly neutral and all colors are rendered without undesired color casts. Scroll further down the menu to reveal more options.

16. Tap to enable or disable an onscreen grid that can help you with composition of the photo. Scroll down to the bottom of the list of options.

17. Tap Storage to determine whether the photos you capture are stored on an optional memory card or on your Tab.

18. Tap Reset to return the Camera settings to the default settings.

19. An image that is too light or too dark degrades the appearance of your photos. To take full advantage of the camera feature of the Galaxy Tab, you must adjust the exposure level for various bright or dark lighting conditions. Swipe up in the list and then tap Exposure Value.

20. Drag the exposure level up to achieve a proper exposure level in a low-light shooting environment, or drag it down for a very bright shooting environment. After you set the exposure level, the slider bar disappears after a few seconds.

21. Tap the up arrow icon at the bottom of the screen to add camera effects to your videos as you capture them. Your choices are Grayscale, Sepia, and Negative.

22. Tap the down arrow icon to close the Effects area.

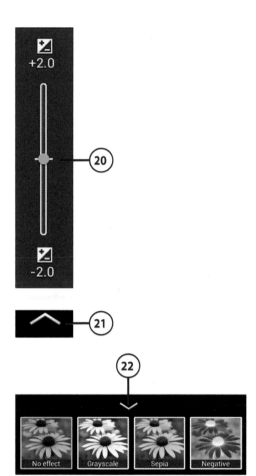

Adding Camera Effects

Keep in mind that when you use any of the video effects, such as Grayscale, Sepia, and Negative, they become a permanent part of your videos. To give yourself more choices in the future as to how you use your images, consider purchasing a video-editing app that enables you to perform such effects but still maintain your original video.

23. Tap the Settings icon.

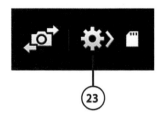

24. Tap the Timer icon to designate how long the Tab should wait before the camera starts to record. This is great for allowing time for you to set up the shot and then place yourself in the frame.

25. Tap the Recording mode icon to optimize your video for being sent as an email attachment and limit the size of the video you record to 50 megabytes.

26. Tap to switch between the rear-facing and front-facing cameras.

27. Tap the Video button to begin recording. When you finish, tap the Stop button.

28. The video you just recorded appears in the Image Viewer in the lower left of the window. Tap the Image Viewer to review the recorded video in the Gallery app.

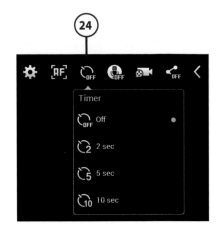

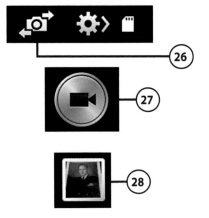

Purchasing Music

The Galaxy Tab 3 includes two preinstalled apps for finding, purchasing, and downloading music to your Tab 3: The Samsung Music Hub and the Google Play Music App. These two apps aren't the only ones you can use, however—there are plenty of other music apps available for download in the Google Play Store. This chapter describes how to download and use the Spotify music service on the Tab 3.

Use the Samsung Music Hub

The Music Hub app is a great place to shop for music online, download and listen to your music, and also listen to audio files that are already stored on your Galaxy Tab 3. Samsung has partnered with 7digital to provide music tracks for the Music Hub app, and this task explains how to shop the 7digital online catalog from within the app.

USING MUSIC HUB ON AN ONGOING BASIS

>>Go Further

You can use the Music Hub app for seven days without charge. Every time you start the Music Hub app, it reminds you that you can extend your trial until a certain date if you submit your credit card. If you decide against using the full version after the trial expires then you are limited in what you can do with the app. After you submit your credit card and you don't cancel the service when the trial period is over, Samsung charges your credit card $9.99 (plus any applicable taxes) each month for full access to the Music Hub.

1. Tap Apps on the Home screen.

2. Tap Music Hub.

3. Tap Start.

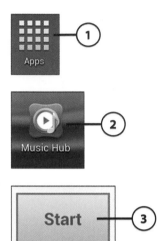

What If I Don't Have a Samsung Account or I'm Not Logged Into My Samsung Account?

If you didn't log into or set up a Samsung account when you set up your Galaxy Tab 3, you see the Samsung Account screen after you tap Start so you can either sign in or create a new account. After you sign in or create a new account, the Music Hub app continues to sign you in to the service.

4. Tap OK to acknowledge that your free 7-day trial is starting. Tap the next screen to dismiss the introductory information. (This information won't appear when you open the Music Hub app in the future.)

5. Tap Catalog to shop for songs.

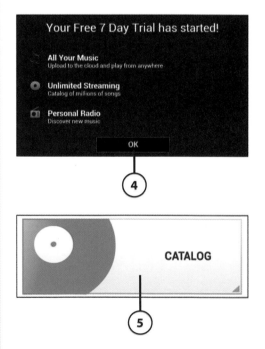

6. Categories within the catalog appear as tiles on the screen; swipe up and down the page to view all the category tiles. Open a category page by tapping on the tile.

7. Swipe up and down in the screen to view 30 songs that you can listen to within the Music Hub app. Some songs have the 30-second icon included in the description to indicate that you can only listen to a 30-second snippet of the song.

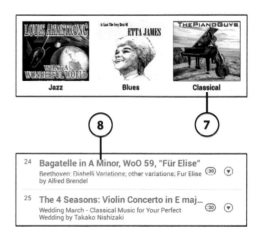

8. Tap a song name to listen to the song.

9. The name of the song appears in the bar at the bottom of the screen.

10. Tap the Rewind icon to begin playing at the beginning of the song.

11. Tap the Pause icon to pause playback.

12. Tap the Fast Forward icon to move to the end of the song.

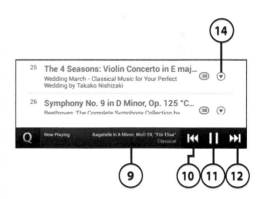

13. When the Music Hub finishes playing the song, the Music Hub begins to play the next song in the list.

14. View more information about the song by tapping the down arrow to the right of the song.

15. You can add the song to your queue for later playback, buy the song, view the album, get more information about the artist, and find similar music.

16. Tap Buy Song.

What Happens When I Buy a Song?

After you buy a song, the entire song is downloaded to your Tab 3 so you can listen to it in the Music Hub or the Music Player app anytime you want.

17. Type your Samsung account password in the Purchase Confirmation window.

18. Tap Buy to purchase the song. For now, tap Cancel.

19. Tap Albums.

20. Swipe up and down the list to view a list of albums. View more information about the album by tapping on the album cover.

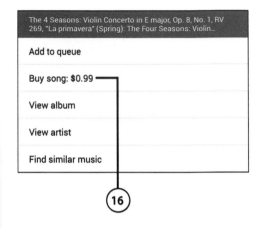

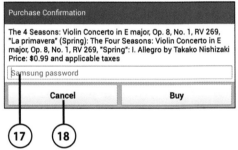

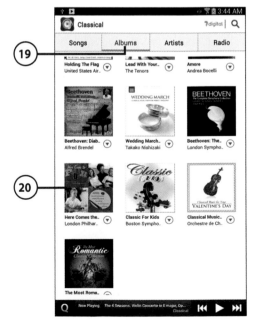

21. Swipe up and down the list of songs in the album. If the song listing includes the 30 second icon, you'll only be able to hear a 30-second snippet before the Music Hub plays the next song in the album list.

22. Tap the down arrow icon to the right of the album name to purchase all songs in the album.

23. Tap the down arrow icon to the right of a song name to purchase the song and more.

24. You can add the song to your queue, your playlist, and to your My Music database. You can also purchase the specific song.

25. Return to the album page by tapping the Back touch button.

Change Music App Settings

1. Tap the Menu touch button to open the Settings menu.

2. Tap Equalizer to modify your sound settings including bass, treble, and volume.

3. Tap Download to view your downloaded songs and albums.

4. Tap Settings to change your settings, including how you store the songs on the device and the audio quality.

5. Tap Help to get quick answers to common questions.

6. Tap About to learn more about the Music Hub app.

7. Tap Exit to close the app.

8. Return to the Music Hub home page by tapping the Music Hub icon.

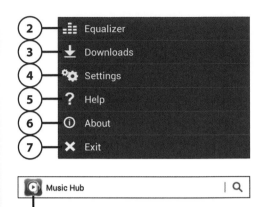

Search for Music

1. Tap the Search icon on the Music Hub home screen, Catalog screen, and Albums screen to search for songs.

2. Start typing your search terms in the Search field.

3. As you type, suggestions for what you're trying to search for appear in the drop-down menu underneath the field. Tap the appropriate term in the list, which, in this example, is an artist.

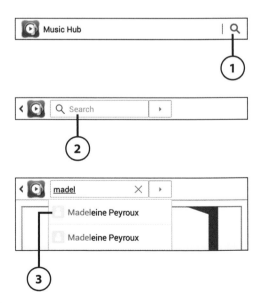

4. Songs recorded in part or in full by the artist appear on the Artists screen. Tap the song to begin playing it.

5. Tap the down arrow icon to the right of the artist name and then tap More in the window.

6. A list of albums the artist has recorded as well as albums that contain song(s) recorded by the artist appear on the Albums page.

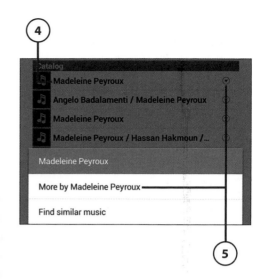

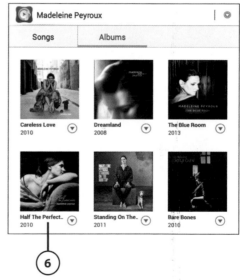

Shop in the Google Play Music App

The Play Music app is one of four Google Play apps pre-installed on your Galaxy Tab 3 and allows you to shop for, preview, purchase, download, and play songs and albums.

1. Tap Apps on the Home screen.

2. Move to the second page in the Apps screen by swiping from right to left on the screen.

3. Tap Play Music.

4. Tap Try It Free to play any song in the Google Play music catalog free for 30 days. After the 30-day trial period, you can choose to purchase a membership for $9.99 per month.

5. For now, tap Not Now to continue.

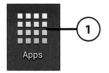

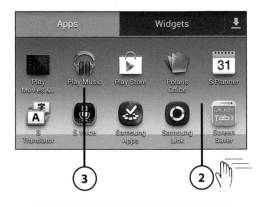

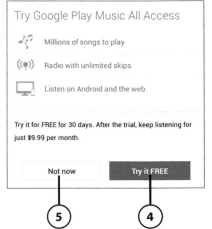

6. Tap Learn More to discover more about adding songs and copying music to your phone.

7. Tap Shop if you want to shop for tracks.

8. For now, tap Done.

9. Tap Shop on the Google Play Music home screen.

10. The Music screen shows the latest releases on the Home page. Swipe up and down the screen to view more featured songs and albums in a variety of categories.

How Do I Know if a Song Has Explicit Lyrics?

If you don't want to listen to songs with explicit lyrics (and/or don't want your kids to listen to them), you can easily see which songs and albums have explicit lyrics by looking for the Explicit warning within the song or album tile.

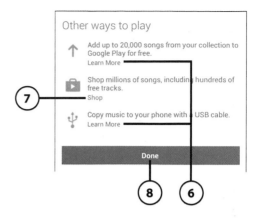

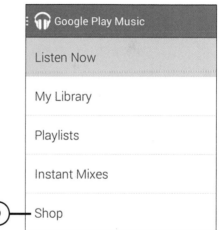

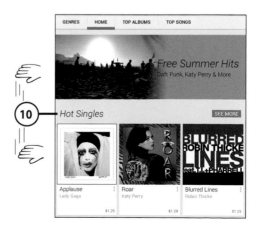

11. Tap See More to view more songs and albums in the category.

12. Tap Top Albums to view the best-selling albums in Google Play.

13. Tap Top Songs to view the best-selling songs in Google Play.

14. Tap Genres to view categories of music you can choose from.

15. View all the genres by swiping up and down in the list. When you find a genre you want, tap the genre name in the list.

16. Swipe up and down the screen to view different sections of the genre page.

17. Tap a category to view top selling albums in the genre, top selling songs in the genre, and picks from the Google staff.

The Explicit warning label in the album tile

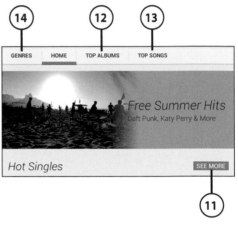

18. Swipe left to right in the menu bar and tap New Releases to view new songs and albums within the genre.

19. Swipe left to right in the menu bar and tap Genres to view a list of subgenres within the main genre.

20. Tap a subgenre in the list.

21. Top selling albums in that subgenre appears on the screen. Scroll up and down the screen to view all the top albums.

22. Tap Top Songs to view the bestselling songs in the subgenre.

23. Tap New Releases to view newly released songs and albums within that subgenre.

24. Tap the Back touch button to return to the genre page.

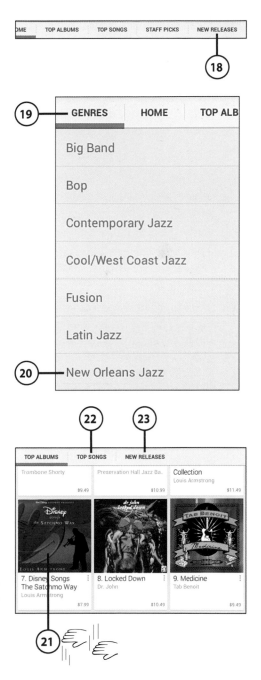

25. Tap the album or song tile on the screen to view more information.

26. The title and album cover appears at the top of the screen. You can purchase the entire album by tapping the purchase button that contains the album price.

27. Tap a song name to play a 90-second snippet that song.

28. Tap Play All to play all the snippets in the album.

29. Purchase a song on the album by tapping the purchase button that contains the price of that specific song.

30. Swipe from bottom to top on the page to view the remaining songs, reviews from other Google Play users who downloaded the songs or album, see more albums by the artist, and also view similar artists.

31. Purchase the album by tapping the purchase button at the top of the screen.

32. The Google Play window appears with the price of the album and the credit card Google Play will use to process the transaction.

33. Tap Buy to purchase the album.

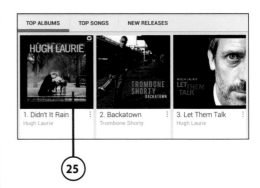

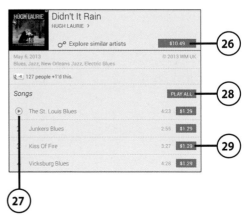

34. After you purchase a song, a Shopping bag with a check mark appears in the Status bar, which tells you that you have downloaded the song to your Tab 3 successfully.

35. Tap the Listen button to the right of the song you've purchased to listen to the song.

Playing Songs

In the Music Hub app, you can play songs you added to your play queue within the app. You can also listen to music you downloaded from the Google Play Store within the Play Music app.

The Music Player app on your Galaxy Tab 3 was designed to make it easy for you to browse and play your music collection downloaded onto your Tab 3. A great set of headphones can enhance the enjoyment of your favorite music. The ability to browse your music library and understanding your playback options are a big step toward getting the most out of your many entertainment possibilities on the Tab 3.

Play Music in the Music Hub App

1. Tap Apps on the Home screen.

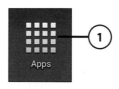

2. Tap Music Hub.

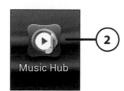

3. Tap the Queue icon to view all music in the Play Queue window.

4. The most recent song you listened to appears at the top of the queue. Swipe up and down in the screen to see other songs in the queue.

5. Tap Clear to clear the Play Queue.

6. Tap the Close button to close the Play Queue screen.

7. Tap a song in your queue to listen to that song in the Music Hub Player.

8. Tap the Play icon to play the song.

9. Tap the Pause icon to pause playback.

10. Tap the Rewind icon to begin playing at the beginning of the song.

11. Tap the Fast Forward icon to move to the end of the song.

12. Tap and hold your finger on the button in the timeline to move to different points in the song.

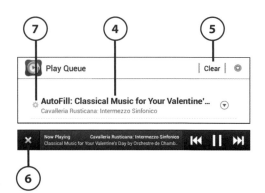

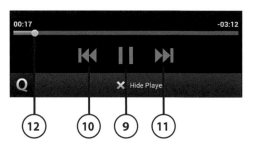

Play a Song Even When Music Hub Is Closed

After you add a song to your playlist in Music Hub, you see the song icon in the Status Bar at the top of the screen. Play the song by opening the Quick Settings and Notifications screen and then tapping the song to play it in the Music Hub Player. You can read more about opening the Quick Settings and Notifications screen in Chapter 3, "Setting Up the Galaxy Tab 3."

The song icon in the Status Bar

13. Tap Shuffle to have the Music Hub player play songs in your Play Queue at random.

14. Tap Repeat to repeat all songs or repeat the current song.

15. Tap Similar to view songs that are similar to the one you're listening to.

16. Tap the Back touch button to go back to the Player screen.

17. Tap Share to share a link to the song on the 7digital website through Twitter or email.

18. Tap Add to add the current song to your playlist.

19. Tap Hide Player to go back to the previous screen.

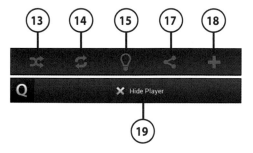

Playing Music in the Google Play Music App

1. Tap Apps on the Home screen.

2. Move to the second page in the Apps screen by swiping from right to left on the screen.

3. Tap Play Music.

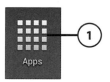

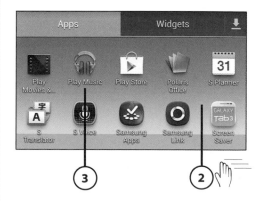

4. If you see the Welcome to Listen Now tile at the top of the screen, close this tile by tapping Got It.

5. View more songs you can play by swiping up and down in the screen to view the list of album tiles that contain songs in your Play Music library.

6. View songs in the album by tapping the album tile in the list.

7. Swipe up and down the list of songs in the album (if necessary) and then tap on the song title in the list.

8. Tap the Pause button while you're playing the song to pause playback.

9. Tap the Play button to resume playing the song.

10. Tap the Rewind icon to begin playing at the beginning of the song.

11. Tap the Fast Forward icon to move to the end of the song.

12. Rate the song so other Google Play users can view it by tapping the thumbs up (good) or thumbs down (bad) icons.

13. View more song options by tapping the menu icon to the right of the song title in the list.

14. Have the Play Music app play all songs in the album randomly by tapping Start Instant Mix.

15. Download the song to your Galaxy Tab 3 by tapping Add to Queue.

16. Add the song to a new playlist by tapping Add to Playlist.

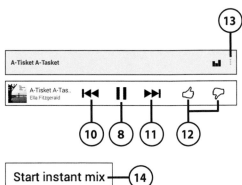

17. Within the Add to Playlist window, tap a playlist to add the song to a playlist in the Recent or All section.

18. Tap New Playlist to add the song to a new playlist.

19. Type the playlist name in the Playlist Name window.

20. Tap OK. A pop-up box appears at the bottom of the screen that informs you that Play Music added the song to your playlist. Open the song options menu again by tapping the Menu button to the right of the song title.

21. View all the artist's albums that you've added to your library by tapping Go to Artist.

22. Tap Delete to delete the song from your Galaxy Tab 3 and from your playlist within the Play Music app.

23. Tap Share to share the music file with other Google+ users in a Google+ post.

24. Tap Shop This Artist to shop for more music from the artist in the Google Play Store.

25. Tap the Back touch button to return to the main Play Music screen.

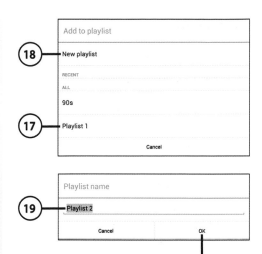

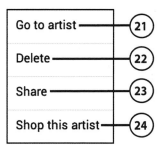

Play Music in the Music Player App

1. Tap Apps on the Home screen.

2. Tap Music Player.

3. Music Player automatically shows a list of songs on your Tab 3.

4. Tap the Menu touch button.

5. In the menu you can delete a song, scan for nearby devices, set an alarm tone, access more Music Player settings, or end Music Player operations.

6. Tap the Search icon to search the Music Player library.

7. Tap the Shuffle icon to play all songs on your Tab 3 in random order.

8. Create a new playlist by tapping the Create Playlist icon and then tapping Create Playlist in the menu. Read more about creating playlists later in this chapter in the "Creating Your Own Playlists" section.

9. Tap the appropriate category to filter the music in the Music Player library.

10. Tap a song to play it. The playback controls automatically appear at the bottom of the screen.

11. Tap the cover of the song that is currently playing to play the song on the entire screen.

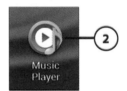

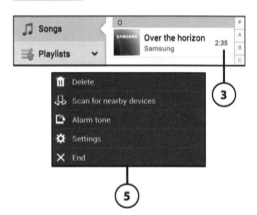

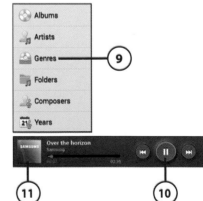

12. Tap the AllShare Play icon and then select the device to share the song with another device that uses the AllShare Play app.

13. Tap the volume icon to change the volume.

14. Tap, hold, and drag on the slider button to adjust the volume.

15. Tap the star icon to mark the song as a favorite.

16. Tap to enable or disable shuffling during playback.

17. Tap and hold your finger on the button in the timeline to move to different points in the song.

18. Tap to enable or disable looping of a song or album.

19. Tap to view information about the song.

20. Tap the Menu touch button to add a song to a playlist, share a song with another device, scan for nearby devices, use a song to set an alarm tone, access more Music Player settings, and end Music Player operations.

21. Return to the Music Player home screen by tapping the Minimize icon.

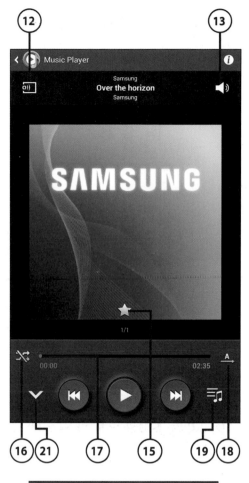

Creating Your Own Playlists

Playlists are a great way to create a compilation of your favorite songs for playback in the Music Player app. Use playlists as an opportunity to organize the best songs from your favorite artists, acoustic selections, party music, classic rock, orchestral masterpieces, relaxation tracks, and more.

1. Tap Apps on the Home screen.

2. Tap Music Player.

3. Tap the Add Playlist icon.

4. Tap Create Playlist.

5. Type the name for your new playlist.

6. Tap OK.

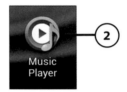

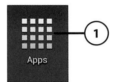

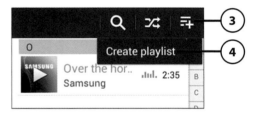

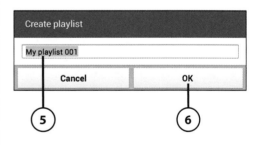

7. A plus icon appears to the right of each song.

8. Tap the songs that you want to appear in the playlist.

9. The songs you choose appear at the bottom within the Playlist.

10. Tap the minus icon to delete the song from the playlist.

11. Tap Done when you are finished creating the playlist. Alternatively, tap Cancel to cancel the new playlist.

REMOVING AND ADDING SONGS IN A PLAYLIST

You can remove songs from a playlist by selecting the playlist and then tapping Delete in the application menu at the top of the screen. Select the track(s) you want to remove by tapping the check box next to each item, tap Remove, and then tapping OK in the Delete window. You can add a song to a playlist by opening the playlist to which you want to add the song and then tapping the Add Music icon in the application bar. You can then select additional music from the library.

>>>Go Further

Adding a Podcast App

One popular podcast manager is BeyondPod for Tablets, and the lite version of it is free. The lite version has all of the features of the Pro version except scheduling of updates is disabled, you can update only one feed at a time, and you can download only one podcast at a time.

During the first 7 days after installation you can use the full version of Beyon-dPod at no charge. If you decide you want all the bells and whistles Beyon-dPod has to offer, you can purchase an unlock key for $6.99. If not, you can continue to use the free lite version indefinitely.

1. Find the BeyondPod for Tablets app in the Google Play Store and install it. (Read Chapter 16, "Find-ing and Managing Apps," for more information on getting apps from the Google Play Store.) After you have installed the app, tap Open to launch the app.

2. Tap Continue in the Welcome screen.

3. Scroll up and down the feeds list on the left side of the BeyondPod home screen; tap a podcast to view the episodes.

4. Slide up and down the list of episodes on the right side of the screen. View episode notes in the episode screen by tapping on the episode title or summary description.

5. Tap and hold on the episode title to open the menu bar at the top of the screen so you can perform more tasks.

6. Tap Add to Playlist to add the episode to your playlist.

7. The number of episodes in your playlist appears in the upper-right corner of the podcast tile in the feeds list. View all episodes in your playlist for that feed by tapping on the playlist number.

8. Tap the episode's image to play the episode.

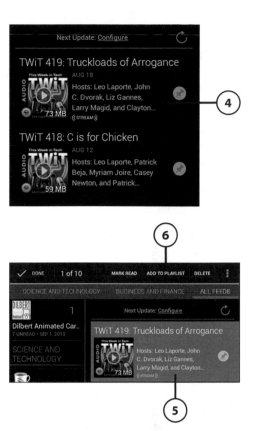

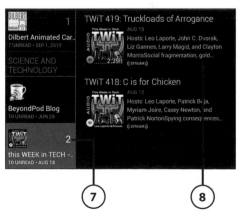

9. Tap anywhere in the screen while you're watching the episode to view the playback controls. Use the playback controls to pause or jump forward or backward in the video.

10. Use the slider to shuttle through the video. When the video ends, BeyondPod begins to play the next episode in the playlist, if any.

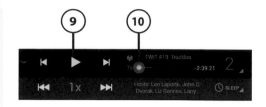

11. Tap to browse popular feeds and add a new feed in the Add Feed page.

12. Tap to refresh all feeds on the page.

13. Tap to refresh the current feed on the page.

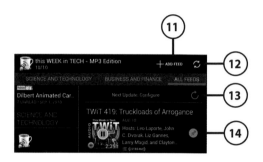

14. Tap the pushpin icon to download the episode to your Tab 3.

15. View a menu with more options by tapping the Menu touch button.

16. Tap Mark All Read to mark all episodes in the feed as read.

17. Tap Hide Read to hide all read episodes in the feed.

18. Tap Feed to update the feed, edit feed settings, or delete the feed.

19. Tap Purchase Unlock Key to get the unlock key for the full version of BeyondPod for Tablets.

20. Tap Search to search for a feed in the BeyondPod database.

21. Tap Help to find answers to your questions and get more support from BeyondPod.

22. Tap More to change BeyondPod settings, manage feed categories, view the app update log, export feeds to a file, suggest a new feature to the BeyondPod team, and get information about BeyondPod.

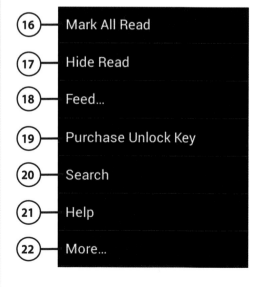

Automatically Updating Feeds

By default, feeds are set to automatically update on a configurable interval. You can change the interval by tapping Menu in the status bar, tapping More, tapping Settings, and then tapping Feed Update Settings to change the interval.

Deleting Feeds and Episodes

If you want to delete a downloaded episode, tap the orange pushpin icon to the right of the episode description and then tap Yes in the window that appears. If you want to delete a feed, tap and hold your finger on a feed on the left side of the screen. A pop-up menu displays that includes a Delete Feed option.

Purchase and read books with Play Books

Purchase and read magazines with Play Magazines

Find out how to purchase books and magazines using the preinstalled Play Books and Play Magazines apps and how to read them on your Galaxy Tab 3. Topics in this chapter include:

→ Logging in to your account

→ Purchasing books

→ Using reading aids

→ Adding bookmarks, highlights, and notes

→ Organizing your books and magazines

→ Finding other book and magazine readers in the Play Store

Reading and Managing Books and Magazines

Your Galaxy Tab 3 offers a great outlet for you to enjoy books and magazines. The Play Books app that is installed on your Tab 3 offers a stylish e-reader that enables you to browse, purchase, download, and read e-books on your device. The Tab 3 also includes the preinstalled Play Magazines app so you can read the latest magazines on your device.

Both the Play Books and Play Magazines apps enable you to enhance your reading experience by offering reading aids such as the ability to increase font size and change background color. If you prefer a different e-reader, you can shop Google Play for other apps and then download and add books from other sources. Consider trying out a few of the available readers to see which one you like the best.

Using Google Play Books

When you open the Play Books app, you can start shopping for books in the Google Play Store right away. Books are available for purchase or available for free, and after you download (and purchase, if necessary) a book you can read it within the Play Books app. You can also use built-in reading aids such as changing how the page appears on the screen.

Browse the Catalog

1. Tap Apps on the Home page.

2. Tap Play Books.

3. Tap Shop to begin shopping for books.

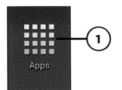

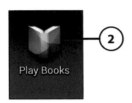

4. Swipe up and down the screen to view recommendations and books in various categories. View more books in a category by tapping See More.

5. Tap New Arrivals in Fiction to view the newest fiction books.

6. Swipe from right to left within the menu bar to view books in the New Arrivals in Nonfiction, Top Selling, and Top Free section.

7. View a list of book categories by swiping from left to right on the menu bar and then tapping Categories.

8. Tap a category in the list to view featured books within the category.

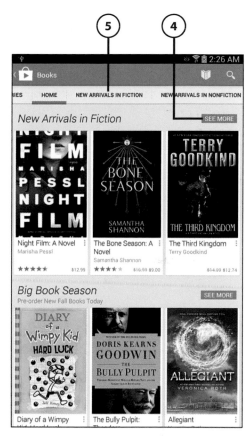

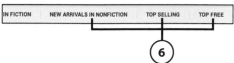

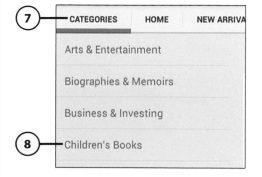

9. View the entire list of featured books by swiping up and down the screen.

10. Tap New Arrivals to view all the latest books Google has added in the category you're viewing.

11. Open a book in a subcategory by tapping Categories, swiping up and down the category list, and then tapping a category name in the list.

12. Tap a book cover to open the book description page.

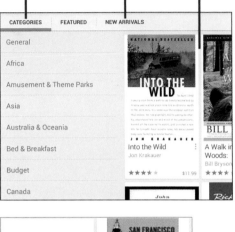

Purchase a Book

From a book's description page, you can purchase books that are currently available as well as pre-order books that will be released soon so you will receive the book on your Galaxy Tab 3 as soon as possible.

1. The title of the book, the book cover, and the Buy button appear at the top of the page.

What if the Book Isn't Available Yet?

If the book hasn't been published yet, the estimated publication date appears above the purchase button. When the book is available, a notification icon displays in the Status bar. You can read your delivered book in the Play Books app by opening the Quick Settings and Notification screen and then tapping the notification on the screen.

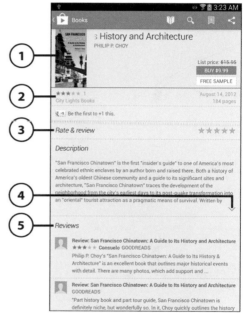

2. Ratings, the publication date, and the number of pages appears at the top of the description area.

3. Add your own rating and review to the book by tapping Rate & Review.

4. View the entire description by tapping the down arrow in the Description area.

5. Read the entire review by tapping on the review summary entry in the Reviews section.

6. Swipe upward on the screen to view more books by the author, related books, and an author biography.

7. View more information within a section, such as related books, by tapping the See More button.

8. Tap the Buy button to begin the purchase process.

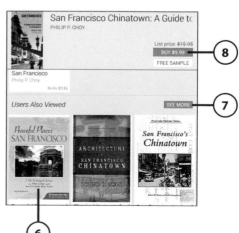

DOWNLOADING A FREE BOOK SAMPLE

Some books give you the opportunity to download a free sample of the book so you can read some of what the book is about before you decide to buy it. If a free sample is available, the Free Sample button appears below the Buy button. You can then read the free sample in Play Books as you would with any other book.

9. Tap the price to access more payment options.

10. Tap Payment Options to change or add a credit or debit card, redeem Google Play credits, or buy Google Play credits.

11. Tap Buy to purchase the book. After you purchase the book, you will see the book in the Play Books app so you can read it as described in the next section.

Download and Read a Book

There are plenty of free books you can download from the Google Play Store so you can start reading classics and favorites right away.

1. Open the Play Books app as you did earlier in this chapter.

2. Swipe from right to left in the menu bar and then tap Top Free.

3. View all books in the list by swiping down. Tap the tile of the book you want to download.

4. Get information about the book, read reviews, add your own rating and review, and see related books as described in the previous section.

5. Tap the Add to Library button to add the book to your Play Books library.

6. The first page of the book appears in the Play Books app. Move to the next page by tapping on the right side of the screen.

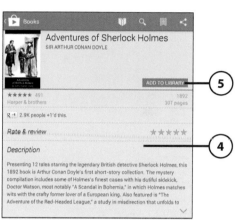

Changing Settings

If you need to change settings before you start reading the book, such as if you want the screen to rotate when you rotate the Galaxy Tab 3, tap the Menu touch button and then tap Settings in the menu. You can then view or add a Google account to use with Play Books, change the auto-rotation setting for the Play Books app only, determine how you download book files, change how you turn pages, and tell Play Books to automatically read the book aloud if the correct accessibility setting is on. Return to the book page by tapping the Back touch button.

Adventure I

A SCANDAL IN BOHEMIA

I

TO Sherlock Holmes she is always *the* woman. I have seldom heard him mention her under any other name. In his eyes she eclipses and predominates the whole of her sex. It was not that he felt any emotion akin to love for Irene Adler. All emotions, and that one particularly, were abhorrent to his cold, precise, but admirably balanced mind. He was, I take it, the most perfect reasoning and observing machine that the world has seen; but, as a lover, he would have placed himself in a false position. He never spoke of the softer passions, save with a gibe and a sneer. They were admirable things for the observer —excellent for drawing the veil from men's motives and actions. But for the trained reasoner to admit such intrusions into his own delicate and finely adjusted temperament was to introduce a distracting factor which might throw a doubt upon all his mental results. Grit in a sensitive instrument, or a crack in one of his own high-power lenses, would not be more disturbing than a strong emotion in a nature such as his. And yet there was but one woman to him, and that woman was the late Irene Adler, of dubious and questionable memory.

I had seen little of Holmes lately. My marriage had drifted us away from each other. My own complete happiness, and the home-centred interests which rise up around the man who first finds himself master of his own establishment, were sufficient to absorb all my attention; while Holmes, who

Use Reading Aids

The Play Books app contains many options for enhancing your e-book experience, including changing background color, font size, jumping to locations within the book, and organizing your book titles.

1. Open the Play Books app as described earlier in this chapter.

2. Open the book by tapping the book cover image in the Recent section.

3. Tap the right side of the book page to progress to the next page. Tap the left side of the page to revisit the previous page. You can also flick left or right to turn pages.

4. Go to a page with text and then tap the middle of the screen to access reading aid controls.

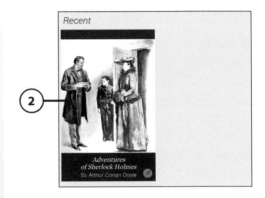

Recent

Adventures
of Sherlock Holmes
Sir Arthur Conan Doyle

ADVENTURE I

A SCANDAL IN BOHEMIA

I

TO Sherlock Holmes she is always *the* woman. I have seldom heard him mention her under any other name. In his eyes she eclipses and predominates the whole of her sex. It was not that he felt any emotion akin to love for Irene Adler. All emotions, and that one particularly, were abhorrent to his cold, precise, but admirably balanced mind. He was, I take it, the most perfect reasoning and observing machine that the world has seen; but, as a lover, he would have placed himself in a false position. He never spoke of the softer passions, save with a gibe and a sneer. They were admirable things for the observer —excellent for drawing the veil from men's motives and actions. But for the trained reasoner to admit such intrusions into his own delicate and finely adjusted temperament was to introduce a distracting factor which might throw a doubt upon all his mental results. Grit in a sensitive instrument, or a crack in one of his own high-power lenses, would not be more disturbing than a strong emotion in a nature such as his. And yet there was but one woman to him, and that woman was the late Irene Adler, of dubious and questionable memory.

I had seen little of Holmes lately. My marriage had drifted us away from each other. My own complete happiness, and the home-centred interests which rise up around the man who first finds himself master of his own establishment, were sufficient to absorb all my attention; while Holmes, who

5. Tap the Contents icon to access the table of contents for the book. You can jump to a chapter by tapping its title in the contents.

6. Tap About This Book to read an overview of the book.

7. Close the Chapters list by tapping the Back touch button.

8. Tap the Search icon to search for text in the book.

9. Type the search term(s) in the Search in Book field.

10. Tap the Search button in the keyboard.

11. View all the results and the page number on which each result appears by swiping up and down in the list.

12. View the page that contains your desired passage by tapping on the entry in the list.

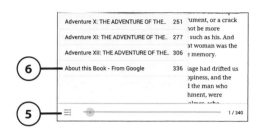

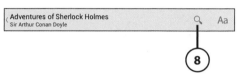

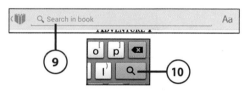

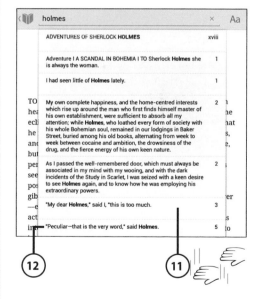

13. The search term(s) appear highlighted on the screen.

14. Return to the previous page in the book that contains the search term(s) on that page by tapping the left arrow icon.

15. Go to the next page that contains the search term(s) by tapping the right arrow icon.

16. Return to the search results list by tapping the Google Play icon in the menu bar.

17. View reading aid controls by tapping the Back touch button.

18. Drag the slider to jump to different pages in the book.

19. After you drag the slider to jump to a different location, you can tap the arrow to jump back to where you were last reading.

20. Tap the Style icon at the right side of the menu bar to access more options.

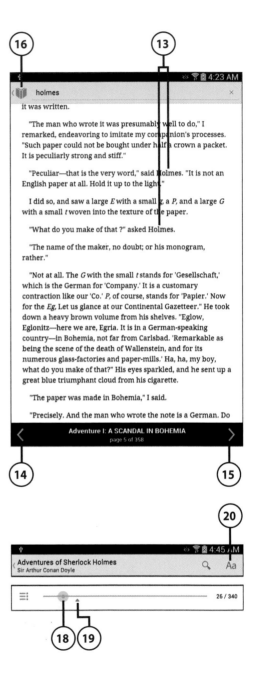

21. Tap to change the text and background color theme for the page. Your choices are Day (black text on a white background), Night (white text on a black background), and Sepia (black text on a beige background).

22. Tap to change the overall font style for the book. Your choices are Default, Sans, Serif, Merriweather, Sorts Mill Goudy, and Vollkorn.

23. Tap to change the overall text alignment for the book. Your choices are Default, Left, and Justify.

24. Change the screen brightness in the Brightness slider. Set the brightness level to its default level by tapping the Auto checkbox.

25. Tap the T- and T+ buttons to decrease and increase, respectively, the size of the book font on the screen.

26. Tap the decrease button to decrease the size of the height between lines in the book.

27. Tap the increase button to increase the size of the height between lines in the book.

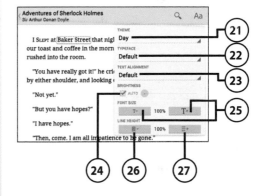

Add Bookmarks, Highlights, and Notes

Play Books provides the convenience of placing a bookmark where you stopped reading so you can begin at the right location later. You also have the capability to highlight text in a book and to leave notes.

1. When you close a book, a book-mark is automatically placed on the page where you stopped reading. When you open the book again, the book opens to the bookmarked page.

2. You might want to specify a block of text in a block as a point of interest by highlighting it. Press your finger on the screen and hold. Blue handles appear on either side of the word.

3. A dictionary definition appears at the bottom of the screen.

4. Drag the handles of the arrows to specify the text you want to high-light.

5. Tap the Highlight icon in the menu bar.

Removing Highlights from Text

You can remove the highlight from text by pressing your finger to the highlighted text, select-ing the text that includes the highlight you want to remove, and then tapping the Delete Highlight icon (it has a box with an X inside).

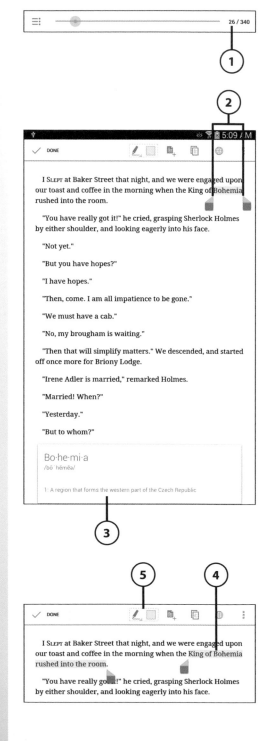

6. The highlighted text appears on the page.

7. You can leave a note for an excerpt of text. Press your finger on the screen and hold. The highlighted word appears with handles on either side of the word.

8. Tap the Add Note icon.

9. Type the note in the Add Note field.

10. Tap the book page when you're finished typing.

11. The passage of text is highlighted and an icon of a note sheet appears at the right side of the screen.

Deleting a Note

To modify or delete a note, you can tap the icon of a note sheet that appears at the right side of the screen to reveal the notes on that page. You can then edit your notes or select the text in the note that you want to cut and then tap Cut in the menu bar.

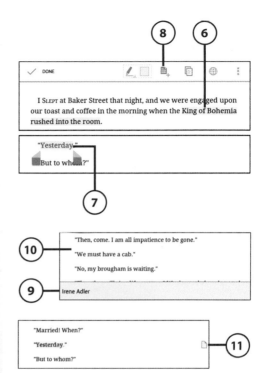

VIEWING ALL NOTES AND MARKS

Your Galaxy Tab 3 offers a quick and convenient way to view and jump to all notes and highlights you have made in a book. Tap the middle of the screen to reveal the book options. You can then tap the Contents icon. On the left side of the screen you can view all of your highlights and notes.

Organize Your Books

After you have accumulated many titles in your Play Books library, you need a method to the madness of organizing your books. By default, your books are ordered by the most recently downloaded on the Play Books home page. You have a couple other sorting options to choose from.

1. Tap the Play Books icon in the menu bar.

2. Tap My Library to view all the books in your library.

3. Tap the Menu touch button.

4. Tap Sort to choose from the sorting options. Your choices are Recently Read, Title, and Author.

5. Tap Refresh to update your library with all of your latest, purchased content.

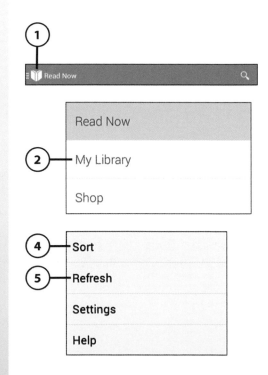

REMOVING AND ARCHIVING BOOKS

You can access the option to remove books from your device by tapping your finger on the menu icon that appears to the right of the book title. A menu opens from which you can choose the Delete from Library option. The book is removed from the library page, but remains archived in your Play Books account.

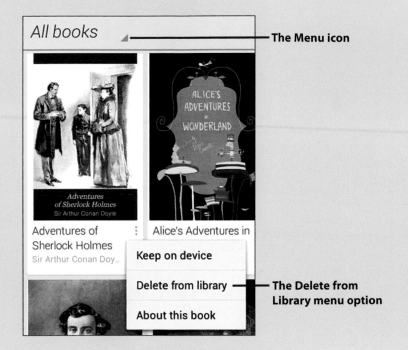

Using Google Play Magazines

If you want to read magazines without wasting paper then the preinstalled Play Magazines app on the Galaxy Tab 3 is for you. This app enables you to shop for magazines in the Google Play Store, purchase one or more issues of the magazine, and then read the magazine within the app.

Shop for Magazines

1. Tap Apps on the Home page.

2. Tap Play Magazines.

3. Tap the Play Magazines icon in the menu bar.

4. Tap Shop.

5. Swipe up and down the screen to view recommendations and magazines in various categories. View more magazines in a category by tapping See More.

6. Tap Top Selling to view top-selling magazines in the Play Store or tap New Arrivals to view the newest magazines.

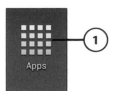

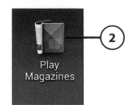

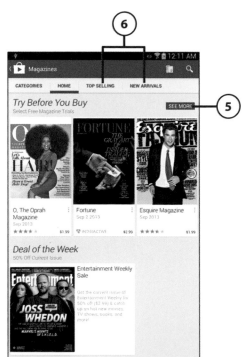

7. Tap Categories to view a list of magazine categories.

8. Tap a category in the list to view featured magazines within the category.

9. View the entire list of featured magazines by swiping up and down the screen.

10. Tap New Arrivals to view all the latest magazines Google has added in that category.

11. Tap a magazine cover to open the magazine description page.

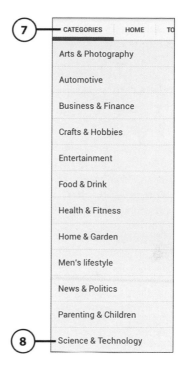

Purchase a Magazine

1. The title and issue of the magazine, the cover of the current issue, the Subscribe button, and the Buy button appear at the top of the page.

2. Ratings and the number of issues published in a specific timeframe (such as 13 issues per year) appear at the top of the description area.

3. Add your own rating and review to the book by tapping Rate & Review.

4. View the entire description by tapping the Down arrow in the Description area.

5. Swipe upward on the screen to view reader reviews, similar magazines, and back issues.

6. Tap See More to view more information within a section, such as back issues.

7. Tap the Buy button to begin the purchase process.

8. Tap the price to access more payment options.

9. Tap Payment Options to change or add a credit or debit card, redeem Google Play credits, or buy Google Play credits.

10. Tap Buy to purchase the issue. After you purchase the issue, you will see the issue in the Play Magazines app so you can read it as described in the "Read an Issue" task later in the chapter.

Subscribe to a Magazine

You can also subscribe to the magazine so you can receive new issues on your Galaxy Tab 3 over a period of time

1. Open a magazine page as described in the previous section.

2. Tap the Subscribe button to begin the subscription purchase process.

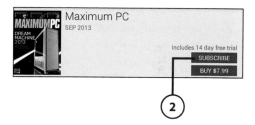

Can I Preview a Magazine Subscription?

If there is a free trial for your subscription, you will see the length of the free trial above the Subscribe button. Some magazines make it free for you to purchase if you're already a print subscriber. Some magazine subscriptions also offer a limited time free trial, although you have to agree to start paying for the magazine after the trial period. You can cancel the subscription before the trial period is over.

3. Tap the subscription option in the Purchase Options window; you can pay for your subscription monthly or yearly.

4. At the top of the Address window, the app asks if you want to receive information about additional product services from the publisher, and allow third parties to send you information about additional products and services. The check boxes for both these options are checked by default, so if you want to deselect one or both of them, tap the appropriate check box(es).

5. The first name appears in the First Name field. Type a different first name if necessary, or just keep the name as is without typing anything.

6. Tap Next in the keyboard.

7. The last name appears in the Last Name field. Type a different last name if necessary, or just keep the name as is without typing anything.

8. Tap Next in the keyboard.

9. Tap the Country field and then select your country in the pop-up menu if you do not live in the United States.

10. Type your street address in the Street Address field. As you type, address suggestions appear in the drop-down list underneath the area. You can narrow options in the list further by typing a comma and then typing the name of the city or town, for example, "123 Main Street, Anytown" (without the quotes). When you find your address, tap it in the list.

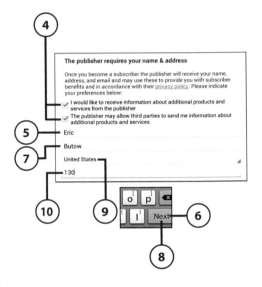

11. The app adds your city, state, and ZIP code information into the appropriate fields automatically.

12. Tap Continue.

13. Tap the price to access more payment options. If the magazine includes a free trial, you see the date the trial expires.

14. Tap Payment Options to change or add a credit or debit card, redeem Google Play credits, or buy Google Play credits.

15. Tap Subscribe to purchase the magazine subscription. After you purchase the subscription, you will see the most recent issue in the Play Magazines app so you can read it as described in the next task.

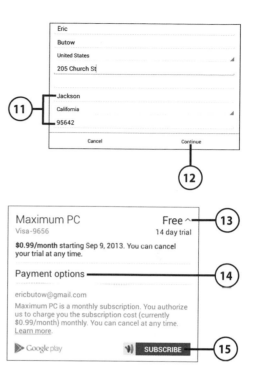

Read an Issue

1. Open the Play Magazines app as described earlier in this chapter.

2. Tap the magazine cover in the Recent section on the app home screen.

Pushpin icon

3. The magazine issue cover appears in the Play Magazine app. Move to the next page by swiping from right to left on the screen.

③

ADDING AND REMOVING A DOWNLOADED MAGAZINE

>>>Go Further

When you purchase the magazine, you have the ability to download it to your Galaxy Tab 3 so you can read it even when you're not connected to the Internet. Download the magazine by tapping the Play Magazines icon in the menu bar, tapping My Library, and then tapping Download underneath the magazine cover. After you download a magazine, you'll see a blue pushpin icon (a blue circle with a white outline of a pushpin) in the lower-right corner of the magazine cover. You can remove the magazine from your magazine library by tapping the pushpin icon. After you tap the pushpin icon, a pop-up window reminds you that you won't be able to read the magazine until you download it again from the Play Store. Remove the magazine by tapping OK in the window.

**The Play
Magazines icon**

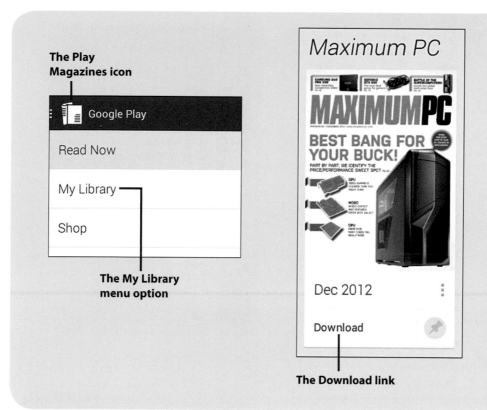

**The My Library
menu option**

The Download link

Use Reading Aids

The Play Magazines app contains
several options that make reading a
magazine easier for you.

1. Open the Play Magazines app as
   described earlier in this chapter.

2. Open the magazine by tapping
   the magazine cover image in the
   Recent section.

3. Tap the right side of the magazine page to progress to the next page. Tap the left side of the page to revisit the previous page. You can also flick left or right to turn pages.

4. Tap the middle of the screen to access reading aid controls.

5. Tap the Contents icon to access the table of contents for the book.

6. Tap an article's entry in the Contents list to jump to that article.

7. Tap the Back touch button to close the Contents list.

8. Navigate to another page in the magazine by swiping from right to left in the thumbnail area. Each thumbnail page contains two facing pages in the magazine and the pages appear in the order in which they appear in the printed magazine. The only exceptions to this facing pages layout are the front and back covers; there is only one page for each cover.

9. Tap a thumbnail page to open it.

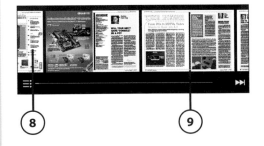

10. The left side of the facing page appears on the screen. View the right side of the facing page by tapping on the right side of the screen.

11. Go to the next thumbnail page by tapping the Fast Forward icon.

12. Your current location within the magazine is represented by the slider bar.

13. If you're on a page that contains text, you can view the text version of articles on the page by tapping View Text.

14. If there is more than one article on the page, tap the article's title to read in the Flowing Text Articles window.

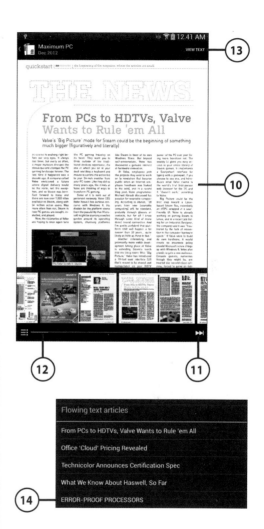

15. Move to the next page in the article by tapping on the right side of the screen. Move to the previous page by tapping on the left side of the screen.

16. View the table of contents by tapping the Contents icon. You can then swipe up and down in the contents and then read the article on the magazine page by tapping on the article in the list.

17. Return to the text article by tapping the Back touch button.

18. The slider icon shows you where you are in relation to the entire article.

19. Move to the next text article on the page by tapping the Fast Forward icon.

20. Return to the magazine page screen by tapping the Back touch button.

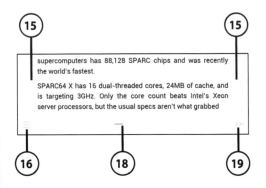

supercomputers has 88,128 SPARC chips and was recently the world's fastest.

SPARC64 X has 16 dual-threaded cores, 24MB of cache, and is targeting 3GHz. Only the core count beats Intel's Xeon server processors, but the usual specs aren't what grabbed

Organize Your Magazines

After you have accumulated many titles in your Play Magazines library, you need a method to the madness of organizing your magazines—just as you do with books in the Play Books app. By default, your magazines are ordered by the most recently downloaded on the Play Magazines home page. You have a couple other sorting options to choose from.

1. Tap the Play Magazines icon in the menu bar on the Play Magazines app home page.

2. View all the magazines in your library by tapping My Library.

3. Tap the Menu touch button.

4. Tap Refresh to update your library with all of your latest, purchased content.

5. Tap On Device Only to view only those magazines that have been downloaded onto your device.

6. Tap Manage Subscriptions to manage your magazine subscriptions on the Google Play Store website within either the Internet or Chrome browser.

Deleting a Magazine from the Library

You can delete a magazine from the library by tapping the menu button to the right of the issue month and date within the magazine cover tile. After you tap the menu button, tap Delete from Library in the menu. If you downloaded the magazine to your Tab 3, the magazine will remain stored on the Tab 3.

The Menu icon

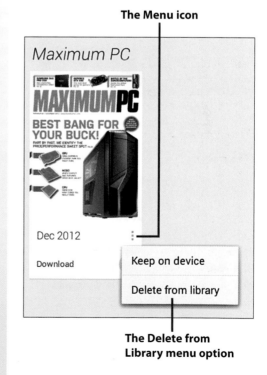

The Delete from Library menu option

Shopping for Book and Magazine Readers

If you prefer to use another book or magazine reader, you can shop the Google Play Store for other cloud storage apps that are optimized for the Android operating system.

1. Tap Play Store on the Home page.

2. Tap Apps.

3. Tap the Search icon in the menu bar.

4. Type "book readers" (without the quotes) in the Search Google Play field.

5. Tap the Search button in the keyboard.

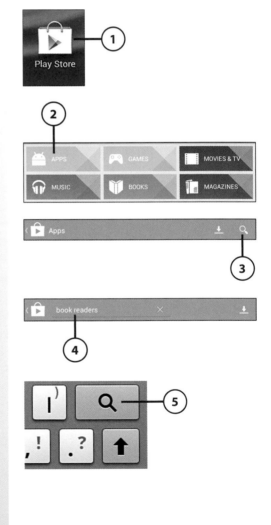

6. Swipe up and down within the list of apps in the search results screen; you also see the Google Play Books app in this list. Tap a tile to view more information about the app. Read more about shopping for apps in the Google Play Store in Chapter 16, "Finding and Managing Apps."

7. Tap the X icon in the Search Google Play field.

8. Type "magazine apps" (without the quotes) in the Search Google Play field.

9. Tap the Search button in the keyboard.

10. Swipe up and down within the list of apps in the search results screen; you also see the Google Play Magazines app in this list. Tap a tile to view more information about the app. Read more about shopping for apps in the Google Play Store in Chapter 16.

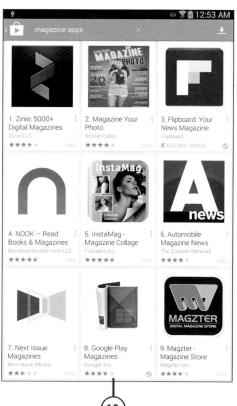

Browse, manage, and share photos

Capture photos

Edit and share photos

In this chapter, you find out how to capture photos and screenshots, share photos via email and slideshows, and view and manage photos with Gallery:

→ Using the camera

→ Navigating Image Viewer

→ Tips for capturing photos

→ Working with Gallery

→ Editing and sharing images

→ Performing screen captures

14

Capturing and Managing Photos

Along with transferring images from other sources, such as your computer or Micro SD card, to your Galaxy Tab 3, you can also take high-quality photos with your Tab 3, which can house thousands of photos organized in categories. You also have the capability to take screenshots of the Tab's interface.

Your Tab's high-resolution screen offers a great way to showcase photos to friends and family, but you don't have to stop there. You can also use Photo Editor and Photo Studio, which are accessible from Gallery, to perform basic photo edits. You can even share pictures via AllShare, Bluetooth, Gmail, Messaging, Picasa, and more.

Using the Camera

All Galaxy Tab 3 models use a rear-facing camera located on the back of the device to take photos along with a 1.3 megapixel front-facing camera that you can use for self-portraits. However, each of the three Galaxy Tab 3 models use rear cameras with different resolutions:

- The Tab 3 7.0 uses a 3.0 megapixel rear camera.

- The Tab 3 8.0 uses a 5.0 megapixel rear camera.

- The Tab 3 10.1 uses a 3.2 megapixel rear camera.

Taking a photo can be as simple as choosing a subject, composing your shot, and pressing a button. The Galaxy Tab 3 is also equipped with some helpful features commonly found on dedicated photo cameras, including shooting modes, scene modes, manual exposure, white balance, flash, manual exposure, and ISO settings.

1. Tap Camera on the Home screen.

2. If you have a micro SD card inserted, you can either tap OK to change the storage settings to the SD Card or tap Cancel to use your Tab's storage to store photos and videos.

3. Tap the Settings icon to customize camera settings.

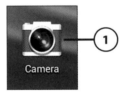

Order of Menu Options Differs

If you are using the 7.0 Tab, it is important to note that the order within the Settings menu is slightly different than what is described here.

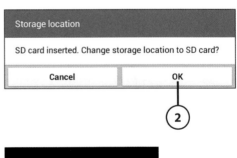

4. Five icons appear underneath the Settings icon so you can customize the first five camera setting shortcuts in the menu: Focus Mode, Timer, Voice Control, Recording, and Share.

5. You can swap out these settings with others that appear when you tap the Menu touch button and then tap Edit Quick Settings in the menu. Just drag a new setting on top of an old one to replace it.

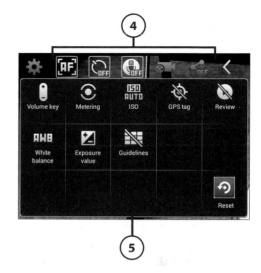

6. Tap the Back touch button after you've finished replacing your quick setting icons.

7. Change the scene mode by tapping the Mode button and then swiping back and forth between the tiles; the selected tile appears at the top of the tile stack and a description of the mode appears above the tile for a few seconds. The default mode is Auto.

8. Tap the mode tile you want to use.

>>>Go Further

EXPLORING SCENE MODES

The scene mode options optimize your camera for special shooting situations. For example, Panorama mode enables you to take a picture and then use the onscreen guide to move the viewfinder and take seven more shots. This is a great mode for capturing wide vistas, such as landscapes and cityscapes.

Night mode uses a flash in combination with a slow shutter speed to brighten dark backgrounds. Sports mode uses a fast shutter speed to capture moving subjects without blurring.

9. Tap the Menu touch button and then tap Settings in the menu.

10. Tap the Settings icon.

11. Tap GPS Tag to enable or disable GPS tagging of the photos you capture. Embedded GPS information can come in handy if you use a photo-editing and managing application such as iPhoto 9 and later, which enables you to use the location information to manage and showcase photos.

12. Tap Timer to designate how long the Tab should wait before the camera takes a picture. This is great when you want to set up the shot and then place yourself in the frame.

13. Tap to adjust the white balance for the camera. The white balance features help accurately reproduce colors when you are shooting in various lighting situations so that neutral colors, such as white and gray, are truly neutral and all colors are rendered without undesired color casts.

14. Swipe down the list to view more options.

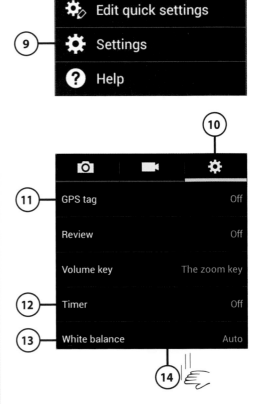

15. Tap Guidelines to enable or disable an onscreen grid that can help you with composition.

16. An image that is too light or too dark degrades the appearance of your photos. To take full advantage of the camera feature of the Tab 3, you must adjust the exposure level for various bright or dark lighting conditions. Tap Exposure Value.

17. Drag the exposure level up to achieve a proper exposure level in a low-light shooting environment, or drag it down for a very bright shooting environment.

18. When you're finished changing the exposure level, return to the Settings menu by tapping the Menu touch button and then tapping Settings in the menu as you did in Step 9.

19. Swipe down the list until you can tap Storage to determine whether the photos you capture are stored on an optional memory card or on your Tab.

20. Tap to reset the Camera settings to the default settings.

21. Tap the Camera icon.

22. Tap to set how the camera measures or meters the light source. This setting determines how the camera factors light in a scene to achieve the proper exposure.

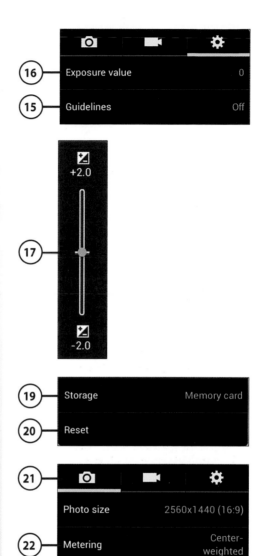

>>Go Further

TALKING ABOUT CENTER-WEIGHTED AND SPOT METERING

The default Metering setting is Center-Weighted. Your other choices are Matrix, which measures light intensity in several points to achieve the best exposure, and Spot, where only a small area in the scene is measured. Matrix metering is usually considered the most accurate form of metering because it measures the entire scene and then sets the exposure according-ing to an average. Spot measuring is generally used to capture very high contrast scenes, such as when a subject's back is to the sun.

23. Return to the Viewer by tapping the Back touch button.

24. Tap to switch between the rear-facing and front-facing cameras.

25. Compose the subject in the Viewer. By default, Camera auto-matically focuses on what is in the center of the Viewer.

26. Hold your finger on the Camera button, level the shot, and then remove your finger from the button to capture the image. A thumbnail of the image appears in the Image Viewer.

27. Tap the Image Viewer to review the image you just captured. You can also access your photos by tapping the Gallery icon under Applications from any Home screen.

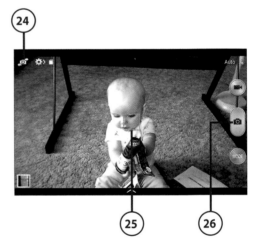

Navigating Image Viewer

Image Viewer provides a quick-and-easy way to review the photos that you have just taken. It also enables you to quickly share your pictures as soon as you capture them or set them as wallpaper. You can also edit and delete unwanted photos in Image Viewer.

As soon as you take a picture, a thumbnail of that photo appears next to the camera button. You can tap that thumbnail to review the picture you have taken and browse other photos.

1. Tap the Image Viewer to review the image.

2. The image opens full screen, the controls appear, and then they fade away. Tap the middle of the screen to access the controls again.

3. Tap the AllShare Play icon to share your photo with another device that has an AllShare Play account.

4. Tap the Share Via icon to access many options for sharing your photos through services such as Group Play, ChatON, Dropbox, Wi-Fi Direct, Picasa, Google+, Flipboard, Hangouts, Bluetooth, Gmail, and email. The button next to the Share Via icon displays the last option you used to share photos.

5. Tap to edit the currently displayed photo.

6. Tap to delete the currently displayed photo.

7. Flick the image from left to right or tap the thumbnail representations of photos at the bottom of the screen to navigate through all the photos you have captured.

8. Tap the Menu touch button to access more options.

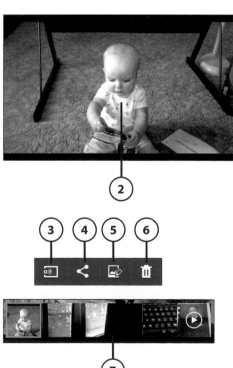

9. Tap Favorites to add the photo to your Favorites album. If the photo is already one of your favorites, then tap Unfavorite to remove the photo from your Favorites album.

10. Tap to begin a slideshow of your photos. After the slideshow begins, you can tap anywhere onscreen to end the slideshow.

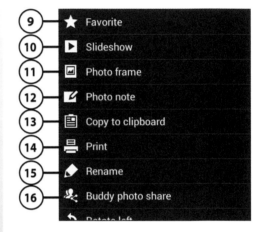

11. Tap to edit your photo and place it within a frame image.

12. Tap to edit your photo to make it look like the back of a printed photo.

13. Tap to copy the current image to the clipboard.

14. Tap to print the photo, such as to a Bluetooth printer.

15. Tap to give the currently displayed image a new name.

16. Tap to share the photo using face detection.

17. Swipe down the list to view more options.

18. Tap to rotate the photo to the left.

19. Tap to rotate the photo to the right.

20. Tap to crop the currently displayed photo.

21. Tap to connect to other nearby devices, such as someone else's smartphone.

22. Tap Set As to set the current picture as a contact photo, Home and lock screens, lock screen, or wallpaper.

23. Tap to view details about the photo including the time it was taken, aperture, and exposure settings upon capture.

24. Close the menu by tapping the Back touch button.

25. With the menu closed, double-tap the image to enlarge it. You can double-tap it again to return it to its normal size. You can also touch the screen with two fingers and then move them apart to enlarge an image.

26. Tap the Back touch button to return to the Camera app and take more pictures.

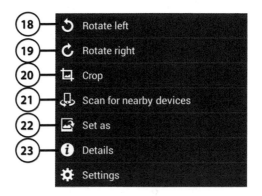

Tips for Capturing Photos

Shutter lag is the amount of time that elapses between your press of the shutter release button and the moment the picture is captured. A longer shutter lag is common among most compact cameras and also the Galaxy Tab 3. What this means for you is that is that you have to be particularly mindful of timing your shots when recording moving subjects. Shutter lag can cause you to miss out on a key action if you do not anticipate the shot.

One important thing to know about your Tab is that the shutter does not fire as you place your finger down on the Camera button; the shutter fires when you lift your finger off the button. Use this knowledge to your advantage by pressing your finger on the shutter button and holding while you frame the shot and focus on an object about the same distance as where the subject will pass, to anticipate the shot, and then lift your finger. This means you need to hold your Tab completely still for a little bit longer. Anticipating moving subjects to capture dynamic, moving shots can take some practice.

The Tab 3's slow shutter makes it prone to producing blurry photos if you do not remain perfectly still during capture. Even the smallest movement can have an adverse effect on your photographs; this is especially true in low-light situations. A photo might appear to be fine when you review it on the Tab display, but when you download it and view it on a larger display, you can see the problem.

Working with Gallery

Gallery offers a more robust photo and video management system than Image Viewer, but it has similar options for viewing, sharing, and editing photos.

Manage Photos with Gallery

By default, you can access the Gallery icon by flicking the main Home screen from left to right, or you can access it from the Apps menu.

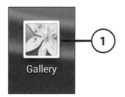

1. Tap Gallery on the Home screen.

2. Content is arranged in categories/ albums. If you have downloaded videos, such as video podcasts or recorded videos, with your Tab and transferred images from your computer, they are in here, too. Tap the camera icon to access the Camera feature from Gallery.

3. Tap the Albums menu to group your photos and videos in other ways. The name of this particular menu changes depending on which grouping method you have selected.

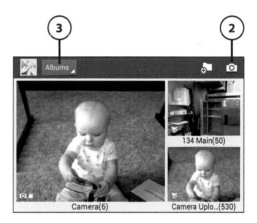

4. Tap the Albums option to arrange photos based on the folder in which they are stored.

5. Tap All to arrange all photos on the Galaxy Tab 3 based on the time they were captured from newest to oldest; the newest photos appear at the top of the screen.

6. Tap Time to arrange photos based on the time they were captured. The most recent photos appear in the row at the bottom of the screen.

7. Tap Locations to arrange photos based on their GPS location.

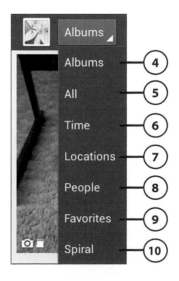

8. Tap People to arrange photos based on pictures where a face was detected.

9. Tap Favorites to arrange photos in your Favorites album.

10. Tap Spiral to display your photos in a fun spiral pattern on the screen.

11. Close the menu by tapping the Back touch button.

12. Tap the Menu touch button.

13. Tap to select one or more complete albums to stream to another device, share, or delete. On the Gallery home screen, you can also hold your finger on an album cover photo for a few seconds to select it.

14. Tap to view a slideshow of photos. The first frame of any video that you have shot also plays in the slideshow. You can tap the screen again to stop the slideshow.

15. Tap to view all albums by All Content, Content in Device, Content in Dropbox, Content in Facebook, or Content in Picasa.

16. Tap to share photos with nearby devices, such as a friend's smartphone.

17. Close the menu by tapping the Back touch button.

18. Tap an album to view all photos in it.

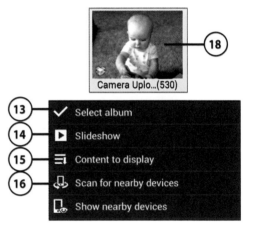

19. After you have captured many photos and videos, the thumbnail representation of images in this category becomes long. Flick the screen up and down to view all thumbnails in the album.

20. Tap the Camera icon to capture another photo.

21. Tap the Menu touch button to reveal the options Select Item and Slideshow. Select Item enables you to select one or more items that you want to stream to another device, share, or delete. The Slideshow option enables you to view a slideshow of pictures within the album.

22. Touch and hold your finger to a photo to reveal more Gallery options.

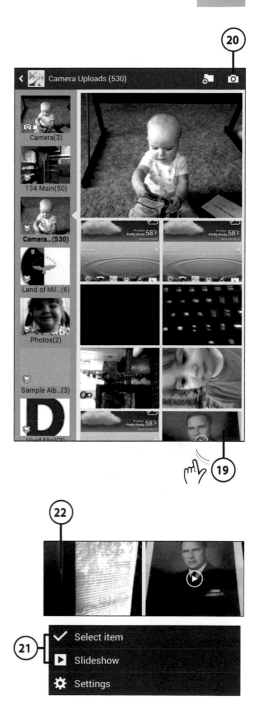

23. To delete images within an album, touch each image you want to delete (the check box in the upper-right corner of the image is checked) and then tap the Trash icon.

24. You can touch the number of selected images to reveal the option to Select All photos in the album.

25. Tap the Menu touch button and then tap Slideshow to show your selected photos as a slideshow.

26. Tap to copy or move your photos to a different album or to your external SD card.

27. Tap Share to view options for sharing the displayed image with friends and family via Group Play, Dropbox, email, Gmail, Google+, Picasa, YouTube, or to another device via a Bluetooth or Wi-Fi Direct connection.

28. Turn off the image selection feature by tapping the Back touch button, and then tap a photo in the album to open it full screen.

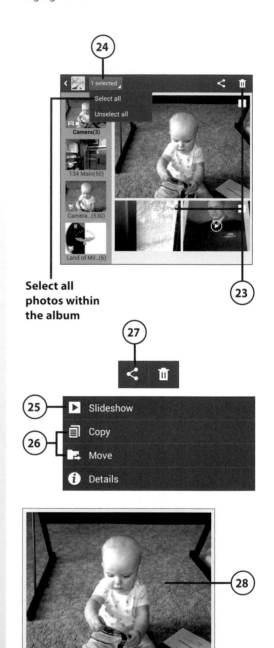

Select all photos within the album

Viewing the Tag Buddy Window

You might see the Tag Buddy window that tells you if you tag someone in a picture then some information, such as the location, person's name, and the picture date, will appear briefly when you view the picture. Close this window for good by tapping the Do Not Show Again check box and then tapping the OK button.

29. Touch the middle of the screen to reveal the controls.

30. Tap the Gallery icon in the menu bar to return to the previous screen.

>>>Go Further

MORE PHOTO EDITING OPTIONS

The Photo Editor and Paper Artist apps offer many more options for enhancing your photographs. You can send your photos from Gallery and Image Viewer to Photo Editor or Paper Artist by opening a photo full screen, tapping the Menu touch button, and then selecting Edit. Paper Artist is installed on your Tab when you purchase the device, and you can download Photo Editor to your Tab 3 when you tap Photo Editor. In Photo Editor you find options to rotate, resize, crop, color, and add effects. Spot healing is also an option that enables you to retouch blemishes in your photographs. Paper Artist enables you to apply different paper effects to your photo including Watersketch, Pen and Pencil, Oil Painting, and Mosaic.

Email Photos from Gallery

Emailing your photos to friends and family can be accomplished in just a few taps on your Galaxy Tab 3.

1. Open the album that has the photo you want to email, and then touch and hold your finger to that photo to access more Gallery options.

2. Touch more photos that you want to share. A green check mark appears within the check box that appears in the upper-right corner of each photo, letting you know that it is selected. Email providers have varying file size limitations, so make sure you are aware of your provider's limitations before emailing photographs.

3. Tap the Share icon to access the options in the Share Via menu. You can access these same Share options even if you are viewing a single photo in full screen mode.

Additional Sharing Options

Keep in mind that as you add an email account or Facebook account on your Tab 3, those options also display in the Share Via menu.

4. Tap on the Gmail or Email icon. This example uses Gmail. The Gmail application opens with the images you selected attached.

5. Tap the X located to the bottom-right corner of a photo to remove the attachment. Keep in mind that you do not have the option to attach a new image at this stage, if you choose to remove an attachment.

6. Type the recipient's email address into the To field. If you see the name of the recipient in the drop-down list as you type, tap the name of the recipient. After you add a recipient to the list, you can add another one by typing the recipient name; you don't need any separator characters, such as a semicolon.

7. Tap in the Subject field and then type a subject for the email.

8. Tap in the Compose Email field to compose a message.

9. Tap Send to send the message.

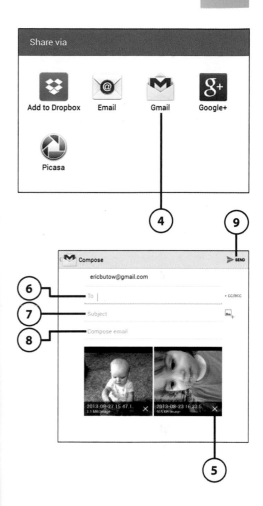

EMAILING FROM CAMERA

You can also email a photo from Camera within Image View. After you tap the Camera button to capture the image, a thumbnail of the image appears in the Image Viewer. Tap the Image Viewer to review the image, and then tap the Share icon to access your email. Email providers have varying file size limitations, so make sure you are aware of your provider's limitations before emailing photographs.

>>>Go Further

Creating Screen Captures

You Galaxy Tab 3 has a very helpful feature that enables you to take screen captures of its interface. The ability to take screenshots can come in handy for educational purposes, especially if you want to post a few Galaxy Tab tips online.

1. Open the screen that you want to take the screen shot of and position the Tab into the orientation in which you want to grab the screen capture: vertical or horizontal.

2. Press and hold the Power button and Home button at the same time. You hear the shutter sound effect as it takes the screen capture.

3. The screenshot is saved to the Screenshots folder in the Gallery app, and the image is also saved to the clipboard.

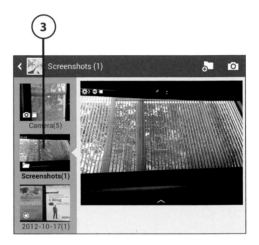

It's Not All Good

DIFFICULTIES TAKING SCREEN CAPTURES

It might not be possible to capture some of your Tab's menus using the Screen Capture function. For example, if you access the Quick Settings menu by tapping the notification icons at the bottom right of the screen and then tap the Screen Capture button, the Quick Settings close and the screenshot is not captured.

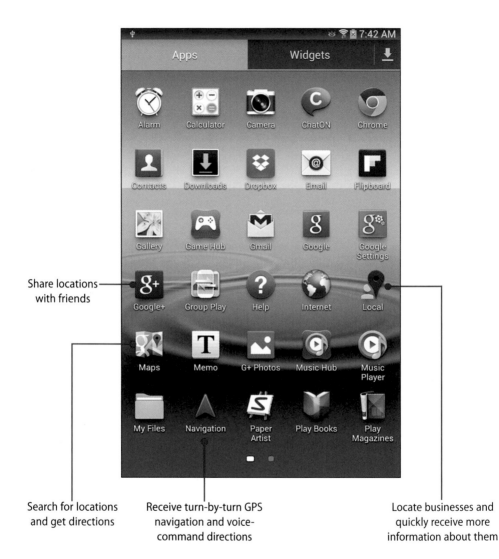

Share locations with friends

Search for locations and get directions

Receive turn-by-turn GPS navigation and voice-command directions

Locate businesses and quickly receive more information about them

In this chapter, you find out how to use the Maps, Navigation, Local, and Location Sharing apps to find locations, get directions, and connect with friends. Topics include:

→ Enabling GPS

→ Getting around with maps

→ Getting voice-command directions

→ Getting to know Local

→ Enabling wireless networks

→ Sharing locations with Google+ friends

Using Maps, Navigation, Local, and Location Sharing

Your Galaxy Tab 3 is equipped with four apps that can help you get where you need to go: Maps, Navigation, Local, and Location Sharing. Each app helps you accomplish a unique task, yet most of their collective feature base is accessible within each app. Maps can supply detailed destination directions for a specific address. Navigation can provide voice-guided turn-by-turn directions to a location. You can use Local to quickly locate local businesses and access contact information, coupons, and customer reviews. Location Sharing enables you to share your location with Google+ friends and view their locations on a map.

Enabling GPS

Before you can begin to use the many features of your Galaxy Tab 3 that utilize GPS, you must first enable your Tab's GPS capabilities.

1. Open the Quick Settings and Notifications page by tapping and holding on the Status Bar at the top of the page and then swiping down the screen.

2. Tap GPS into the On position if it isn't on already. The icon turns green and a green bar appears beneath the setting to indicate that GPS is on.

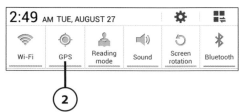

Getting Around with Maps

Maps is great when you're planning a trip across town or the nation. You can change your map view by adding layers that include traffic, terrain, satellite imagery, transit lines, and more. You do not even have to have an address for Maps to help you get where you need to go. Just specify the general area on a map and let the Maps app generate directions.

Find a Location with Maps

The Maps app on your Galaxy Tab 3 gives you the capability to find locations, get directions, and pinpoint locations. It also gives you access to features in other apps, such as Navigation, Local, and Location Sharing. The Maps app can help you pinpoint your exact location if you ever find yourself in an unfamiliar place. As soon as you launch Maps, your Tab uses GPS to pinpoint your current location.

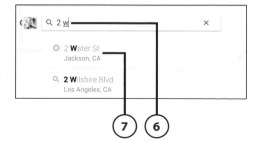

1. Tap Apps on the Home screen.

2. Tap Maps.

3. Tap the Accept & Continue button.

4. Tap Yes, I'm In if you want Google to improve your search suggestions. A map displaying your current location opens.

5. Tap the Search field at the top of the screen to find a location. If you see a message asking you to store your personal data on the Tab 3, tap OK.

6. Type the address of the location you want to find. As you type, a list of possible locations displays.

7. Tap the correct address in the list. Your Tab 3 displays the location on the map. If you cannot find the address you need in the list, Maps might not have complete data for that area or the information Google Maps has might be outdated.

Welcome to Google Maps

By using this application, you agree to the Terms of Service and Privacy Policy.

Close   Accept & continue

Skip for now   Yes, I'm in

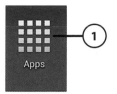

>>>Go Further

INACCURATE OR INCOMPLETE DATA

The Maps application is not always correct. Some of the directions and navigation data that it presents might be inaccurate or incomplete due to change over time. Complete information might not be available for some locations. Always use your best personal judgment and pay attention to road signs, landmarks, traffic conditions, and closures when following directions generated on your Tab 3.

8. Tap the location overlay.

9. Tap Save to save this location for future searches. There are many options you can access from this window, including Share, Directions, and Street View.

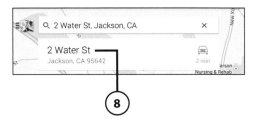

10. Tap the Google Maps icon to close the window.

11. Tap the Menu touch button to add additional layers of information to the current map.

12. Tap the layer of information that you want to add to the map in the menu. The information is added to the map, changing map view.

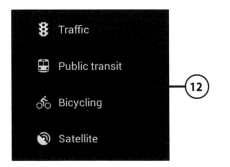

>>>Go Further

SWITCHING MAP VIEWS

You can view a location map as a satellite image by tapping Satellite in the menu. You can also overlay a traffic, public transit, or bicycling layer on top of the map or satellite image.

13. Pinch outward to enlarge the map. You can also double-tap your finger in a specific location on the map to enlarge the area. As you move in closer on the map, you start to notice that new information appears in the map, such as the name of banks and restaurants.

14. Use your finger to physically move the map and pinpoint locations.

Get Directions with Maps

Maps can help you get from point A to point B by providing detailed directions. You can get step-by-step driving, public transportation, biking, and walking directions to a specified destination by designating addresses for a starting location and a desired destination.

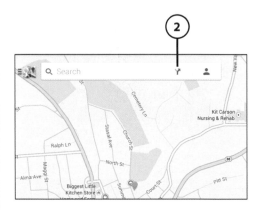

1. Tap Apps on the Home screen and then tap the Maps icon. A street map opens, displaying the last searched location.

2. Tap the Directions icon.

3. By default, your Tab 3 is able to pinpoint your current location, which appears as My Location in the top field. You can also type a different starting address in the top field. As you type, suggested addresses appear in a list below the box; you can tap an address in the list to place that address in the box.

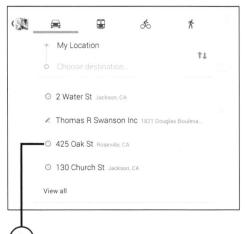

4. By default, the address you searched for appears in the End Point box. You can change the address by tapping in the box and typing a new address. As you type, suggested addresses appear in a list below the box; tap an address in the list to place that address in the box.

5. By default, the car button is selected so you can determine how long your trip will take by car. You can also select how long the trip will take by bus, bicycle, or walking.

6. Tap the estimated travel time to receive directions. A screen of detailed directions appears as a list. The estimated travel time appears above the list.

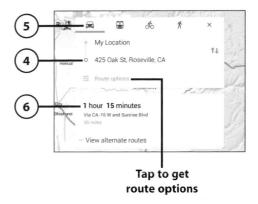

Tap to get
route options

BOOKMARKING LOCATIONS

Each time you generate directions within maps, they are bookmarked and appear underneath the My Location field with a pencil icon to the left of the address or contact name. To use these bookmarked directions, tap the location for which you want to generate directions.

7. Swipe up and down the Directions list to move through each step in the directions.

8. Tap any step in the directions to review it on the map.

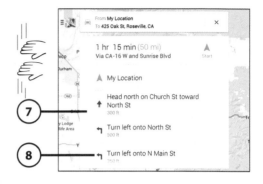

UPDATING/MODIFYING DIRECTIONS

After Maps generates the directions, you can can instruct Maps to generate new directions that avoid highways and toll roads. Tap Route Options that appears underneath the destination location to designate which options you want. Tap OK for updated directions.

Specify Locations with Maps

Maps can also help you find locations for which you do not have an address. For example, you might know that a café that you would like to visit is located downtown, but you do not know how to get downtown from your hotel. Maps enables you to specify a vicinity on a map where you want to go and generates directions from your current location.

1. Tap Apps and then tap the Maps icon.

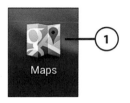

2. Use your finger to move the map to your desired location.

3. Tap and hold on the location until the pin appears on the location.

4. Tap the location address.

It's Not All Good

CURRENT LOCATION UNAVAILABLE

Occasionally, your Tab might not be able to pinpoint your current location because of lack of area coverage or a temporary disruption in the system. If for some reason Maps gives you the "Your Current Location Is Temporarily Unavailable" warning, you might have to enter your location by hand.

5. The location appears on the map so you can save the location, share it with someone else, or get driving directions. Tap the car icon to get driving directions.

6. Get driving directions by tapping the estimated travel time.

7. Swipe up and down the Directions list to move through each step in the directions.

8. Tap any step in the directions to review it on the map.

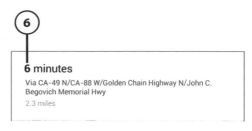

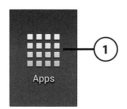

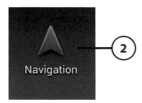

Getting Voice-Command Directions

The Navigation app is a subset of the Maps app and enables you to turn your Galaxy Tab into a turn-by-turn voice-command GPS device.

1. Tap Apps on the Home screen.

2. Tap Navigation.

3. Driving directions are selected by default. Tap your destination in the list or type the location by tapping Choose Destination.

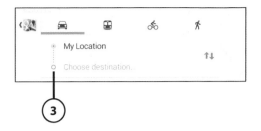

4. Type the name of the destination for which you need directions in the Choose Destination field.

5. Tap the correct destination in the list.

6. Your Galaxy Tab 3 searches for a GPS signal. After a connection is made, a street map appears with a highlighted route and the Navigation app speaks the first set of directions.

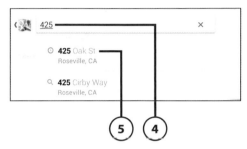

7. If you have a vehicle mount in your car, attach the Tab 3 to the vehicle mount. Appendix A, "Finding Galaxy Tab 3 Accessories," has more information about vehicle mounts.

8. Drive the route. Much like a dedicated GPS, your Tab senses where you are on the route and proceeds to give you instructions, verbally and graphically.

9. Tap Route Options and View Alternate Routes to view information about the route and alternative routes, respectively.

10. Tap the estimated travel time to view directions as a step-by-step list.

11. Tap the Google Maps icon to access more navigation options.

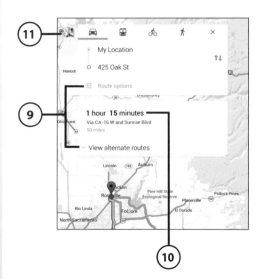

Exploring Route Options

You can access alternative routes by tapping View Alternate Routes. You can compare different route options by reviewing their distances in miles as well as overall travel times and highlighted map routes. View more information about the alternative route by tapping the route travel time on the screen.

>>>Go Further

VIEWING THE MAP

You can find the current step in the directions highlighted within the directions list. Within each direction entry in the list you can view the direction you are supposed to travel in the current step, as well as the estimated traveling distance for completing the step. Directions take the form of a left turn arrow, straight arrow, right arrow, or a U turn. On the map, you find the direction for your next move.

12. Tap to overlay a traffic status layer on the map.

13. Tap to overlay a public transit route layer on the map.

14. Tap to overlay a bicycling route layer on the map.

15. Tap to view a location map as a satellite image.

16. Tap to download the Google Earth app and then view your map within the app.

17. Tap Settings to view your account information, edit your home or work address, change location information, view your maps history, change distance units, send feedback, get tutorials and help, and to read the terms, privacy policy, and notice information.

18. Tap to launch tutorials and help for the app.

19. Tap to send feedback about the app to Google.

20. Tap to learn more about location sharing features in Google+, which replaced the Latitude app that was discontinued in August 2013. You find out how to use location sharing features in Google+ later in this chapter.

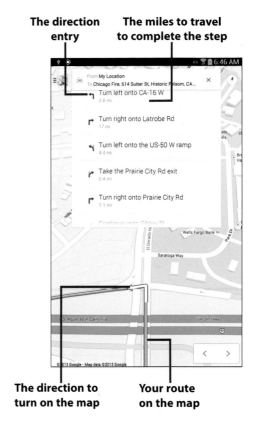

The direction entry

The miles to travel to complete the step

The direction to turn on the map

Your route on the map

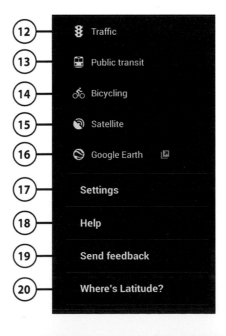

Getting to Know Local

Local is a preinstalled app on your Galaxy Tab 3 that enables you to locate places of interest with Google Maps and retrieve information, such as addresses, hours of operation, and phone numbers for those places. You can use Local to pinpoint the exact locations of restaurants, bars, ATMs, gas stations, and more, or you can create a new location, such as a pharmacy or hospital. Local offers a great way to explore nearby areas with which you might not be familiar.

1. Tap Apps on the Home screen.

2. Tap Local.

3. Local pinpoints your current location and displays a list of local establishments in your area. Tap the Search field to enter a new address to search what is nearby that location.

4. Tap a category for a place you would like to find in your area and a list of places displays.

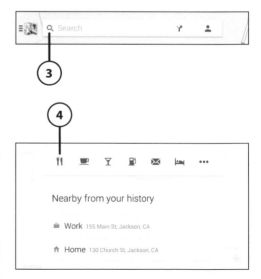

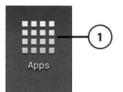

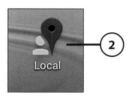

5. Tap Results List to view all the results in that category.

6. Swipe up and down the list to view all the results. When you want to find more information about an establishment, tap the appropriate tile.

7. The business type, address, and hours of operation appear underneath the business name.

8. Tap Save to save this location for future searches.

9. Tap Share to share information about this business to other users on Dropbox, ChatON, email or Gmail, via a Bluetooth or Wi-Fi Direct connection, Flipboard, Google+, or in a memo.

10. Tap to get driving directions to the business location.

11. The aggregated review ranking based on the number of written reviews appears in the Review Summary tile. Ratings vary from 1 star (bad) to 5 stars (great).

12. Tap to view a map of the location on the entire screen.

13. Tap to view a street view of the location so you can see what the business looks like before you drive there.

14. Tap to add a photo of the business location that will help fellow Google Maps users decide if they want to visit the business.

15. Swipe down the screen to view more options.

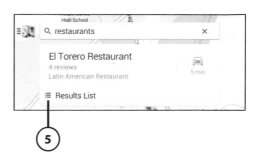

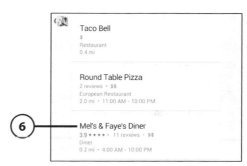

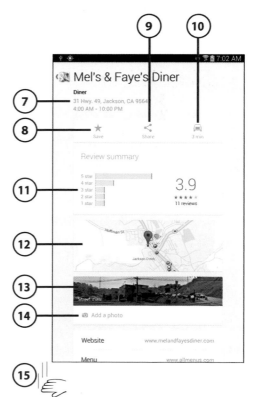

16. Tap to open the business website in the Internet or Chrome browser app.

17. If you're viewing a restaurant and a menu is available, tap to view the menu in the Internet or Chrome browser app.

18. Tap to get more information about the business.

19. Tap to report a problem with the business so Google can update the business entry in Google Maps. For example, if the business listing has the wrong contact details you can send the correct details to Google. You can also ask Google to notify you when the problem has been resolved so you can check the revised listing for accuracy.

20. Tap to rate and review the business. Your review will be read by other Google Maps users who are interested in visiting the business. Swipe down the screen to read other user reviews.

21. Return to the map by tapping the Google Maps icon.

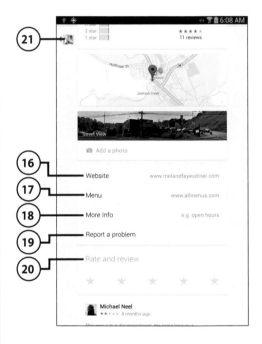

Sharing Locations with Friends

The Google Maps app enables you to see the location of your Google+ friends on a map or as a list. You can set up Google+ to share your location with individual friends or circles of friends.

Enable Location Settings

Before you can use Google Maps, you must first configure your Galaxy Tab 3 to use wireless networks and enable Wi-Fi. Use the following steps to turn on the Use Wireless Networks option.

1. Tap Settings on the Home screen.

2. Swipe down in the Settings list and then tap Location Services.

3. Tap Use GPS Satellites to enable the setting so Google Maps knows where you are.

4. Tap Use Wireless Networks to enable the setting.

5. Swipe up in the Settings list until you see Wi-Fi.

6. Slide the Wi-Fi button to the On position.

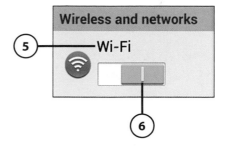

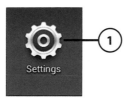

Share Locations in Google+

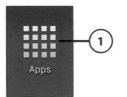

Now that you can use Google Maps, you need to set up Google+ to share locations with others.

Where Can I Learn More About Google+?

If you want to learn how to use the Google+ social networking site beyond the specific application discussed in this section, refer to Chapter 11, "Using Apps for Learning, Creating, and Sharing."

1. Tap Apps on the Home screen.

2. Tap Google+.

3. Tap Next.

4. Tap Done to back up the photos stored on your Galaxy Tab 3 onto Google+.

I Don't See the Screens in Steps 3 and 4

If you don't see the screens shown in Steps 3 and 4, that means you've already set up Google+. In this case, after you tap the Google+ icon you will see your news feed on the Google+ screen.

5. Tap the Google+ icon.

6. Tap Locations.

7. Turn on location sharing by tapping Yeah, Turn It On.

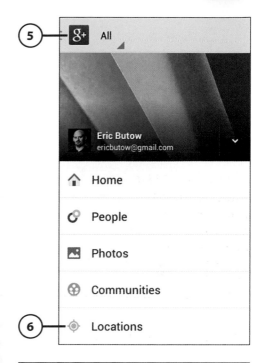

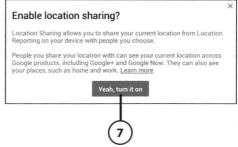

8. Tap Choose People to Share With in the Pinpoint Location tile if you want to share your exact location with others.

9. Alternatively, tap Choose People to Share With in the City Location tile if you only want to share your city. This example uses the city location.

10. Swipe up and down in the screen to view the circles and individual friends with whom you want to share your location information.

11. Select a circle or friend by tapping the check box to the right of the circle or friend name.

12. The circles and friends you added appear above the circles list.

13. Tap OK when you've made all your selections.

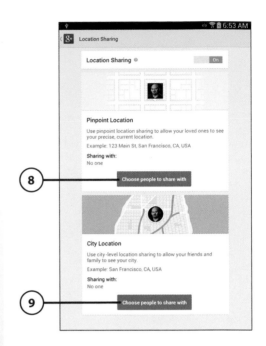

14. Tap Edit to edit the list of people you're sharing with.

15. Return to the map page in Google+ by tapping the Google+ icon in the menu bar.

16. The name and photo of the person who appears nearest you and is sharing his contact information appears at the bottom of the screen. The information includes the person's current location and how long ago the person checked in at that location.

17. The person's photo appears above the person's current location in the map.

18. See a list of more contacts who are sharing their locations by tapping the Contact icon.

19. Tap the name of a person in the list.

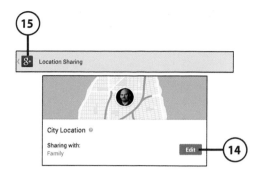

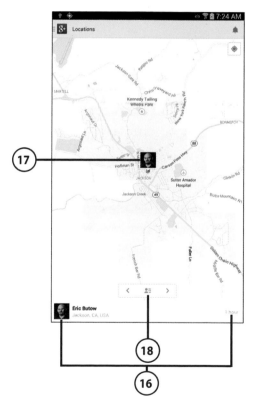

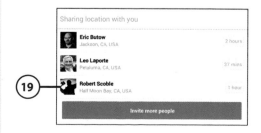

20. The person's current location appears on the map and more information about the person appears at the bottom of the screen.

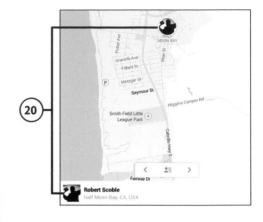

>>>Go Further

INVITING MORE PEOPLE TO SHARE THEIR LOCATIONS

If you want to find out where someone is currently but that person isn't sharing their location, you can ask that person to share her location by tapping Invite More People in the Sharing Location with You window. In the message composition screen is a default message so you can select the circle(s) or friend(s) to whom you want to send the invitation. Your message will be sent to all your recipient(s) on Google+.

Search the Google Play Store for thousands of useful, educational, and entertaining apps

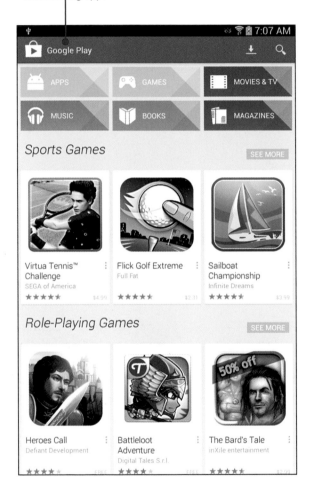

In this chapter, you discover how to expand the capabilities of the Galaxy Tab 3 by installing new apps. You also find out how to browse and make purchases in the Google Play Store and organize application icons on your Galaxy Tab. Topics covered in this chapter include:

16

→ Searching for Android applications
→ Purchasing Android applications
→ Rating applications
→ Getting help with apps
→ Arranging app icons on your Galaxy Tab 3
→ Adding and removing Home pages
→ Adding a dictionary and thesaurus
→ Adding an RSS reader
→ Using the Note Everything app

Finding and Managing Apps

The Galaxy Tab 3 is not just about superior hardware craftsmanship. Your Tab's true strength lies in the incredible software that is developed for it. The Galaxy Tab 3 comes with some truly amazing, preinstalled apps right out of the box, but you can expand its capabilities even further by downloading new apps from the Google Play Store. You can choose from thousands of innovative apps, ranging from games to productivity apps. The number of apps optimized for use on your Tab is growing rapidly.

Getting Apps in the Google Play Store

The Google Play Store makes it easy for you to browse apps and games that you can download to your Galaxy Tab 3. If this is your first time shopping in the Google Play Store, you will find the interface quite intuitive. A great way to become acquainted with the Google Play Store is just to start browsing. Many reviews of apps and games are available, so you can make an intelligent choice before downloading. A Google, Bing, or Yahoo! search for "Best Android apps for Galaxy Tab 3" can help you identify the most popular apps. Tab 3 users from around the world are writing articles about their experiences with apps that you might find useful. After you download and try out an app, consider giving your feedback so that new Tab 3 users can learn from you.

Search for Android Applications

To access the Google Play Store for the first time, you must use your Google account to sign into the Google Play Store. After you launch the Google Play Store app, there are several ways for you to search apps from the home page. The home page search options change position on the page, depending on which orientation you hold your Tab 3: vertical or horizontal.

1. Tap Play Store on the Home screen.

2. Tap Accept if you see the Google Play Store Terms of Service.

Terms of Service
The Terms of Service appear only the first time you launch the Google Play Store.

3. Tap Apps on the Google Play Store home page. A page of featured apps displays.

4. Scroll up and down the page to review groups of apps as well as individual apps. You can view more apps in a group by tapping See More.

5. Tap a category to browse the list of results for that category.

6. If you know the name of the app, book, magazine, or movie you want, tap the Search icon to specify a search term.

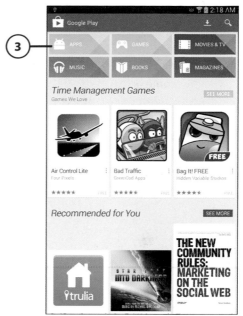

7. Type a search term into the Search Google Play field. Possible matches for your search appear in the list below the search field.

8. Tap the app in the list if the product you want is listed as an option.

9. Read more about the product. You can purchase—or download, if the app is free—the app on the description page. In this example, install Where's My Perry? Free by tapping Install.

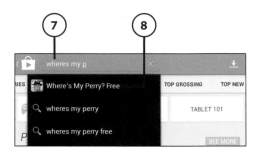

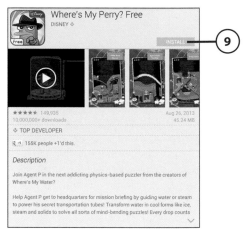

More About Product Descriptions

The description page for an app is chock full of useful information so you can make an educated decision about whether you want to purchase the app. Sample screenshots of the app are featured on this page along with customer reviews and information about the developer.

Other Ways to Search for Apps

Your Galaxy Tab 3 also has the Samsung Apps application preinstalled on the Home screen. You can find many popular free and paid apps for your particular Tab 3 with Samsung Apps. You access Samsung Apps by tapping the Samsung Apps icon on the main Home screen.

Find Great Apps

There are thousands of apps that you can download to your Galaxy Tab 3, so use your storage space wisely by finding the great ones. Finding the best apps might be the biggest challenge of all as you wade through your many options. This task gives you some tips on how to locate the highest-performing apps.

1. Tap Apps in the Google Play Store app.

2. Take a look at the featured apps on the Play Store home page. Keep in mind that large companies, usually with well-established names, tend to dominate the featured list. Lesser-known developers are also producing outstanding apps, so look deeper.

3. Some apps have trial versions you can test drive before purchasing. Look for Lite or Free versions of applications to test before you buy.

4. Tap an app in the Apps list that you want to learn more about.

5. Scroll down to check out customer reviews for products, but don't trust everything you read. Some reviews might not be in-depth or unbiased, and therefore they are less helpful.

6. Scroll to the bottom of the page and take a look at the Users Also Viewed list. You see apps that are similar along with their ratings next to them. You might find a higher-rated app that you want to look into.

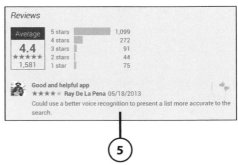

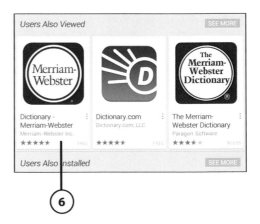

USING OTHER RESOURCES TO FIND APPS

You can use other solid resources outside the Play Store for finding great apps.

- **Perform a Google search**—For example, if you are looking for an app suited for taking dictation, type "Galaxy Tab 3 App Dictation."

- **Search for sites that feature and post reviews for apps**—Be aware that some of these sites are sponsored by the developers and might not convey completely objective views.

- **Find a Galaxy Tab forum**—There are many of these popping up every day. In a forum, you can post questions to other Galaxy Tab 3 owners regarding apps. Be aware that experienced Tab users might not moderate all of these forums, and the advice you receive can be questionable.

Purchase Android Applications

Software developers from around the world have developed thousands of apps for you to take advantage of with your Galaxy Tab 3. You can choose from many free apps in the Google Play Store, and you can also purchase a variety of more sophisticated apps for a fee. The process for downloading free apps and paid apps is similar, but you need to designate a payment method to make purchases.

1. Tap Play Store on the Home screen.

2. Locate and then tap the app that you want to download. The product description page opens.

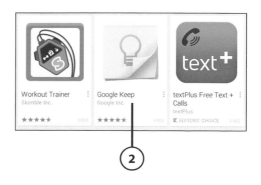

3. Tap the price of the app to see the permissions for this app. If this app is free, as in this example with Google Keep, tap the Install button. A page that lists the permissions the app is requesting opens.

4. Tap See All to review all permissions for the app.

5. Tap Accept to begin installing the app.

Accepting Permissions

If the application you have selected requires control of your Tab or access to data, the Google Play Store displays the information in this area. The list of permissions changes from app to app. When you accept permissions, you are essentially allowing the application you are purchasing to access your Galaxy Tab 3, including Internet access.

6. Tap Open to launch the application.

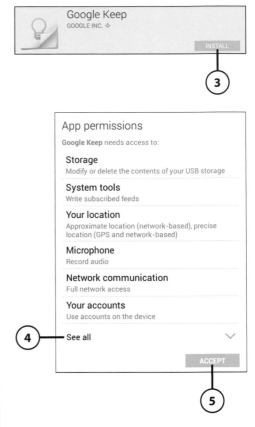

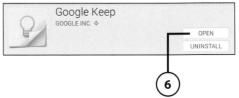

UPDATING APPS

The Google Play Store periodically searches for updates for apps that have been downloaded to your Galaxy Tab 3. If an update has been found, a notification appears in the Status bar. You can open the Quick Settings and Notifications screen and then tap the item in the Notifications list to be taken to the Google Play Store so you can begin the update. You can learn more about opening the Quick Settings and Notifications screen in Chapter 3, "Setting Up the Galaxy Tab 3."

DISABLING UPDATE NOTIFICATIONS

If you prefer to manually check for updates, you can configure the Google Play Store to stop notifying you about updates. Just launch the Google Play Store app and then tap the Menu touch button. Select Settings in the menu, and then deselect the Notifications option. You can tap the Download icon in the top-right corner of the Apps Bar to view a list of installed apps in the My Apps screen. The list of installed apps also lets you know which apps have an update that is available. You can also enable the Allow Automatic Updating setting within this list.

>>>Go Further

Rate Applications

Rating content you have purchased on Google Play Store helps others make educated decisions about their purchases. The Google Play Store uses a five-star rating system to rate all content. Much of the content on the Google Play Store features reviews that you can read to see how others like the product.

1. Tap Play Store on the Home screen.

2. Tap the Download icon to see the list of apps you have previously downloaded.

3. Tap the app that you want to rate.

4. Tap Rate & Review.

5. Tap OK if you see a window with information about Google Play reviews using Google+.

6. Enter a title for your review in the Summary field.

7. Enter your comments in the Comment field.

8. Tap a rating star on a scale from one to five. For example, if you tap the second star from the right the first four stars from left to right are highlighted in blue, which signifies that you give the app four stars on a five-star scale.

9. Tap OK.

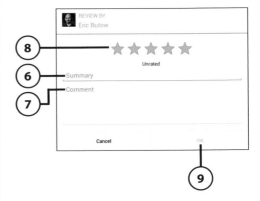

Get Help with Apps

Many new apps are being added to
the Google Play Store daily from well-
known companies, small companies,
and individual developers. Bugs and
other problems are likely to arise in
such a fast-moving market. There are
ways for you to contact developers
so that you can ask questions.

1. Tap Play Store on the Home
    screen.

2. Tap the Download icon to see the
    list of apps you have previously
    downloaded.

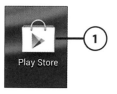

3. Tap the app for which you need
    help.

4. Tap the down arrow icon to view
    the entire description.

5. Scroll down and then tap Send
    Email in the Developer section to
    compose an email message ask-
    ing your question(s).

6. Tap Visit Webpage to visit the
    developer's site and search for
    information.

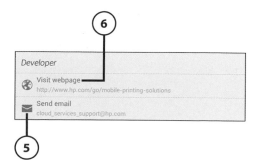

Managing Apps Through Your Home Pages

You begin many of your activities on the Home screen of the Galaxy Tab 3. As you purchase new apps, the number of icons in your Applications menu multiplies, which might prompt you to rearrange them according to the ones you use the most. You can manage your apps through your home pages by creating new home pages, deleting existing home pages, and grouping and arranging apps as you see fit on respective pages.

By default, when you download an application from Google Play Store, a shortcut is placed in the Applications menu, which is accessible from any Home screen. You can easily move shortcuts from the Applications menu to a Home screen and then rearrange them.

1. Tap Apps on the Home screen.

2. Swipe from right to left on the screen to view the app you added on the second page of the Apps screen.

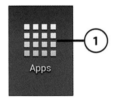

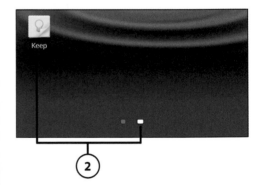

3. Locate the application shortcut, or widget, that you want to use, and then press and hold your finger on it. An overlay of the main Home screen appears on the page and overlays of all three Home pages display below the main Home screen overlay.

4. Move the shortcut to the desired Home screen overlay. Your selected Home screen appears as an overlay on the screen.

5. Move the shortcut to your desired location on the Home screen.

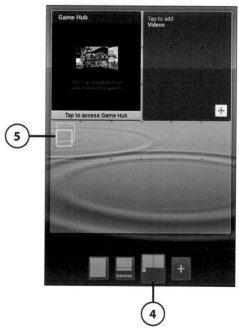

6. Release your finger. The shortcut is placed on the Home screen.

7. Repeat Steps 2 and 3 to move more App shortcuts from the Applications menu to the Home screen.

ADD TO HOME SCREEN

A quick way to add widgets, apps, folders, and new pages is to use the Add to Home feature. Press your finger on an empty space on a Home screen and hold until the Home screen menu pops up. Tap Add to Home screen and then choose the options that you want and follow the prompts to complete the task.

>>>Go Further

8. By default, your Galaxy Tab has three Home screens. Press your finger on a shortcut on a Home screen (in this example, Home screen 3) that you would like to move to another Home screen.

9. Drag the icon with your finger to the edge of the screen to move to another Home screen (in this example, Home screen 2).

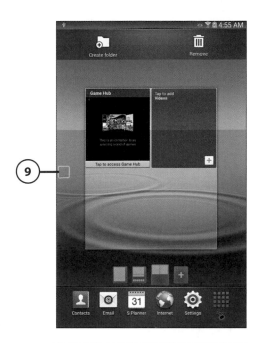

10. Remove your finger from the shortcut when you reach the spot where you would like to leave the shortcut.

CUSTOMIZING HOME SCREENS

Each Galaxy Tab 3 can be customized to be as unique as its individual owner. You can arrange your icons on any Home screen for shortcuts or widgets that you frequently use. For example, you can arrange all your games on one Home screen panel and all your productivity apps on another. You can even create new panels by tapping the Menu touch button on your Tab 3 from any Home screen, and then tapping Edit.

>>>Go Further

11. When you hold your finger on a shortcut and after it pulsates once, the Remove icon (a trash-can) appears in the top-right of the screen. Drag a shortcut to the Remove icon to remove it from a Home screen.

Removing Shortcuts and Widgets

When you remove a shortcut or widget icon, it does not delete or uninstall the app from your Galaxy Tab 3; it simply removes it from that panel. If you want to create a shortcut for that application again, it is still located in the Applications menu, or you can use the Add to Home Screen function.

UNINSTALLING APPS FROM YOUR TAB

>>>Go Further

After you purchase an app from the Google Play Store, you own it forever. You can uninstall a paid app from your Galaxy Tab 3 and then choose to reinstall it later (at no additional charge) in the future. To uninstall an app, tap the Apps icon on a Home screen and then tap Settings. Tap Applications Manager, and choose All to view a list of your applications. Tap the app that you want to uninstall to open the App Info screen and then tap Uninstall. You can also uninstall apps by using the Uninstall option for the application in the Google Play Store.

Adding Useful Apps

The true power of the tablet revolution lies not only in the simplification of computing, but also personalization. Apps enable you to optimize your Galaxy Tab for your unique lifestyle. Your Galaxy Tab 3 can be a virtual dictionary or thesaurus. Add an RSS reader and transform your Tab into a news-gathering device so that you are always up to date on current news and events. Many practical apps on the market enhance the capabilities of your Galaxy Tab 3, freeing you from having to purchase and carry a second device such as a digital audio recorder or scanner. There are too many options to list them all here, but let's explore a few practical apps that you might want to consider.

Use the Merriam-Webster Dictionary App

Adding a simple dictionary app to your Galaxy Tab is a very handy and practical solution for having to lug around an actual paper reference book.

The Merriam Webster Dictionary app is free on the Google Play Store and delivers content that is trusted. The following steps presume you have already downloaded the Merriam Webster Dictionary app from the Google Play Store.

1. Tap the Merriam-Webster app on the Home screen. If you see the End-User License Agreement on the screen, tap Accept.

Use Any Dictionary App

There are many other free options for dictionary and thesaurus reference apps. If you prefer another, don't hesitate to use it. This is just a recommendation for the usefulness of such a reference to exist on your Galaxy Tab 3. The Dictionary.com app is also a great application and gets the job done.

2. Tap in the Search field and enter a word to look up. Search suggestions appear in the list beneath the field.

3. Tap the correct word in the list. The definition(s) for the entry appear.

4. You can tap the speaker icon to hear the pronunciation of the word.

5. Tap to speak a new word to search.

6. Tap to view a list of recently searched words.

7. You can learn a new word every day. Tap to view the word of the day.

8. Tap to view all words you have marked as Favorites.

9. Tap the star to add this word to your Favorites.

10. Tap to provide Feedback to the developers of this app, rate this app, and share this app. You also find information about Merriam-Webster and list of similar recommended apps such as the Britannica Encyclopedia.

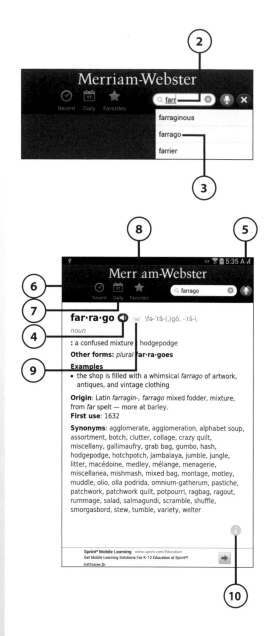

Use the Pulse RSS Reader

If part of your daily routine includes reading news websites and blogs, adding an RSS reader can help you manage your news sources from one app in the form of feeds instead of visiting multiple websites. Pulse News is a free RSS feed reader that you can download from the Google Play Store; it enables you to acquire and manage multiple news feeds as an interactive mosaic. The following steps presume you have already downloaded the Pulse News app from the Google Play Store.

1. Tap Pulse on the Home screen.

2. Pulse is loaded with predefined news feeds to get you started. Each row represents an individual news feed. Flick down in a news feed to view the rest of the news items for the feed.

3. Tap to choose a new feed to add to the page.

4. After you tap the topic(s) you want, tap Start Reading.

5. Tap a news story to open it. The story opens.

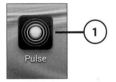

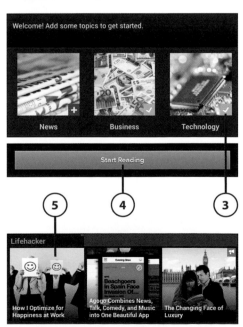

Refreshing Automatically

You can choose an automatic refresh option by tapping the Pulse icon on the menu bar at the top of the screen. Next, tap Settings, and then tap Edit Application Settings to access the Applications Settings screen. Then you can make changes to refresh settings including the automatic refresh frequency in the Background Source Refresh section.

6. Open a menu to change your viewing options by tapping the Menu icon.

Landscape or Portrait Orientation

The Pulse interface options change, depending on whether you hold your Tab in landscape orientation or portrait orientation as shown in these steps. Try holding your Tab in various orientations to see which you prefer.

7. Tap to select a new font size and style for the article text as well as the brightness level for the page.

8. Tap to open the article in the Internet or Chrome browser.

9. Tap to open the article on the main website where the article is found.

10. Tap to mark the article as a favorite.

11. Tap to share the article on Linked, Facebook, Twitter, and/or Google+.

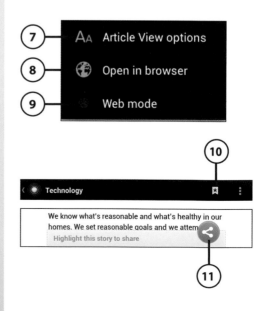

12. Tap to share the article with other apps including email, Gmail, ChatON, and Dropbox.

13. Tap to return to the Pulse home screen of various feeds.

14. Return to the category news feed page by tapping the Back touch button.

15. Tap Edit.

16. Press your finger to the name of a news feed and drag it to reorder feeds.

17. Tap the X to delete a feed.

18. Tap Done when you finish editing your feeds list.

19. Scroll down the screen and then tap Add Content to add a new category page.

20. Search new categories and then tap the category name you want to add.

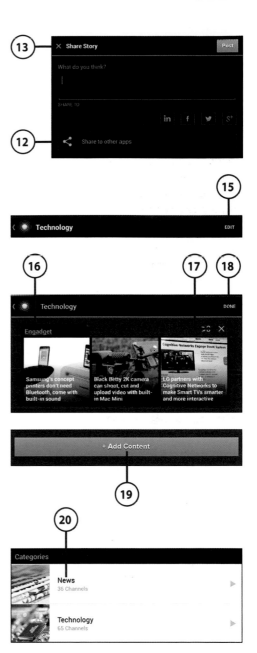

21. Search the feed you want to add in the category and then tap the plus icon to the right of the feed name you want to add.

22. Tap to add the feed to a new page.

23. Type the new page name in the Enter Page Name field.

24. Tap Done.

25. Tap the Back touch button twice to return to the feeds page.

26. Tap the Pulse icon.

27. View the feeds on the new page by tapping the page name.

Multiple Pages of News Feeds

You can add 50 pages of news feeds within Pulse with 12 feeds per page for a maximum total of 600 feeds. If you choose to populate a new page with feeds you can access the new pages by tapping the various page numbers at the top of each page.

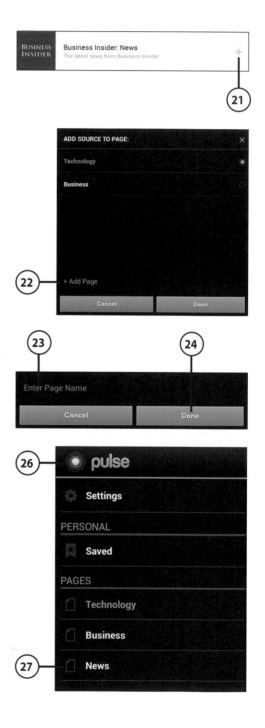

Use Note Everything

A digital voice recorder can be a priceless tool if you ever need to record some notes for yourself. Or have you ever wished you had the capability to scan barcodes on a product so that you could store the information?

Note Everything is a free app that can do all of this and more, including taking handwritten notes and tucking information away neatly in folders. This section presumes you have already downloaded the Note Everything app from the Google Play Store.

1. Tap Note Everything on the Home screen.

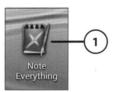

Receiving Help

When you first use certain functions, a help screen appears and provides you with tips.

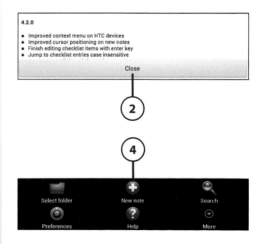

2. Tap Close in the What's New screen.

3. Tap the Menu touch button.

4. Tap New Note.

5. Tap Textnote to leave a note using the keyboard. This is similar to how the preinstalled Memo widget works on your Tab, but you might find it more beneficial to have all your notes in one location.

6. Tap Paintnote to leave a note using your finger as a pen. You can tap the Menu button on your Galaxy Tab and change the color of ink, erase marks, change stroke width, clear colors, work full screen, and more. This is a great option for jotting down a quick visual note.

7. Tap Voicenote to record voice memos. Each recording is stored as an individual file that you can play back on your Tab 3.

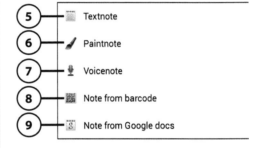

8. Tap Note from Barcode to use your Galaxy Tab 3 camera to read barcodes and note the barcode for later reference. This option requires you to install another free app named Barcode Scanner for it to work. The installation process is streamlined within the Note Everything app and takes only a few moments.

9. Tap Note from Google Docs to import and export text notes from Google Docs. This option requires you to install another free app named Note Everything (NE) GDocs. These two apps can work seamlessly together or independently.

It's Not All Good

NOT ALWAYS ACCURATE

Be advised that not all barcode scanners on your Galaxy Tab 3 are 100% accurate. That goes for any product, not just the one featured here. Sometimes these scanners might not recognize the product, or the price they provide for the product might be way off the mark. Use all these apps with caution. If you don't like this app, you can choose from many other free options.

Recording Voice Notes

After each recording, you can choose whether to use or discard the recording. If you choose to keep it, you are taken to a page with a notepad where you can play back the voice memo and take text notes at the same time.

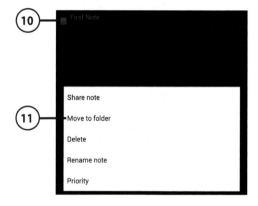

10. After you create a note, it is placed in the main (root) menu. Tap and hold your finger on any note that you would like to move to a different folder, and a pop-up menu appears.

11. Tap Move to Folder.

12. Tap Close after you read the help screen. Help screens appear when you access a function for the first time.

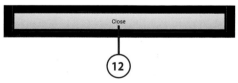

13. Tap the Menu touch button.

14. Tap Create Folder.

15. Type the name in the Foldername field.

16. Tap OK to move the note to the new folder.

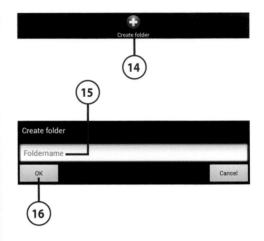

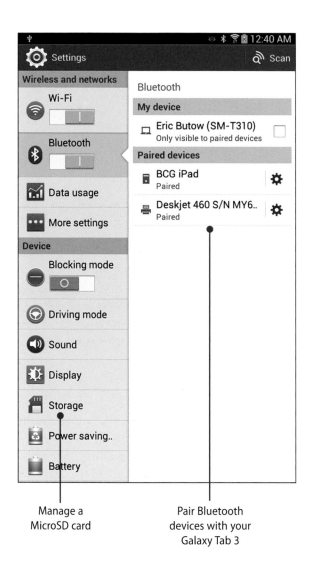

Manage a
MicroSD card

Pair Bluetooth
devices with your
Galaxy Tab 3

This chapter covers how to get the most from your Galaxy Tab 3 using hardware accessories such as Bluetooth keyboards, Bluetooth devices, and memory card options. Accessories covered in this chapter include:

→ Galaxy Tab USB and SD connection kit
→ Bluetooth devices
→ MicroSD cards

Adding New Hardware

Your Galaxy Tab 3 is fully capable of providing an amazing multi-media experience right out of the box, but whether you are viewing movies, capturing photos and video, or composing a long email, you want your Galaxy Tab to be versatile. Accessories such as Bluetooth headsets, desk docks, Bluetooth keyboards, and extra memory cards can offer some much needed practical support for your Tab use.

You can find accessories for the 7", 8", and 10.1" Galaxy Tab 3 models in electronics stores such as Best Buy, or you can try your local electronics store. Online stores, such as Samsung.com and Amazon.com, are also great places to find hardware accessories for the Galaxy Tabs. Always make sure that you pick the right accessory for your Tab 3 model. As of this writing, none of the previous Galaxy Tab accessories work with the Tab 3.

Limited Accessories to Date

This section covers accessories that were available as the book was written for both the Galaxy Tab 3 8" and 10.1" devices. I am sure that shortly after this book finds its way onto shelves that there will be new accessories that are not mentioned in this chapter. For example, Samsung does not offer a multimedia desk dock or keyboard dock for the Galaxy Tab 3. I encourage you to keep up to date on what is available for your device by periodically checking the Samsung website, Amazon.com, and tech forums.

Galaxy Tab 2013 USB Connection Kit

Samsung offers a USB connection kit that is small enough to put in your pocket, and it enables your Galaxy Tab 3 8" or 10.1" to connect with compatible USB accessory devices including mice, keyboards, and thumb drives.

Bluetooth Keyboards

Your Galaxy Tab 3 comes with Bluetooth 3.0 technology, which enables you to use devices such as wireless headphones and wireless keyboards. There are limited third-party companies that produce accessories such as the Bluetooth keyboard for both the 8" and 10.1" Tab 3 devices. (One such company is eWonder.) A Bluetooth keyboard provides the convenience of typing with a physical keyboard, which makes it easier to write a lengthy message. This accessory provides a typing experience similar to using a computer keyboard, so inputting information is easier than using the onscreen keyboard. Users who perform extensive writing tasks might find the more ergonomically pleasing Bluetooth keyboard a better alternative to the onscreen keyboard. This accessory is usually in a 2-in-1 package, which means that it serves both as a QWERTY keyboard and also a folding leather case to protect your keyboard. A Bluetooth keyboard case not only protects your Galaxy Tab, but it is also very travel-friendly. You can find eWonder accessories by performing a product search on Amazon.com.

Pairing Bluetooth Devices

Along with the many other comfort features and conveniences found with the Galaxy Tab 3, your Tab gives you the capability to connect some external hardware devices wirelessly. The Tab 3 is equipped with Bluetooth 3.0

technology, enabling you to connect cable-free with Bluetooth-capable keyboards and headphones. By default, Bluetooth is disabled on your Tab. If you
have already played with this setting, you can tell if Bluetooth is turned on by
verifying that the Bluetooth symbol is visible in the status bar at the top of
the screen.

Pair a Bluetooth Device

You can easily connect your Tab 3 to
a Bluetooth device in two phases:
discovering and pairing.

1. Turn on the wireless device that
   you want to pair with your Galaxy
   Tab and make it discoverable.

Discoverability

Bluetooth devices broadcast their
availability only after you instruct
them to do so. If necessary, refer
to your device's manual to learn
how to make it discoverable.

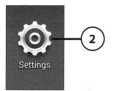

2. Tap Settings on the Home screen.

3. Tap Bluetooth to view the
   Bluetooth options to the right of
   the screen.

4. Swipe the Bluetooth slider to the
   right to place the Bluetooth setting in the On position. The switch
   turns green and any detectable
   Bluetooth devices are listed to the
   right.

5. Tap your Bluetooth device in the
   list. Your Tab attempts to pair with
   the device.

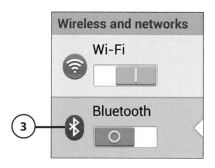

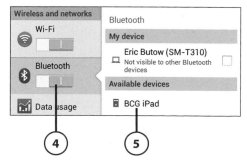

6. The device then appears under a newly created Paired Devices list.

Paired Bluetooth Device Settings

After you have successfully paired your device to your Tab 3, a Settings icon appears next to the name of the Bluetooth device within the Paired Devices list. Tap that Settings icon to rename, unpair, or further configure your device.

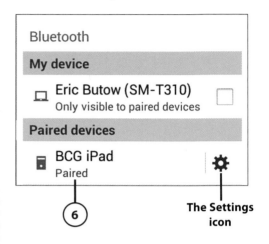

6

The Settings icon

When Paired

When a device is paired with your Galaxy Tab, you never have to configure the devices again.

MicroSD Cards

Your Tab supports MicroSD and MicroSDHC memory cards that come in the following sizes: 4GB, 8GB, 16GB, 32GB, and 64GB. Increasing the storage capacity of your Galaxy Tab 3 is a convenient way to store more music, photos, videos, and other files.

Formatting MicroSD Cards

If you buy a new card, you need to format it for your Tab 3. Whether you are upgrading a MicroSD card or adding a new card, follow these steps to format your new memory card:

1

1. Tap Settings on the Home screen.

2. Tap Storage.

3. Insert the MicroSD card into your Tab 3. All of the MicroSD Card information appears under the SD card category to the right.

4. Tap the Format SD card option located at the bottom of the SD card category.

5. Read the warning and then tap Format SD Card.

6. If you type a password to log into the Tab 3, type the password in the Confirm Password screen.

7. When you finish typing the password, tap Continue.

8. Read the warning and then tap Delete All. The SD card is formatted and becomes instantly available for use.

Unmount Before Removing

It is very important that you first unmount the MicroSD card before removing it from the slot. Failing to do so can result in damage to the MicroSD card. Simply tap Unmount SD Card in the SD Card category.

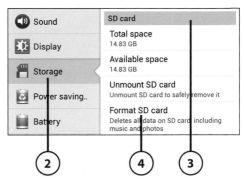

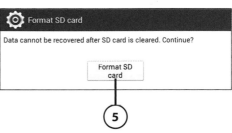

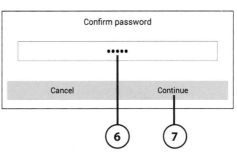

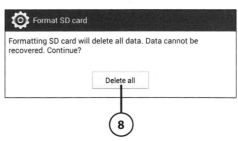

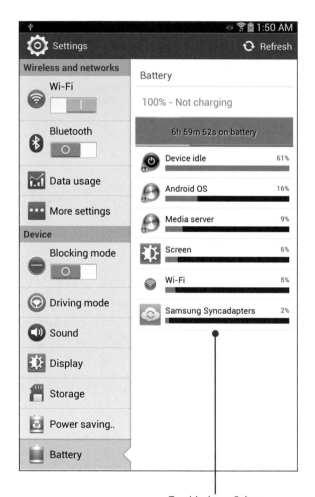

Troubleshoot Galaxy
Tab software, hardware,
and accessories

This chapter covers ways that you can properly maintain your Galaxy Tab 3 and troubleshoot basic software or hardware problems. Topics covered in this chapter include:

→ Maintaining your Galaxy Tab 3
→ Updating the Galaxy Tab software
→ Backing up and restoring your Galaxy Tab 3
→ Extending battery life
→ Solving Galaxy Tab issues
→ Troubleshooting connected devices
→ Getting help

Troubleshooting Your Galaxy Tab 3

Although problems concerning the Galaxy Tab 3 software, hardware, and accessories are rare, on occasion you might experience incidents where your Tab does not perform properly. There are a few fixes you can try if you experience the occasional glitch that can occur with any hardware device.

Although your Galaxy Tab 3 is a sophisticated piece of hardware, it is less complex than an actual computer, making any issue that might arise more manageable.

Maintaining Your Galaxy Tab 3

Regular maintenance of your Galaxy Tab 3 not only helps extend the life of your Tab, it also helps ensure peak performance. It's important that you make sure your Galaxy Tab 3 software is up to date and understand basic troubleshooting concepts. Properly cleaning and protecting your Tab's body can be equally important. The Tab 3 was designed to be sturdy, but, like any other electronic device, it can collect dust, and a simple drop on the sidewalk can prove disastrous. The first step in maintaining your Galaxy Tab is prevention. You can start by purchasing a protective case.

A sturdy case designed for the Galaxy Tab 3 is important for the overall protection of your device. A number of companies have created a variety of cases for the Tab, so search the Internet or go to Amazon.com to see what's out there. The more padded the case, the better it can absorb a shock if you happen to drop your Tab. A case can also help protect your Tab from dust and keep it dry if you happen to get caught in the rain. Make sure that you keep the inside of your case clean. Dust and sand can find its way into even the most well-constructed cases. Instead of using your sleeve to wipe off your Galaxy Tab's display, invest in a microfiber cloth; you can find them in any office supply or computer store.

Your first instinct might be to wet a cloth to clean your Galaxy Tab touchscreen. Don't use liquids to clean the touchscreen, especially if they include alcohol or ammonia. These harsh chemicals can cause irreparable damage to the touchscreen, rendering it difficult to see. Consider purchasing a screen protector at a local store or your favorite online retailer to keep the touchscreen dust and scratch free. Some screen protectors also come with a microfiber cleaning cloth.

Updating Galaxy Tab 3 Software

Every so often, Google releases software updates for your Galaxy Tab's Android operating system. To get the most from your Galaxy Tab 3, it is good practice to update soon after an upgrade has been released. When an update is available, you receive a notification that indicates that you can download a system upgrade. At that point, you have the option to initiate the software update. You can also check for system updates manually by tapping Settings in the Apps menu, tapping About Device, and then choosing Software Update. You are given an option to Check for Updates. If your system is up to date, your Tab alerts you to this fact. If an update is available, follow the provided directions to upgrade your software.

The Android operating system is not the only software you need to update on your Galaxy Tab. Your Tab also uses software, called *firmware*, to run its internal functions. When an update is available, use your own discretion as to whether you want to update right away, just in case there are any issues with the update.

Backing Up and Restoring Your Galaxy Tab 3

Backing up the contents of your Galaxy Tab 3 is a good practice for securing your important information and multimedia content. You can ensure that your contacts, photos, videos, and apps are copied to your PC or Mac in case something happens to your Tab.

Ensuring Automatic Google Account Backup

Your Google account information—such as your Gmail inbox, Contacts list, and Calendar app appointments—automatically sync with Google servers, so this information is already backed up for you. To ensure that your Google account information is being automatically backed up, follow these directions.

1. Tap Settings on the Home screen.

2. Scroll down the Settings list until you view all the accounts in the Accounts section.

3. Tap a Google account.

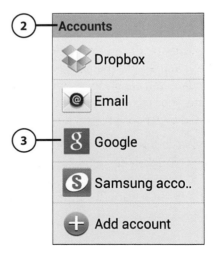

4. Tap the Google email account in the list of accounts.

5. Ensure that all the account settings in the list have a green check mark to the right. If they don't, tap the box to place a green check mark within the box.

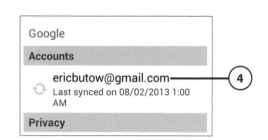

Multiple Google Accounts

If you have multiple Google accounts, repeat Steps 1 through 5 for each account.

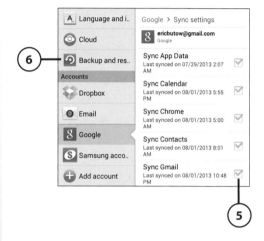

6. Tap Backup and Reset.

7. Ensure that a green check mark appears next to Back Up My Data and Automatic Restore. If not, tap the box in each field to place a green check mark within the box. The information associated with your Google address is now automatically backed up.

8. Tap Backup Account to immediately begin backing up your Google account data.

The Automatic Restore Option

When checked, the Automatic Restore option ensures that any data or settings placed on third-party apps are restored when you restore those apps to your Galaxy Tab.

Syncing and Using Manual Backup

There are multiple ways for you to back up content that is outside of your Google account information on your Galaxy Tab 3, such as your apps and multimedia content, onto your computer. Connect your Galaxy Tab 3 to your PC as a mass storage device and manually drag and drop files. You can use the Samsung Kies software to transfer data, synchronize files, and update firmware while connected to a PC or Mac.

When connected to your PC as a mass storage device, you can view all of the data on your Tab's internal storage and optional MicroSD card. The content is categorized into specific folders that you can copy from your card and internal storage such as DCIM, Download, Music, Pictures, Movies, Podcasts, and more. You can also copy all folders with the names of apps installed on your Galaxy Tab 3.

You can also use the Samsung Kies software for PCs and Macs to sync your content. See Chapter 12, "Playing Music and Video," to learn how to exchange content between your Galaxy Tab 3 and your computer by connecting as a mass storage device and by using Samsung Kies.

Extending Battery Life

Your Galaxy Tab 3 is capable of up to at least 7.5 hours of battery life depending on the model you have. Battery life can also vary depending on how you use the Galaxy Tab. Strenuous tasks, such as playing HD video, dramatically lower your battery life more than surfing the Web does. You can monitor your battery power at the top of the screen in the Status area. The green battery status icon located in the lower right of the status bar lets you keep an eye on how much battery power you have left. When the battery gets low, a warning appears, informing you of the percentage of battery power you have left and instructing you to connect the charger. When the battery is too low, your Tab automatically shuts down. There are a few things you can do to extend the life of your Tab's battery.

Monitor Power Usage

On the Galaxy Tab 3 you can use the Battery Usage screen to see which of the apps you use consumes the most power, and then you can reduce the use of those apps. Your battery power savings are small, but if you're running low on power with no way to recharge, every little bit counts. Follow these directions to access the Battery Usage screen.

1. Tap Settings on the Home screen.

2. Scroll down the Settings list (if necessary) and then tap Battery. The screen displays the items that are consuming the most battery power. In this example, 5 percent of the battery power has been used to use the Wi-Fi hardware to communicate with the Internet.

Adjust Screen Brightness

The high-quality touchscreen of the Galaxy Tab 3 can consume plenty of battery power. The higher the brightness level set on your Galaxy Tab 3 the more power the touchscreen uses. If you are viewing the screen in very bright conditions, you probably do not need a very high brightness setting. Consider dimming the screen to extend the battery life.

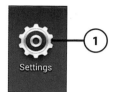

1. Tap Settings on the Home screen.

2. Tap Display.

3. Tap Brightness.

4. Tap the Automatic Brightness check box to deselect the Automatic Brightness setting.

5. Slide the slider to the left to lower the brightness level.

6. Tap OK.

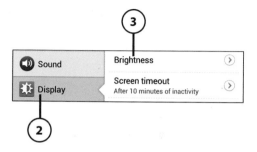

Automatic Brightness

When the Automatic Brightness checkbox is checked, your Tab uses sensors to determine your current light conditions and then adjusts the screen brightness automatically. In bright conditions, the screen is dimmed, and vice versa.

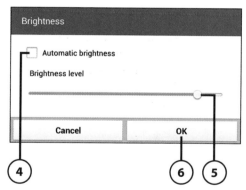

Quick Settings for Brightness

The Galaxy Tab 3 offers a quicker way for you to access the brightness controls by providing quick settings in the notification panel. Simply tap in the far-right corner of the status bar located at the bottom right of your Tab's screen, deselect the Auto setting, and then use the slider to adjust screen brightness.

Utilize Sleep Mode

Your Galaxy Tab 3 goes to sleep after a specified period of inactivity, but you don't have to wait for it to fall asleep, you can put it to sleep manually. When your Tab is awake, it is consuming battery power. Press the sleep button on the side of your Tab when you have finished using the device to conserve battery power.

Conserve Power by Turning Off Wi-Fi

When the Wi-Fi antenna is activated on your Galaxy Tab, your device is incessantly looking for available Wi-Fi networks to join, which uses battery power. To see if Wi-Fi is turned on, check the status bar in the top-left corner of your Galaxy Tab for the Wi-Fi symbol. If you do not need a Wi-Fi connection, turn it off to conserve battery power. If you are not wandering and are using Wi-Fi in a single location, look for a power outlet and plug in your Tab.

1. Tap Settings on the Home screen.

2. Tap Wi-Fi to view Wi-Fi networks available to you.

3. Turn off Wi-Fi by sliding the Wi-Fi slider to the right. The slider button displays an O (for Off) with a gray background, and the right side of the screen asks you to turn on Wi-Fi to see available networks.

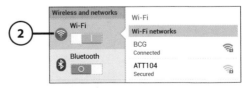

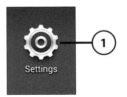

Quick Settings for Wi-Fi

The Galaxy Tab 3 offers an even quicker way for you to access the Wi-Fi setting by providing quick settings in the notification panel. Simply tap in the far-right corner of the status bar located at the bottom right of your Tab's screen and tap the green Wi-Fi setting to turn it off.

Conserve Power by Turning Off Bluetooth

When Bluetooth is activated on your Galaxy Tab, your device is constantly checking for other Bluetooth devices, which drains battery power. To see if Bluetooth is turned on, check the status bar in the top-left corner of your Galaxy Tab for the Bluetooth symbol. If you are not using a Bluetooth device, turn this function off. There are also security reasons why you should turn off Bluetooth when you are not using it, so get in the habit of turning Bluetooth off as soon as you finish using a wireless device with your Galaxy Tab. You can easily deactivate Bluetooth in the Notifications panel.

1. Tap Settings on the Home screen.

2. View all Bluetooth devices to which the Galaxy Tab 3 is connected by tapping Bluetooth.

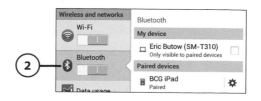

3. Turn off Bluetooth by sliding the Bluetooth slider to the right. The slider button displays an O (for Off) with a gray background, and the right side of the screen asks you to turn on Bluetooth to see available devices.

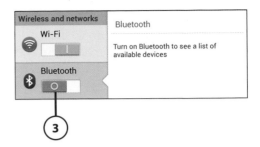

Quick Settings for Bluetooth

The Galaxy Tab 3 offers an even quicker way for you to access the Bluetooth setting in the Quick Settings and Notifications screen. Turn off Bluetooth by simply tapping the green Bluetooth tile in the far-right corner of the status bar located at the top right of your Tab's screen.

Solving Random Galaxy Tab Issues

The occasional hardware or software glitch happens to even the best of electronic devices. You might encounter an issue, although rare, where an app you are using freezes, a wireless device proves difficult to pair with your Galaxy Tab 3, the touchscreen becomes unresponsive, or landscape orientation is not available at all times. Fortunately, it is not very difficult to troubleshoot some of these issues. If you should happen to come across a problem that you can't solve yourself, there are plenty of channels for you to find technical support.

Difficulty Turning Your Tab On or Off

On rare occasions, you might find your Galaxy Tab 3 stubborn when you try to turn it on or off. It might appear that the device has locked or become unresponsive. If this happens to you, hold the Power button for 8 seconds to see if it responds. If this does not work, you might need to let your Tab sit for a few seconds before you again try holding the Power button for 8 seconds.

Touchscreen Becomes Unresponsive

This tip assumes that your Galaxy Tab 3 and any app you are using is responsive, but the touchscreen is not responding to your touch. If you attempt to use your Galaxy Tab 3 touchscreen while wearing conventional gloves, it does not work. This can prove inconvenient on a very cold day, so you might want to consider a capacitive stylus for your Galaxy Tab.

Your Tab uses a capacitive touchscreen that holds an electrical charge. When you touch the screen with your bare finger, capacitive stylus, or special static-carrying gloves, it changes the amount of charge at the specific point of contact. In a nutshell, this is how the touchscreen interprets your taps, drags, and pinches.

The touchscreen might also be unresponsive to your touch if you happen to have a thin coat of film on your fingertips. So no sticky fingers, please.

Force Stop an App

Sometimes an app might get an attitude and become unruly. For example, an app might provide a warning screen saying that it is currently busy and is unresponsive, or it might give some other issue warning to convey that a problem exists. If an app is giving you problems, you can manually stop the app.

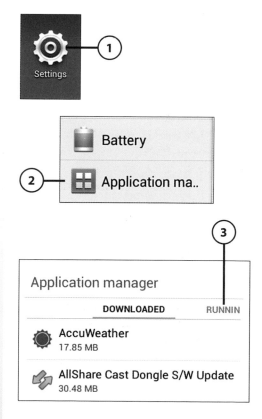

1. Tap Settings on the Home screen.

2. Scroll down the Settings list (if necessary) and then tap Application Manager.

3. Tap Running at the top of the screen to view only the apps that are currently running.

4. Tap the problem app.

5. Tap Stop. The app stops running.

6. Tap Report to send a problem report to the app's developer.

Battery Does Not Charge

If you find that your battery is not charging, first start with the power outlet. Is the outlet supplying power? Is the power strip turned on? Plug something else into the outlet to see if it works, or try another outlet.

Make sure that everything is connected properly. Is the adapter secure on both ends? If the outlet supplies power and the cables are connected properly, but the battery still does not charge, try another cable. If this does not solve the issue, your battery might be defective. Contact Samsung technical support. (See the "Getting Technical Help" section later in this chapter for more information about how to contact Samsung.) There is no way for you to remove the battery yourself.

Overheating

Overheating is rare, but if your Galaxy Tab becomes too hot and regularly turns itself off, you might need to replace the battery. You can tell if your Tab is getting too hot by holding it in your hands. Use caution.

Horizontal Screen Orientation Does Not Work

The orientation setting on your Galaxy Tab 3 could be set so that your Tab stays in either vertical or horizontal mode, regardless of how you hold the device. If your Tab no longer utilizes horizontal orientation, first check the setting for screen orientation.

The Galaxy Tab 3 has an Auto-Rotate setting that must be selected for the screen to adjust from vertical to horizontal mode, depending on how you hold the device. You can easily confirm that the Auto-Rotate setting is selected from the Settings menu.

1. Open the Quick Settings and Notifications screen from the Home screen by tapping and holding on the top edge of the screen and then swiping downward.

2. Locate the Screen Rotation setting button and confirm that the icon and bar underneath the Screen Rotation text is green. If the icon and bar are gray, activate the setting by tapping the button. Your Galaxy Tab screen should now adjust to the orientation in which you hold the device.

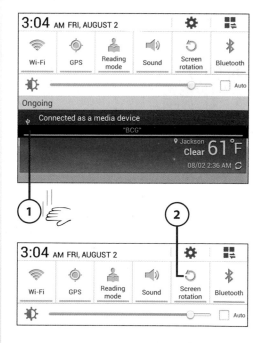

Changing Orientation on the Tab 3 10.1"

For the 10.1" Tab, you need to go into the settings under Screen and ensure that the Auto-Rotate Screen option is enabled. A green check mark next to this setting means that it is enabled.

Horizontal Orientation and Apps

Not every app in the Google Play Store was developed to take advantage of the horizontal orientation of your Galaxy Tab. If you notice this issue while using an app, close the app and then see whether your Tab can situate itself in horizontal orientation.

Troubleshooting Wi-Fi Accessibility Problems

Your Galaxy Tab 3 provides you the convenience and flexibility of wireless Internet access via Wi-Fi connectivity. Along with this convenience and flexibility comes the potential for connectivity issues regarding wireless networks. If you are unable to access a Wi-Fi network, or if your connection is sporadic, there are some troubleshooting tips you can use to pinpoint basic accessibility options.

Make Sure Wi-Fi Is Activated

First and foremost, make sure that the Wi-Fi antenna is on. You can determine this by looking in the right corner of the system bar at the top of your Galaxy Tab screen to see whether the Wi-Fi icon is visible. If it is not on, you can open the Quick Settings and Notifications screen and then activate Wi-Fi by tapping the Wi-Fi button.

Wi-Fi Antenna

Check Your Range

If Wi-Fi is activated on your Galaxy Tab 3 and you still cannot connect, take note of how far away you are from the Wi-Fi access point. You can be only 115 feet from a Wi-Fi access point before the signal becomes weak or drops altogether. Structures such as walls with lots of electronics can also impede a Wi-Fi signal. Make sure you are close to the access point or turn on the access point's range booster, if it has one, to improve your connection.

Reset Your Router

The issue might not be your distance from the Wi-Fi access point, a signal-impeding barrier, or your Galaxy Tab 3. As a last resort, you might need to reset the router. After you reset your router, you have to set up your network from the ground up.

Reset the Galaxy Tab 3 Software

If all else fails and your technical problems still persist, as a last ditch effort you might need to reset the Galaxy Tab software. Resetting your Galaxy Tab software restores your Tab to the factory defaults, just like when you took it out of the box for the first time. Consider contacting support before you reset your Tab, but if you must, follow these directions to reset the device.

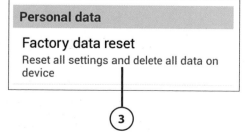

1. Tap Settings on the Home screen.

2. Scroll down the Settings list and then tap Backup and Reset.

3. Tap Factory Data Reset.

4. Tap the Reset Device button.

5. If you use a password to log into your Tab, type the password in the Confirm Password field.

6. Tap Continue.

7. Tap the Delete All button to confirm. Your Tab is returned to its factory state.

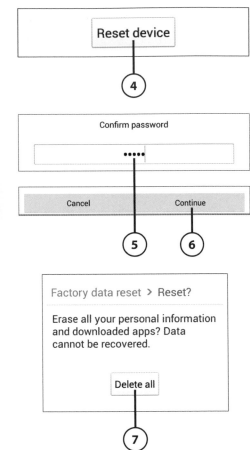

Getting Technical Help

There are many outlets available where you can find help if you run across a Galaxy Tab technical problem that you can't seem to beat. Although limited, the user's manual is a good place to start. You can download the correct manual for your Galaxy Tab model online from the Samsung website (www.samsung.com), in the form of a PDF, and scan the table of contents or perform searches in the document for words that pertain to your problem. In most user manual PDFs, topics in the Table of Contents are often linked to the section they pertain to within the document, so when you find what you are looking for, click the topic and jump to the page.

Websites and Galaxy Tab forums are also a great way for you to get support for your device. Type a search phrase, such as "Galaxy Tab Google Calendar sync problem," into Google. Chances are there are plenty of people who are experiencing the same issue. Doing some online research of your own could save you a few minutes on the telephone with technical support and help you solve your problem more quickly.

Contact Your Cellular Provider or Samsung

The Samsung website is a great resource for getting help with technical issues with your Galaxy Tab 3. The Samsung website (www.samsung.com/us/support/) offers support via Twitter, Facebook, Google+, as well as by phone (1-800-726-7864). Before you call, you need to have your device's model number so that you can give it to the technical support representative.

Locate Tab Model Number

You can find the model number on the box that your Tab shipped in, and you can also find it in the Settings menu.

1. Tap Settings on the Home screen.

2. Scroll down the Settings list and then tap About Device.

3. Locate your Tab's model number in the About Device field on the right of the screen.

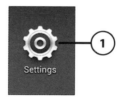

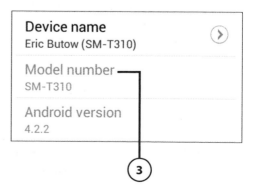

Index

A

accepting permissions, 398
accessing
    web bookmarks with S Bookmarks
        widget, 166-168
    Widgets screen, 79
accessories
    adapters, 446
    Bluetooth devices, 421-422
    Bluetooth keyboards, 420
    power chargers, 445-446
    protective cases, 443-444
    Samsung Car Adapter, 445
    screen protectors, 445
accounts
    Contacts accounts, 194
    News360 accounts, 187
AccuWeather app, 180
Active Apps Manager, 81
adapters, 446
    Samsung Car Adapter, 445
Adapt Sound, 81
adding
    apps, 404
    attachments to email, 127
    bookmarks, Play Books app,
        328-330
    contacts, 195-198
    Dictionary app, 407
    hardware, 419
    notes in ebooks, 329
    RSS readers, 409
    songs to playlists, 311
    videos to Video Player widget,
        161-163
    widgets to Home screen, 90-93
adjusting
    brightness level, 75
    screen brightness, 430-431
Alarm app, 81
alarms for calendar events, 205
albums (photo), creating, 358
alert sounds
    configuring, 69-71
    notification ringtone, setting, 71
alternative routes
    in Maps app, 374
    in Navigation app, 378
alternatives to protective cases, 444
Android, 4
Android operating system
    button bar, 39
    keyboard, 42-43
    Settings menu, 38
    sliders, 38
    Tab areas, 39
    text, 43
antiglare protective screens, 445
applications screen, Galaxy Tab 3 8",
    34-35
appointments. See events
apps
    AccuWeather, 180
    Dictionary, 407
    disabling update notifications, 399
    Dropbox app, sharing files, 222-229

finding high-quality apps, 395
force stopping, 435
getting help with, 401
Google Maps app, sharing locations, 382-387
Google Play Music
  playing music, 305-307
  purchasing music, 298-303
icons, 402
Internet Explorer 10. *See* Internet Explorer 10
Local, 380-382
Maps, 368-371, 453
  directions, 372-374
  locations, 374-376
Movies & TV, 273
Music Hub
  playing music, 303-305
  purchasing music, 291-296
  searching for music, 296-297
Music Player, 303
  playing music, 308-309
Navigation, 378
  voice-command directions, 376-379
News360 for Tablets, 180, 187
Note Everything, 413
Note Everything (NE) GDocs, 414
permissions, 398
Play Books, 318
  browsing catalogs, 318-320
  downloading books, 322-323
  purchasing books, 320-322
  reading aids, 324- 327
Play Books app
  adding bookmarks, highlights, and notes, 328-330
  organizing books, 330
Play Magazines, 331
  organizing magazines, 342-343
  purchasing magazines, 334-335
  reading aids, 339-342
  reading magazines, 337-338
  shopping for magazines, 332-333
  subscribing to magazines, 335-337
Play Movies & TV, 269
  playing movies and TV shows, 276-277
print apps, downloading, 220
Pulse, 409
purchasing, 397
rating, 400

searching for, 392
S Planner, 203
Stock Alert Tablet, 184
Stock Alert Tablet Edition, 180
troubleshooting, 435
uninstalling, 406
updating, 399
Video Player app, playing videos, 278-281
widgets, 79
archiving books, 331
ArmorSuit Military Shield, 445
arranging ebook library, 330
assigning contacts to groups, 198
attachments, adding to email messages, 127
auto-capitalization, enabling, 73
Automatic Brightness setting, 431
Automatic Restore option, 428
Auto-Rotate setting, 437

B

Back button, 27-28
backing up content, 427
  automatic Google account backup, ensuring, 427
  Automatic Restore option, 428
  manual backups, performing, 429
barcodes, scanning, 414
battery, troubleshooting, 436
battery life, extending, 429-433
Battery Usage screen, 430
BeyondPod, 312
Bluetooth
  configuring, 53
  devices, pairing, 420-422
  keyboards, 420
  turning off, 433
Bluetooth printers, connecting, 219-220
Book app, 81
bookmarking
  locations, 373
  websites, 110
bookmarks
  adding in Play Books app, 328-330
  deleting, 113-114
    from Bookmarks list, 113
    from History list, 114
  syncing, 114
Bookmarks app, 81-82
Bookmarks list, deleting bookmarks, 113
book readers, shopping for, 344-345

books
    archiving, 331
    downloading
        free book samples, 322
        with Play Books app, 322-323
    organizing in Play Books app, 330
    purchasing with Play Books app, 320-322
    reading with Play Books app, 322-323
Briefing, 83
brightness
    adjusting, 75
    settings, 431
browsers, choosing, 82
browsing
    catalogs, Play Books app, 318-320
    the Internet, 105
    web. *See* Internet Explorer 10
built-in camera
    effects, 289
    video, 287-290, 456
button bar in Android, 39
buttons
    Back, 28
    Home, 27
    Menu button, 27
buying apps, 397

C

Calendar, 83
calendar events
    alarms, 205
    creating, 203
calendars
    S Planner (Mini Today) widget, 169-170
    S Planner (Month) widget, 170-171
    views, 207-212
calls. *See* phone calls
camera
    effects, 289
    exposure level, adjusting, 288
    video, 287, 290
Camera app
    metering, 352
    photos, 350-353, 363
    scene modes, 350
    shooting modes, 350
    shutter lag, 356
    white balance, adjusting, 350
capitalizing letters on keyboard, 41
cases, 443-444

catalogs, browsing with Play Books app, 318-320
categories in News360 for Tablets app, 192
Center-Weighted metering, 352
changing date and time, 65-67
changing your password, 62-63
chargers, 445-446
choosing browsers, 82
cleaning your Galaxy Tab, 426
clear protective screens, 445
Clipboard key, 43
Clock (Digital), 83
Clock (Modern), 83
cloud services, finding, 229-230
comparing Galaxy Tab 3 with other Tabs, 9-12
completing web forms, 115
composing email messages, 127
configuring
    alert sounds, 69-71
    Bluetooth, 53
    content filter settings, 64
    ebook settings, 327
    email accounts, 119-123, 133, 136
    Google Hangouts, 142-144
    keyboard settings, 72-74
    parental restrictions, 64
    VPNs, 54, 456
    Wi-Fi, 52
connecting
    Bluetooth printers, 219-220
    to Internet, 50-52
    to Mac computers, 234
    Wi-Fi printers, 217-218
connection issues, troubleshooting, 217
conserving power by turning off Bluetooth, 433
Contact, 83
contacts
    adding, 195-198
    assigning to groups, 198
    display preferences, 198
    email, creating, 124
    joining, 200
    managing, 202
    opening records, 201
    searching, 199
    sending email to, 202
    sharing namecards, 202
    unjoining, 201
    updating, 198

Contacts widget
   accounts, 194
   contacts, 195-202
content filter, configuring, 64
Continue Searching on Server link, 132
conversations (instant messaging),
   starting, 140
copying
   files, 232-233
   images from web pages, 116-117
   media files with Windows Media Player,
     230-232
   text, 43
     from web pages, 116
creating
   email signatures, 130
   folders in Email app, 126
   photo albums, 358-360
   playlists, 310-311
Cupcake, 4
customizing Home screens, 405

D

date and time, changing, 65-67
Day View, 208
deleting
   app icons, 406
   bookmarks, 113
     from Bookmarks list, 113
     from History list, 114
   bookmarks (Internet app), 113-114
   downloaded magazines, 338
   ebooks from library, 331
   email messages, 130-131
   feeds, 315
   highlights, 328
   highlights from ebook text, 329
   Home screen, 100
   magazines from libraries, 343
   notes from ebooks, 329
   songs from playlists, 311
   widgets from Home screen, 100-101
Dictionary app, adding, 407
dimming the screen, 431
directions
   getting, Maps app, 372-374
   voice-command directions, 376-379
Directions & Navigation, 83
disabling
   app update notifications, 399
   wireless Internet connections, 52

displaying features of Galaxy Tab 3, 48-49
display preferences for contacts, 198
double-tapping gesture, 36
downloading
   apps, 397
   books, Play Books app, 322-323
   free book samples, 322
   print apps, 220
   TV shows, 270-272
dragging gesture, 36
DRM (Digital Rights Management), 236
Dropbox app, sharing files, 222-229
Dropbox Folder, 84
Dual Clock (Analog), 84
Dual Clock (Digital), 84

E

ebooks. *See also* books
   organizing, 330
   reading, 324-325
   removing from library, 331
   settings, configuring, 325-326
   text, 328
email
   attachments, 127
   composing, 127
   contacts, 124
   forwarding messages, 128
   messages, 131
     deleting, 130
   reading, 124-126
     with Email widget, 145-146
   replying to messages, 128
   searching through, 131
   sending to contacts, 202
   signatures, 129-130
   spam, 126
email accounts
   configuring, 119-123, 133-136
   IMAP, 120, 452
   POP, 120
Email app, 84
   folders, 126
emailing photos
   from Camera app, 363
   from Gallery, 362-363
Email widget, reading email, 145-146
enabling
   auto-capitalization, 73
   GPS, 368
   password protection, 59-61

ensuring
    automatic Google account
      backup, 428
    Google account backup, 427
error messages, Your Current Location Is
  Temporarily Unavailable warning, 375
events
    alarms, 205
    creating, 203
explicit lyrics, music, 299
exporting Google Docs notes, 414
exposure (Camera app), adjusting, 351
exposure level, adjusting for built-in
  camera, 289
extended keyboards, 42
extending battery life, 429
    Bluetooth, turning off, 433
    screen brightness, adjusting,
      430-431
    Sleep mode, 432
    Wi-Fi, turning off, 432

F

features of Galaxy Tab 3, displaying,
  48-49
feeds, 315
files
    copying, 232-233
    sharing, 222
      Dropbox app, 222-229
finding
    cloud services, 229-230
    high-quality apps, 395
    locations, 368-371, 453
    widgets, 150-151
      on Widgets pages, 151-152
firmware, 426
flicking gesture, 37
Flipboard (Medium), 84
Flipboard (Small), 84
Flipboard widget, 157-159
Flipboard widgets, 151
folders, creating in Email app, 126
font style, setting, 76
force stopping apps, 435
forecasts in AccuWeather app, 180
formatting MicroSD cards, 422-423
forms, completing web forms, 115
forwarding email messages, 128
free book samples, downloading, 322

G

Galaxy Note 8.0, 13
Galaxy Note 10.1, 13
Galaxy Tab 2 7.0, 12-13
    operating system version on, 17
Galaxy Tab 2 10.1, 8
    operating system version on, 18
Galaxy Tab 3
    gestures, 36-37
    Power button, 29
    screen orientation, 37
    setup, 26
    volume control buttons, 30
Galaxy Tab 3 7.0, 5-6, 18
Galaxy Tab 3 8.0, 7
    applications screen, 34-35
    lock screen, 32-33
    physical features, 19-22
Galaxy Tab 3 10"
    lock screen, 33
    physical features, 23-25
    unlocking, 33
Galaxy Tab 3 10.1, 8
Galaxy Tab 7.0, 9
    comparing with Galaxy Tab 2, 9
Galaxy Tab 7.0 Plus, comparing with Galaxy
  Tab 3, 10
Galaxy Tab 7.7, comparing with Galaxy
  Tab 3, 10
Galaxy Tab 8.9, comparing with Galaxy
  Tab 3, 11
Galaxy Tab 10.1, 12-13
    comparing with Galaxy Tab 3, 12
Galaxy Tab USB, 420
Gallery, photos, 357-363
Game Hub, 85
Game Hub widget, 160-161
gestures
    double-tapping, 36
    dragging, 36
    flicking, 37
    pinching, 36
    tapping, 36
Gingerbread, 4
Gmail, widgets, 85
Gmail Label, 85
Google, searching the Web, 107
Google+
    inviting people to share location, 388
    location sharing, 384-387

Google account
  automatic backup, ensuring, 428
  ensuring automatic backup, 427-428
Google Cloud Print, 220
Google Docs, importing/exporting
  notes, 414
Google Hangouts
  configuring, 142-144
  upgrading to, 139-141
Google Maps app, sharing locations,
  382-387
Google Now, 85
Google Play, 269
  apps, 392, 395-401
Google Play Books, 85
Google Play Music, 86
  playing music, 305-307
  purchasing music, 298-303
Google Play Store, 141, 229-230
  content filter, 64
Google+ Posts, 86
Google Search, 86
GPS. *See also* locations
  enabling, 368
  voice-command directions, 376-379
GPS tagging, enabling for photos, 350
grammar. *See* English/language arts apps
groups, assigning contacts to, 198
guitar, learning to play. *See* music apps

H

Hangouts (Google)
  configuring, 142-144
  upgrading to, 139-141
hardware. *See also* physical features
  adding, 419
  Bluetooth devices, 421-422
  Bluetooth keyboards, 420
help with apps, 401
highlighting ebook text, 328
highlights
  adding in Play Books app, 328-330
  removing, 328
high-quality apps, finding, 395
history (Internet app), 112
History list, deleting bookmarks, 114
Home button, 27
Home screen
  app icons, 402
  creating new, 97-99
  customizing, 405
  removing, 100

widgets
  adding, 90-93
  moving, 93-94
  removing, 100-101
  resizing, 95-97
Honeycomb, 4

I

Ice Cream Sandwich, 4
icons
  for apps, 402
  Timer icon (Camera app), 350, 455
images, copying from web pages, 116-117
Image Viewer, 353
  options, 355
IMAP (Internet Message Access
  Protocol), 120
importing Google Docs notes, 414
inaccurate barcode scanners, 415
inaccurate/incomplete data in Maps
  app, 370
incoming email settings, configuring, 137
instant messages, sending and
  receiving, 137
Internet
  connecting to, 50-52
  VPNs, 54, 456
Internet app, 105
  bookmarks, 113
  browsing the Internet, 103
  searching the Web, 105-107
  web forms, completing, 115
  web pages, 107, 111-112, 116-117
inviting people to share location, 388
iTunes, syncing with, 57

J

Jelly Bean, 4
joining contacts, 200

K

keyboard
  capitalizing letters, 41
  Clipboard key, 43
  configuring, 72-73
  special characters, 42
  Skype keyboard, 71
  typing on, 40

L

libraries, deleting magazines, 343
library (ebooks), organizing, 330
links, hunting for, 109
List View, 211
live wallpaper, 69
Local, 380-382
locating Galaxy Tab model number, 441
locations. *See also* GPS
    bookmarking, 373
    finding, 368-371, 453
    inaccurate/incomplete data, 370
    settings, 382-387
    specifying w/o addresses, Maps, 374-376
    Your Current Location Is Temporarily
      Unavailable warning, 375
location sharing, inviting people to do, 388
locking screen orientation, 37
lock screen
    Galaxy Tab 3 8", 32-33
    Galaxy Tab 3 10", 33
lyrics, explicit, 299

M

Mac computers, 234
Mac OS, syncing with Galaxy Tab 3, 56
magazine readers, shopping for, 344-345
magazines
    deleting from libraries, 343
    organizing, Play Magazines app, 342-343
    previewing, 335
    purchasing, Play Magazines app, 334-335
    reading, Play Magazines app, 337-338
    removing, 338
    shopping for, Play Magazines app,
      332-333
    subscribing to, Play Magazines app,
      335-337
maintaining your Galaxy Tab, 425
managing
    contacts, 202
    photos with Gallery, 357-359
manual backups, performing, 429
maps, viewing in Navigation app, 378
Maps app, 368
    directions, 372-374
    inaccurate/incomplete data, 370
    locations, 368-371, 374-376, 453

map views, switching, 371
Mass Storage USB mode, files, 232-233
media files, copying with Windows Media
  Player, 230-232
Memo, 86
memory cards, MicroSD cards, 422-423
messages (email), 127
    deleting, 130-131
    searching through, 131-132
Messenger app, instant messages, 137-138
metering, 352
MicroSD cards, 422
    formatting, 422-423
    unmounting, 423
mirrored protective screens, 445
model number, locating on your Galaxy
  Tab, 441
modifying
    directions, 374
    wallpaper, 68
Moko Slim-Fit Cover Case, 444
monitoring power usage, 430
Month View, 210
movies
    playing in Play Movies & TV app, 276-277
    shopping for, 273-276
Movies & TV app, 273
moving widgets on Home screen, 93-94
Multimedia Sync interface, 234
music
    DRM restrictions, 237
    explicit lyrics, 299
    playing, 303, 308
      Google Play Music app, 305-307
      Music Hub app, 303-305
      Music Player app, 308-309
    playlists, 310-311
    purchasing, 291
      with Google Play Music app, 298-303
      with Music Hub app, 291-296
    sharing, 230
Music Hub, 86
    playing music, 303-305
    purchasing music, 291-296
    searching for music, 296-297
Music Player, 87, 303
    playing music, 308-309
    playlists, 310-311
    songs, 308
Music Playlist, 87

N

namecards, sharing, 202
Navigation app
    viewing map, 378
    voice-command directions, 376-379
network issues, troubleshooting, 439
News360 for Tablets app, 180, 187
news feeds, 409
Note Everything app, 413
Note Everything (NE) GDocs app, 414
notes
    adding in Play Books app, 328-330
    viewing in ebooks, 330
Notification bar, reminders, 205
notification ringtone, setting, 71

O

obtaining technical assistance, 441
opening contact records, 201
operating system version
    on Galaxy Tab 2 7.0, 17
    on Galaxy Tab 2 10.1, 18
organizing
    books, Play Books app, 330
    ebooks, 330
    magazines, Play Magazines app, 342-343
    photos, 357-359
orientation of screen, 37
orientation setting, troubleshooting, 437
outgoing email settings, configuring, 137
overheating issues, troubleshooting, 436

P-Q

paging through ebooks, 324
pairing Bluetooth devices, 420-422
Panorama mode (Camera app), 350
parental restrictions, setting, 64
password protection, enabling, 59-61
passwords
    changing, 62-63
    resetting, 62
pasting text, 43
PCs, Samsung Kies, 234, 452
Peak Schedule, 122
permissions, accepting, 398
photo albums, creating, 358-361
Photo Editor, 361

photos
    emailing
        from Camera app, 363
        from Gallery, 362-363
    exposure level, adjusting, 351
    GPS tagging, 350
    managing with Gallery, 357-361
    organizing, 357
    reviewing, 353
    sharing, 353
    slideshows, 354
    taking, 352, 356
    viewing in Picture Frame widget, 164-165
    white balance, adjusting, 350
Photo Studio, 361
physical features
    Galaxy Tab 3 8", 19-22
    Galaxy Tab 3 10", 23-25
Picture Frame, 87
Picture Frame widget, 164-165
pictures. See photos
pinching gesture, 36
placing widgets, 153
Play, 87
Play Books app, 318
    adding
        bookmarks, highlights, and notes,
            328-330
        organizing books, 330
    browsing catalogs, 318-320
    downloading books, 322-323
    purchasing books, 320-322
    reading aids, 324-327
playing
    movies/TV shows in Play Movies & TV
        app, 276-277
    music, 303
        Google Play Music app, 305-307
        Music Hub app, 303-305
        Music Player app, 308-309
    podcasts, 312-314
    songs, 308
    TV shows, 273
    videos, 278-281
        in Video Player app, 278-281
playlists, 311
Play Magazines app, 331
    organizing magazines, 342-343
    purchasing magazines, 334-335
    reading aids, 339-342
    reading magazines, 337-338

shopping for magazines, 332-333
subscribing to magazines, 335-337
Play Movies & TV app, 269
    playing movies and TV shows, 276-277
Play Recommendations, 87
Play Store, 88. *See also* Google Play
podcasts, playing, 314
POP (Post Office Protocol), 120, 454
power, conserving by turning off
  Bluetooth, 433
Power button, 29
power chargers, 445-446
powering up your screen, 75
power usage, monitoring, 430
Predictive Text slider, 72
preventing spam, 126
preventive maintenance, 425
previewing magazines, 335
print apps, downloading, 220
printers
    Bluetooth printers, connecting, 219-220
    Wi-Fi printers, connecting, 217-218
printing, wirelessly, 217
protective cases, 443-444
    alternatives to, 444
Pulse app, adding, 409
purchasing
    apps, 397
    books, Play Books app, 320-322
    magazines, Play Magazines app, 334-335
    music, 291
        Google Play Music app, 298-303
        Music Hub app, 291-296

R

rating apps, 400
reading
    books, Play Books app, 322-323
    ebooks, 324-325
    email, 124-126, 156
        with Email widget, 145-146
    magazines, Play Magazines app, 337-338
reading aids
    magazines, Play Magazines app, 339-342
    Play Books app, 324-327
rearranging
    app icons, 402
    categories, 192
receiving instant messages, 138
recording
    video, 286-290
    voice notes, 415

refreshing
    news stories in News360 for Tablets
        app, 194
    RSS readers, 410
    stock information, 186
    weather forecasts, 183
reminders, 205
removing. *See* deleting
replying to email messages, 128
resetting
    your Galaxy Tab software, 439-440
    your password, 62
    routers, 439
resizing widgets on Home screen, 95-97
restoring content, Automatic Restore
    option, 428
returning to previously visited web pages,
    111-112
reviewing photos, 353
ringtones, notification ringtone, 71
rotation of screen, 37
routers, resetting, 439
RSS readers, adding, 409

S

Samsung Car Adapter, 445
Samsung Kies, 234, 452
Samsung website, 441
S Bookmarks, 88, 166-168
scanning barcodes, 414
scene modes (Camera app), 350, 454
screen brightness, adjusting, 430-431
screen orientation, 37
    troubleshooting, 437
screen protectors, 445, 454
SD adapter, 420
searching, 104
    contacts, 199
    for apps, 392
    for music, Music Hub app, 296-297
    through email, 131
    Web, 107
searching the Web, 105-107
security
    parental restrictions, 64
    password protection, 59-63
    Wi-Fi Internet access, 52
sending
    email to contacts, 202
    instant messages, 138

Settings menu in Android, 38
Settings Shortcut, 88
setup
    Contacts accounts, 194
    Galaxy Tab 3, 26
Share Via option (Video Player app), 279
sharing
    files, 222
        Dropbox app, 222-229
    locations, 382-387
    music/video, 230
    namecards, 202
    photos, 353
shooting modes (Camera app), 350
shopping
    for book and magazine readers, 344-345
    for magazines Play Magazines app, 332-333
    for movies, 273-276
shuffling songs (Music Player app), 309
shutter lag, 356
signatures (email), creating, 129-130
sleep mode, 30, 432
sliders in Android, 38
slideshows, starting, 354
Slimbook Leather Case, 444
social media, updates with Flipboard widget, 157-159
software, 426
Software Update, 88
songs. *See also* music
    DRM restrictions, 237
    playing, 308
    playlists, 310-311
    shuffling (Music Player app), 309
spam, preventing, 126
special characters on keyboard, 42
S Planner, 88
    calendar events, 203
S Planner (Mini Today) widget, 169-170
S Planner (Month) widget, 170-171
Spot metering, 352
starting
    conversations (Messenger app), 140
    slideshows, 354
Stock Alert Tablet app, 184
Stock Alert Tablet Edition app, 180
stock tracking in Stock Alert Tablet app, 184
Story Album, 88, 172-174
S Travel widget, 175-176
subcategories in News360 for Tablets app, 190

subscribing to magazines, Play Magazines app, 335-337
switching map views, 371
syncing
    Galaxy Tab 2 with Samsung Kies, 234
    Galaxy Tab 3, 55-56
        bookmarks, 114
        with iTunes, 57

T

Tab areas in Android, 39
taking photos, 352, 356
    exposure level, adjusting, 351
    shutter lag, 356
    white balance, adjusting, 350
tapping gesture, 36
Task Manager, 28
Task View, 212
technical assistance, obtaining, 440
text
    copying from web pages, 116
    copying/pasting, 43
    highlighting in ebooks, 328
time display, changing, 65-67
Timer icon (Camera app), 350
touchscreen, troubleshooting, 435
tracking stocks in Stock Alert Tablet app, 184
Travel, 89
travel tips, S Travel widget, 175-176
troubleshooting
    apps, 435-436
    battery problems, 436
    connection issues, 217
    difficulty turning on/off Galaxy Tab 3, 434
    overheating issues, 436
    screen orientation, 437
    settings that won't verify, 123
    technical assistance, obtaining, 440
    touchscreen, 435
    Wi-Fi, 438-439
    wireless printers, 218
TuneSync app, 57
turning off
    Bluetooth, 433
    Wi-Fi, 432
TV shows
    downloading, 270-272
    playing, 273
        in Play Movies & TV app, 276-277
typing on keyboard, 40

U

uninstalling apps, 406
unjoining contacts, 201
unlocking Galaxy Tab 3 10", 33
unmounting MicroSD cards, 423
unresponsive touchscreen,
  troubleshooting, 435
updating
  apps, 399
  contacts, 198
  directions, 374
  feeds, 315
  news stories in News360 for Tablets
    app, 194
  stock information, 186
  weather forecasts, 183
updating software, 426
upgrading to Google Hangouts, 139-141
upgrading software, 426
URLs, browsing, 104-105
User Manual, 89

V

versions of Galaxy tab, 4
Video Player, 89, 279
  playing videos, 278-281
  Share Via option, 279
Video Player widget, 161-163
videos
  adding to Video Player widget, 161-163
  playing, 280-281
    in Video Player app, 278-281
  recording, 286-290
  sharing, 230
  YouTube, 282-285
viewing
  map in Navigation app, 378
  notes in ebooks, 330
  pictures in Picture Frame widget, 164-165
  reminders, 205
  subcategories, 190
  web pages, 107, 111
  YouTube videos, 282-285
views for calendars, 207-212
voice-command directions, 376-379
voice notes, recording, 415
volume control buttons, 30
VPNs
  configuring, 54, 456
  disconnecting from, 55

W

wallpaper
  changing, 68
  versus live wallpaper, 69
weather forecasts in AccuWeather app, 180
Weather widget, 89, 154-156
Web, searching, 104, 107
web bookmarks, accessing with S
  Bookmarks widget, 166-168
web forms, completing, 115
web pages
  copying text and images from, 116
  history (Internet app), 112
  images, copying, 117
  returning to, 111-112
  viewing, 107, 111
websites
  bookmarking, 110
  Samsung, 441
Week View, 209
white balance (Camera app), adjusting, 350
widgets, 79
  Active Apps Manager, 81
  Adapt Sound, 81
  adding to Home screen, 90-93
  Alarm, 81
  Book, 81
  Bookmarks, 81-82
  Briefing, 83
  Calendar, 83
  Clock (Digital), 83
  Clock (Modern), 83
  Contact, 83
  Directions & Navigation, 83
  Dropbox Folder, 84
  Dual Clock (Analog), 84
  Dual Clock (Digital), 84
  Email, 84
    reading email, 145-146
  finding, 150-151
    on Widgets pages, 151-152
  Flipboard, 157-159
  Flipboard (Medium), 84
  Flipboard (Small), 84
  Flipboard widgets, 151
  Game Hub, 85
  Game Hub widget, 160-161
  Gmail, 85
  Gmail Label, 85
  Google Now, 85

Google Play Books, 85
Google Play Music, 86
Google+ Posts, 86
Google Search, 86
Memo, 86
moving on Home screen, 93-94
Music Hub, 86
Music Player, 87
Music Playlist, 87
Picture Frame, 87, 164-165
placing, 153
Play, 87
Play Recommendations, 87
Play Store, 88
removing from Home screen, 100-101
resizing on Home screen, 95-97
S Bookmarks, 88, 166-168
Settings Shortcut, 88
Software Update, 88
S Planner, 88
S Planner (Mini Today), 169-170
S Planner (Month), 170-171
Story Album, 88, 172-174
S Travel, 175-176
Travel, 89
User Manual, 89
Video Player, 89, 161-163
Weather, 89, 154-156
Yahoo! Finance, 89
Yahoo! News, 90
YouTube, 90
Widgets pages, finding widgets, 151-152
Widgets screen, accessing, 79

Wi-Fi
    checking for activation, 438
    security, 52
    settings, 433
    setting up, 50-51
    troubleshooting, 438-439
    turning off, 432
Wi-Fi, disabling, 52
Wi-Fi Alliance, 217
Wi-Fi Connect, 216
Wi-Fi Direct, 215
    setting up, 216
Wi-Fi printers, connecting, 217-218
Windows Media Player, media files, 230-232
wireless keyboards, 420
wireless networks, what to do if you don't
    have one, 50
wireless printers, troubleshooting, 218

Y

Yahoo! Finance, 89
Yahoo! News, 90
Year View, 207
Your Current Location Is Temporarily
    Unavailable warning, 375
YouTube, widgets, 90
YouTube videos, viewing, 282-285

Z

zooming in/out, 36

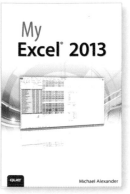

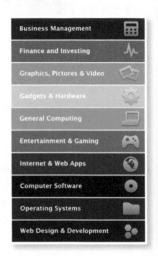